NO-FAULT MARRIAGE

NO-FAULT MARRIAGE

The New Technique of Self-counseling
and What It Can Help You Do

MARCIA LASSWELL &
NORMAN M. LOBSENZ

Doubleday & Company, Inc. Garden City, New York

Library of Congress Cataloging in Publication Data

Lasswell, Marcia E
  No-fault marriage.

  1. Marriage. 2. Interpersonal relations.
3. Marriage counseling. I. Lobsenz, Norman M.,
1919– joint author. II. Title.
HQ734.L336   362.8′2

ISBN: 0-385-04906-4
Library of Congress Catalog Card Number 76-2225

For the ones we love—

TOM . . . and DOROTHEA

CONTENTS

A PREFATORY NOTE

This book is designed to help husbands and wives make their marriages work better. Such books are far from rare, which may underline the extent to which couples need and seek this kind of assistance. We believe this book breaks new ground, however. For instead of doling out prefabricated "solutions" to marital problems, it attempts to show how men and women can develop the self-knowledge, the insights, the skills, and the confidence to deal successfully with their own concerns in their own time and in their own ways.

Marriage has been called our most difficult—if not impossible—social enterprise. Considering how poorly most people are prepared for it, and how immense their expectations of it are, the description more often than not unfortunately proves correct. Self-counseling, then, may seem an anomaly or an illusion; especially in a time when so many of us look to experts for guidance in the realm of human relationships. Yet the paradox is that we know ourselves better than any outsider—no matter how expert—can ever know us. And we are abundantly capable, given the tools and the conviction, of finding our own solutions to the difficulties we may face.

Is it too late to be concerned about making marriage work better? Isn't marriage, as we have known it, being phased out and replaced by new or "alternative" forms of pairing? Half a century ago a world-renowned psychologist predicted that marriage would no longer exist by the year 1977. Well, here we are. And after a decade or so of disillusion with conventional marriage, the institution has reasserted its popularity by accommodating to fit the needs of those who marry. There are approximately fifty million married couples in the United States today—an all-time high. Over ninety of every hundred Americans marries at least once; four of every five divorced persons rewreds within five years of his or her breakup. It would seem there is no adequate substitute for the stable and committed relationship between two individuals that a good marriage implies.

What *have* changed, of course, are the patterns of marriage. The traditional model—in which men and women carry out fixed role-behavior and exchange practical duties and responsibilities—has given way to a flexible and equalitarian linkage which emphasizes the giving and receiving of emotional satisfactions. Many men and women have not been fully able to adjust to meet the demands that the new-model marriage makes.

Moreover, counselors have learned that there is not just one marriage in a lifetime between a husband and wife, but many. For example, young couples who marry today may expect to be wed for fifty years. During that span a couple passes through many stages of the marital life-cycle: they are successively newlyweds, young parents of young children, middle-aged parents of adolescents, mutual victims of their own mid-life crises, "empty nesters," senior citizens. Each stage in the cycle brings its unique conflicts and challenges. Each must be dealt with differently. No one can say any longer: "This is what to do, and all your problems will disappear." As the problems change, so must the ways in which one meets and solves them. Prescribed solutions won't work. What works is the flexibility of self-counseling: the skill to formulate one's own new approaches to each new situation, to choose the best and to implement it.

Many people give lip service to the idea of change. But they fear both to confront it, or to make use of it. Once a marriage "works," even though poorly, they will do almost anything to *prevent* change. Change itself becomes a threat. Thus the most inadequate marriage is considered "all right" so long as it preserves a façade of harmony and the *status quo;* but a good marriage may well be viewed as suspect if a couple begin working to improve it. Yet to those who truly seek growth and satisfaction from marriage, change is not a threat but a promise. Self-counseling, we feel, is a way to make that promise bear fruit.

The twin concepts of "no-fault" marriage and self-counseling are an outgrowth of one author's long experience as a marital therapist—not only with troubled couples but also with those seeking to make an already good marriage better—and as a professor of developmental psychology; and the other author's work as a professional writer in the field of marital relationships. Both are equally responsible for the viewpoints presented. The case histories which are described, or from which husband-wife-counselor interchanges are quoted, are derived from actual cases counseled by Marcia Lasswell. Various nonessential details have been altered to protect the privacy of the persons involved. All names used in case histories are, of course, fictitious.

The authors owe a considerable debt to all those teachers, editors, colleagues, clients, and friends who have provided so much information and wisdom, inspiration and support along the way. More specifically, we are grateful for the early encouragement for this project we received from C. Ray Fowler and Leta Shattuck of the American Association of Marriage and Family Counselors; from our editor, Carolyn Blakemore; and from our trusty literary agent, Robert Lescher. Thanks are also due our longtime friends and editors Robert Stein, Sey Chassler, Geraldine Rhoads, and Rebecca Greer; they will surely recognize their contributions to the sharpening of our ideas and insights. Special appreciation must go to Barbara Blakemore, not only for suggesting our title but also for shepherding so expertly the publication of portions of this book in *McCall's* magazine. And the rigors of a transcontinental collaboration were eased by the excellent secretarial services of Margaret Riemer in New York and Dorothy Winkel in California.

I

"WHY DO WE DO THIS TO EACH OTHER?"

From the outside it looks like one of those television-commercial homes, where the sun slants through curtained windows into a bright kitchen and a smiling family is eating breakfast so cheerfully that the aura of good will is overpowering. Inside this particular house, however, cheer is noticeable chiefly for its absence. The emotional remains of last night's argument still hang almost palpably in the air.

Well-attuned by experience to the atmosphere, the children gobble their cereal and milk and make a fast getaway; school never seems so appealing as on mornings after Mom and Dad have had a fight. Dad drinks his orange juice and coffee standing at the kitchen counter, staring into each liquid as if, somewhere in its depths, he will find the secret of whatever in heaven's name it is that his wife wants from him. Mom makes an effort. In a voice carefully controlled to show no emotion, she inquires whether he wants an egg, or toast.

"Thank you, no," he says, "it's all I can do to get this down." She glares at him in fury. *Does he think he's the only one who gets upset when we argue?* She feels the temple-throb of a headache, not sure whether it's the last gasp of the one that kept her awake most of the night or the early-warning signal of a new one. *Why do we fight about the same stupid things over and over again?* she wonders. She can't even remember how they got from discussing whether to buy an air-conditioner to making mutual accusations of extravagance to squabbling over her parents to a shouting match about—whatever was it?—and, finally, to that long, hostile silence punctuated only by bedspring sounds as they oh so carefully shifted their bodies to avoid touching each other in bed.

He now carefully rinses his cup and glass and puts them in the dishwasher. *See what a good husband I am despite the way you behave,* his action implies. As he goes out the door with no good-by, she says, sarcastically, "Have a marvelous day." He stops, turns, they look at each other—and for an instant it seems they may come together, and kiss, and say it won't happen again, and *Yes, I do love you.*

But they can't . . . or won't . . . or don't know how to—and the instant passes. He leaves, hoping the day's demands of his job will numb his mind. She stirs her coffee, cold inside herself despite the sun and the warmth of the cup in her hands. *God!* she thinks, *Why do we do this to each other? Why can't we get along better? There must be a way.*

The primary aim of this book is to show you just such a way, and to guide you in its use. We believe that most couples can successfully deal with the majority of tensions and conflicts that complicate and sometimes afflict marriage through the new technique of *self-counseling.*

Granted, this is a novel path. Granted, too, it is a demanding one. Nevertheless, learning how to apply on your own the tested methods of professionally trained counselors to problems in your relationship may be one of the most practical and effective approaches to marital well-being. It may be the significant answer for those millions of husbands and wives who are asking themselves not just "Why do we do this to each other?" but the more important "How can we *stop* doing this?"

Some of these couples may battle with the marital equivalent of clubs and broadswords: ranting, screaming, hitting, throwing things. Some may use the rapier of cold-steel words, aimed with cunning precision at the familiar chinks in each other's emotional armor. Others may choose weapons that clearly should be outlawed by some Geneva Convention governing marital conflict: flank attacks via the children, or a subsonic barrage of deadly silence, or the biological warfare of sexual withdrawal. Still others may have ceased open battling altogether and withdrawn into fortified positions, leaving the marriage itself in a no-man's-no-woman's-land.

Yet for the most part these are still loving couples. They still care about their relationship. They want it to continue—to improve if possible, but at least to survive. If they did *not* care they would not expend all that energy in what is, after all, a desperate if misguided effort to reach the other person, to make some sort of emotional contact. They are frightened to let go; yet they make each other miserable when they touch. They say they love each other; but they behave in ways that often leave that in doubt.

Counselors are familiar with this pattern. They have learned that in marriage, love can exist at any of an infinite number of points along a line that ranges from passion to fury—passing on the way through affection, concern, acceptance, mutual tolerance, and, finally, even to open hostility. One case that so dramatically illustrates this paradox was that of the husband and wife who came into the counselor's office and sat side by side hurling the most vitriolic accusations at each other. The interesting thing was that the whole time they sat there the couple held hands . . . their fingers tightly intertwined as if to give the lie to their words, to keep their marriage from slipping away.

Like most couples who bring their problems to a counselor, however, this couple had waited too long. Nearly half of all serious marital problems develop in the first two years of marriage. Yet on the average, couples who seek counseling for the first time have already been married seven years. By then their differences have reached a crisis point, or have hardened and become embedded as permanent irritants in their relationship. The counselor is faced either with an explosive situation that is difficult to defuse, or with a rigid one that defies the possibility of change.

Even more distressing is the fact that *three out of four couples who file for divorce in this country have never consulted anyone about their difficulties*—not a counselor, not a minister, not even a family physician. In effect, lawyers' offices and the courts are filled with men and women who, unable to tolerate or repair their marriage, have decided arbitrarily that the only solution is to end it. "Do not remove a fly from your friend's head with a hatchet," runs a Chinese proverb. Sadly, millions of people use the hatchet of divorce to remove the fly of discontent.

Yet the statistics of divorce are notably confusing and often misleading. We frequently read, for instance, that there is "one divorce for every three marriages," or even that in some states such as California the "divorce rate" is one out of every two marriages. But such figures are the oversimplified result of merely dividing a given year's weddings by that same year's legal uncouplings. Actually, the number of divorces in any given year must be measured against all marriages made over past decades—the last ten, twenty, even thirty years. Without this more sophisticated statistical analysis there is no way to establish accurate "rates" of marital failure. For example, we know that in 1975 (the latest year for which figures are available) more than two million men and women got divorced. That is an appalling number, of course. Yet measured against the knowledge that there were 45 million married couples in the country that same year, it is a far cry from the "one-in-three" divorce rate we have come to accept as the rule of thumb.

The fact is that the overwhelming majority of spouses in unhappy or troubled or unsatisfactory or good-but-not-good-enough marriages do not just "want out." A recent study showed that nine out of ten husbands and eight out of ten wives who sought marital counseling strongly desired to save their marriages. Only a small minority were motivated by religious reasons, or a sense of duty, or the fear of loneliness, or concern about money, or worries about what friends and family would think. Most wanted to rescue and preserve their marriage because, they said, they loved their wife or husband and wanted to make a happy home for their family.

These couples yearn—not for separation or divorce—but for a way to understand, to deal with, and to resolve their differences. They want very much to achieve a reasonably workable relationship. Or to make one that is already workable into one that is more rewarding. Or to make one that is fairly good into something still better.

What stands in their way?

In our view there are three major obstacles.

One is the notion that what is comfortable in marriage should never change, or be changed.

A second is what we call "the need to blame."

A third is the myth of the self-improving marriage.

None of these, taken singly, is a startling new element in marital malaise. Together, however, they form a syndrome that tends to generate its own resistance to treatment and to cure. How this barrier develops can be seen in the following excerpts from an initial counseling session with a couple who, after four years of marriage, had made virtually no progress on their own toward coping with their problems. Their first session revealed a clear tendency to resist change both in themselves and in each other.

MARCIA LASSWELL: I'd like it if you could each tell me how you see your problem.

HUSBAND: I think it's a problem of communication. I'm on FM and she's on AM.

WIFE: I don't think he even listens to me. If it isn't said his way, he turns me off. Sometimes he just walks out of the room.

ML: What have you been trying to tell him that you wish he would listen to?

W: A lot of things. I feel stuck with the kids and the house. It wasn't so bad until the second child came along. Now I feel as if I'm running an endless nursery school.

H: You knew what you were getting into when we got married. You wanted to quit and be a housewife and have children. That was our agreement.

ML: Are you pleased with this agreement, Bob?

H: I would be if Lucy didn't complain all the time. She makes me feel mad and guilty, both at the same time. Sure, I walk out of the room sometimes when she starts up.

ML: If you were comfortable with that kind of agreement when you got married, Bob, I can understand how you wish things would stay the same. But, Lucy, do you go along with what Bob says about your agreement?

W: I guess he's right. But *he* made an agreement, too. He was going to share things with me, carry part of the load. Now he says he's too tired because he has to work so hard to support us.

ML: It sounds to me as if you both ought to think about making some changes.

H: Like what?

ML: Well, we'll have to find out as we go along. It won't be an overnight revolution. But maybe we can make some changes in that "agreement" of yours that will help Lucy with her resentments and you with your guilt and anger.

w: I won't hold my breath. Bob isn't going to give up doing things his way. I've tried for two years to get him to change.

h: Change to do things *your* way, you mean.

ml: Well, a renegotiation probably won't give either of you everything you want because you are pretty far apart to begin with. But both of you could gain something if you could recognize that your marriage is at a different place today than when you made your agreement four years ago. The children for Lucy. Having to work harder and longer to support a growing family for Bob. Marriage doesn't stand still. Just because it was comfortable at one point doesn't mean it will stay that way for both of you indefinitely.

The second obstacle to dealing constructively with marital differences is our need to blame someone for them. Americans are by temperament unhappy with uncertainty, ambiguity, open-endedness. We want definitive answers even when there are none at hand. We seek simplistic reasons for whatever is happening even though there may be many complex causes. We are impatient with indecision. Hung juries bother us; "guilty" or "not guilty"—that is the question we want answered. Who's at fault? Who's to blame?

Every marital therapist is familiar with the complaining wife who says, "Our problem is that my husband drinks too much," or the husband who diagnoses the problem as, "My wife is never interested in sex." The hidden message in these blaming statements is always the same: *What's wrong is your fault . . . If* you'd *only change* my *problems would be solved.* Blaming the other person not only provides a ready, simple answer; it also avoids the need to make that painful search into oneself for possible causes of the situation.

The following case illustrates a typical blaming sequence. If allowed to continue on its course, it could eliminate any possibility of a constructive solution to this middle-aged couple's problems. Notice particularly how each spouse places blame on the other for what has gone wrong even when the counselor makes it obvious that their situation is no one's fault, or that both are equally at fault.

WIFE: I thought that when we bought the house in Willow Heights we'd be more of a *family* than when we lived in the city. But Jim is home less now than he was then.

HUSBAND: Well, what do you expect? It's a long commute. If I have a late meeting, it makes more sense to stay over in a hotel than get home at midnight and go back at 7 A.M.

W: Do you *have* to have all those night meetings?

H (sarcastically): Don't you want me to move up in the company? Make more money? Anyway, what's to rush home for? Half the time you're not there . . . there's a frozen dinner in the oven.

W: Okay, so I've gotten into some local groups and I go to meetings. But who pushed me to get involved in community activities? You said it would be good for your image in the firm.

MARCIA LASSWELL: I would hope that each of you can understand that part of what bothers you isn't the fault of either of you. You have a new job, a new home, you live in a new town— both of you, and the children, are all trying to adjust. That takes time. Blaming each other won't help.

H: I'm not blaming Claire. I'm just saying that if she wants certain things out of life, she has to put up with whatever's necessary to get them.

W: See, there he goes again! Why does he think *I* want these things. I don't care if we have a new car or not!

In an earlier time it was simpler (if perhaps just as unfair) to judge who was to blame. Marriage then was based primarily on an exchange of identifiable duties. Man built the home and woman tended it. He went to work and she raised the children. He brought home the bacon and she cooked it. Since these male and female "role" assignments were clear-cut, it was easy to place the blame for any failure. A popular turn-of-the-century novelist put it this way: "Marriage is a job," Kathleen Norris wrote. "Happiness or unhappiness has nothing to do with it." No one was distressed by that idea; most people agreed with it. A typical marriage a few generations ago lasted only twenty years or so before death ended it. And that time was filled with hard work and child-rearing. No one really expected "happiness" from marriage.

Today, of course, most people would be horrified by such an attitude—and rightfully so. Except for their biological functions, the line between male and female roles in marriage is blurred and elastic. The traditional sex-linked division of labor is no longer necessary, nor even practical. Few men and women today marry for economic reasons, for sexual availability, for social approval, or out of fear of social *dis*approval.

We marry now for emotional fulfillment, for intellectual companionship, for shared values, for mutual psychological support, for the sense of intimacy that goes beyond superficial sex. We marry, in short, for that host of satisfactions to which we give the label "love."

But it is far more difficult to figure out what is going wrong—and who is to "blame"—when a marriage fails to yield these expected satisfactions than when someone merely fails to "do his job." As every counselor sadly knows, the husband or wife who feels disillusioned, unhappy, or desperate is in no mood for rational thinking or an evenhanded approach to the situation. In most cases, he or she already *knows* that the other partner (or, more rarely, oneself) is to blame; all that remains is to make that person see his or her fault, admit it, and shape up.

For example, a counselor we know tells the story of a woman who sailed into his office several years ago and ticked off a litany of complaints about her husband's behavior. He was sullen, he drank a lot, he went out by himself many nights. "When the woman seemed to have run out of charges," the counselor recalls, "I mildly asked if she could think of any reason why her husband might be acting as she had described. The woman glared at me with a mixture of astonishment and distaste. 'I didn't come here to have you ask *me* questions,' she said. 'I came here so you could find out what's wrong with *him!*'"

In another instance a couple spent an entire session itemizing their mutual accusations. Toward the close of the hour, anxious to create a more fruitful atmosphere for the next meeting, the counselor suggested they both give some thought to the attitudes and feelings that might underlie their differences. In an instant they closed ranks. "We don't think that's necessary," the wife said while her husband nodded agreement—for the first time that day, by the way! "We just want you to tell us which of us is right."

Counselors are not in the blame-packaging business. Indeed, one of their hardest tasks is to convince a client that there is almost never a clearly defined "right" or "wrong" side in marital conflict, but only "different" sides. Nothing is easier than fault-finding. And nothing is more damaging. Not until the "need to blame" has been put aside can a couple begin to make progress toward solving their problem.

The third obstacle to a better relationship is *the myth of the self-improving marriage*. As a colleague, family sociologist David H. L. Olson, observed: "One of the most prevalent illusions in our culture is the belief that if an intimate relationship is not good, it will *spontaneously* improve with time."

Counselors see this attitude at work across the entire spectrum of courtship and marriage. A dating couple who are attracted physically but disagree about values often assume that if they "go steady" they won't argue so much. Steady daters who are having difficulties believe that once they are engaged matters will get better. Engaged couples, made somewhat more secure by the formal link between them, accept each other's flaws on the theory that they can be reformed "once we're married." Newlyweds, surprised by the new areas of conflict that result from living together, take refuge in the assumption that "things will straighten out if we give it a little time." Sometimes having a baby is seen as a solution. There are even couples who, when a first child fails to turn this trick, believe that having a second one will certainly do it.

But neither the passage of time, nor increments of forced commitment, nor additional responsibilities automatically improve a troubled relationship. On the contrary, they merely make differences *more* difficult to deal with. The passage of time hardens positions and attitudes. Increased commitment that is largely forced aggravates resentments. Added responsibilities lock couples into a relationship—creating stress rather than easing it, making rigid what needs to be flexible. In fact, it is not at all uncommon for the same "minor" problems that bother a couple during their dating years to be the very ones that escalate into a major rift.

Much of this symptomatology can be seen in the remarks of a young couple who expected automatic improvement in their sex life:

MARCIA LASSWELL: You two have let these problems go a long time—no sex for four months and not speaking for over a week! Is not speaking a usual pattern with you? And I'm curious: what made you communicate enough to come in together today?

HUSBAND: We clam up when things aren't going well. I just decided I'd finally had enough of this, and we needed help.

ML: And how did you feel when Jim said this, Linda?

WIFE: I was relieved. I never thought Jim would go for help.

H: Well, I kept thinking things would get better. We used to argue before we got married, too, but I thought when we got used to each other we'd agree more.

W: Then we had children and there was more to disagree about. We really fight a lot about how we treat the kids. We fight and then we have days of silence.

ML: And why did you choose to stop having sex?

H: Choose to? *I* didn't choose to. Linda did.

W: Don't blame that on me! You never once approached me in that four months.

ML: And was your sex life good before that?

W: No! It has never been good. That's one thing *I* thought would surely improve, but Jim never has learned what I like.

ML: Did you ever tell him what you liked?

W: No . . . I guess I thought he ought to know. He was the one with all the experience before we were married.

ML: It's the experience with *you* that counts. Jim's experience with other women may have nothing to do with what *you* like.

W: Well, it certainly hasn't gotten better. We can't talk about it at all. Should I have to? It seems that if Jim loves me, he'd know me better.

To recapitulate: For a married couple to deal constructively with their differences, each partner must: 1) be emotionally aware of the problems that exist; 2) at the same time be able to put aside the tendency to blame the other (or, equally unrealistically, to blame oneself); and 3) realize that most problems do not disappear but grow if they are ignored—that a marriage, unlike a cold, will not get better by itself.

To accomplish these three things a couple must think of marriage as a "no-fault" relationship.

Is this possible? Is it within the scope of "human nature" for two people in conflict, or for two people seeking a solution to a mutual problem, to agree at the outset that neither of them is specifically to blame? Or is this concept unrealistic and naïve? We believe it is just as unrealistic to assume that a man and woman are automatically *incapable* of taking an objective approach to their difficulties, and equally naïve to attribute all marital problems to conflict between the personalities or the behavior of the partners themselves. Here are some reasons:

Disagreement in marriage is the rule, not the exception. We've all heard the stories about couples who never argue. "There was never a harsh word between them in all the years," is the usual phrase. Nonsense. There may be couples who for the sake of surface amity—or out of fear—unhealthily repress their antagonisms. There may be children who cherish the illusion that *their* parents never fought. The fact is that *every* couple, at one time or another, have their complaints, their angers and their quarrels. Indeed, it is a reasonable conclusion that a couple who never are at odds are never "at evens" either—they simply have so little emotional investment in each other that they do not care enough to try to improve their marriage.

Conflict can be a positive sign of marital growth. Too often we take it for granted that husband and wife are pitted against each other. Spouses even tend to think of themselves as opponents. Yet not all discord is necessarily a clash *between* the partners, but between their marriage and outside forces and events that impinge upon it. For instance, a couple caught in the squeeze of spiraling living costs finds that money management becomes a source of arguments. Though the issue is not of their making, charges of extravagance or miserliness are easily hurled between them over behavior that would go unnoticed were the bank balance healthier. The conflict is actually a symptom of the couple's efforts to overcome the problem of limited funds, much as fever is a symptom of the body's battle to overcome illness.

Moreover, as we shall see later on, new patterns in marriage—and the wider choices and opportunities they present to both men and women—are increasingly responsible for much disagreement and tension between spouses. To assign the "fault" for this state of affairs to one person or the other ignores the fact that massive social changes are at work—changes that require enormous skill and adaptability to meet. One might as well "blame" one's wife or husband for an avalanche or a tidal wave.

Some areas of conflict are normally to be expected at certain stages in the marital "life-cycle" as a result of certain predictable events. Marriages pass through stages of development just as people do. A marriage—and its stresses—in the newlywed year is as different from one in the child-raising period as that is from another in the retirement part of the cycle. Every husband and wife experience many varieties of marriage in a lifetime. Indeed, the late Sidney Jourard, a well-known marital therapist, pointed out that the term "serial monogamy"—normally used to refer to people who keep marrying, divorcing, and remarrying a new spouse—could also be applied to couples who stay together. For each partner becomes a different kind of person at different points in the marital cycle. A woman wed for twenty-five years, for example, can count three marriages: before the children were born, when the children were growing, after the children left home. Her husband breaks down the middle stage into two separate parts: when the children were preschoolers he felt married to "Mother Earth"; when they were older he saw his wife as "Community Worker"—Scout den mother, PTA officer, church school teacher, and so on. They both look forward to a fourth "marriage" as grandparents.

Because these changes are so gradual few couples are aware of this marital metamorphosis. Nor do they realize that certain characteristic tensions and conflicts are normally (and almost universally) produced at each specific stage. Many of these stress points have been identified. One, for example, is the birth of a first child. Delight and joy at the baby's arrival are real. Yet lurking beneath father's pride and mother's happiness are gray, formless but disconcerting feelings. A man frequently feels shunted aside by his wife in favor of the infant. Gone is the freedom and closeness they knew as a twosome. Sex is somehow less intense—interrupted by the child's cries or needs, or perhaps reflecting a wife's intense emotional involvement with her baby or the husband's worry at suddenly increased financial responsibilities. Schedules replace spontaneity. Things—the astounding amount of sheer *things* an infant seems to need—accumulate: the sports car may have to give way to the station wagon. She worries. Will she be a good mother? Will she be tied down too much? Will she resent being at home while her husband's career advances? Will she feel guilty if she keeps on working too? So disconcerting are these unexpected anxieties and fears that most parents force them back into the unconscious—whence, of course, they eventually erupt, disguised or barefaced, and sow the seeds of disharmony.

The normal family life-cycle is booby-trapped with a whole series of similar events: ordinary in and of themselves, yet so "loaded" emotionally, so filled with potential for threatening or promising change, that they can and do trigger what might be labeled "existential" conflict—clashes that in no way can be made or called one partner's fault. Here are some other examples: getting a promotion to a job that demands more effort, more time, more travel; losing a job; a serious illness; a major change for better or worse in family financial affairs; a move to a different part of the country or even to a different neighborhood; an in-law coming to live with you; a housewife's decision to return to school or to work. Here again, the concept of "no-fault marriage" is reinforced: It is pointless to try to accuse one partner or the other of causing tensions that are inherent in the structure and evolution of marriage.

In recent years the doctrine of "no-fault" has proven remarkably sensible and efficient in dealing with automobile accidents and divorce. No-fault car insurance has eliminated enough red tape to festoon all the nation's highways. Similarly, in the states where no-fault divorce is law (at this writing: Arizona, California, Colorado, Delaware, Florida, Iowa, Kentucky, Michigan, Minnesota, Missouri, Nebraska, Oregon, and Washington), it has gone a long way toward easing the pain and cost of that process. Under no-fault divorce laws, grounds such as adultery, drunkenness, abuse, or willful neglect are no longer necessary. If one partner (or both) declares that there are "irreconcilable differences" in the relationship, a divorce may not be withheld. Indeed, the process is no longer called divorce in many states, but "dissolution"—a kinder term. The main accomplishment of no-fault divorce has been to do away with the "adversary" concept. No longer must husband and wife become legal enemies—an artificial relationship which often turned them into actual enemies as well.

Spouses need first to concentrate on *making marriage right* rather than on who may be "responsible" for what is wrong. They must be then willing to *do* something about improving matters. The secret of dealing with difficulties is to admit that they exist . . . to identify them accurately . . . and to take constructive action against them.

Traditionally, this has involved seeking advice from others. In the past, when a young man or woman more often than not married the girl or boy next door, couples continued to live where they grew up. They could count on a circle of relatives and friends to provide a sense of stability as well as the lessons of experience. These supports do not exist for most couples nowadays. The "extended family" network of aunts and uncles, grandparents and cousins, has given way to the isolated "nuclear family"—the couple themselves and their children, if any. All the responsibility for working out problems falls on this little unit, and the pressures often are great. (Margaret Mead once remarked that it is no wonder we call it the nuclear family—it is so explosive.) Then, too, one out of five families moves to a new community each year. Relatives are scattered, friends are few—and most are reluctant to get involved in a couple's marital difficulties.

Today trained marriage and family counselors have replaced the informal advice-giver. Professional counselors know they are helpful to millions of troubled couples. But they also know that many other millions, similarly troubled, do *not* go to counselors.

There are some valid reasons. Most important, there are not enough trained counselors in all areas of the country to meet the demand for their services. Virtually every individual therapist and counseling center have waiting lists. Too, the bulk of counselors are concentrated in a handful of major cities, usually on the East and West Coasts of the country. If you live in West Virginia or New Mexico your problems are just as real and serious as if you lived in New York or Los Angeles—but help is far less accessible.

Letters by the score arrive each week at the national office of the American Association of Marriage and Family Counselors, each a recital of marital anguish and a plea for help. It is not unusual for a couple to send a homemade tape recording of their arguments in the hope that someone will listen to it and counsel them.

Thousands of smaller communities have no resident professional counselor. In many of these towns ministers and family doctors may offer guidance, but for the most part they have little or no specialized counseling training. Moreover, couples hesitate to confide intimate concerns to them out of embarrassment, fear of gossip, fear of the loss of privacy. In addition, some people cannot (or think they cannot) afford the time or the fees for counseling. Actually, fees are usually geared to a client's income. But since money problems are often a major factor in marital stress, to add counseling costs to the budget seems to be just one more burden to carry.

Other reasons for not seeking help are less valid, but just as real. For example, some spouses neurotically *need* to be locked in an unhappy relationship. Unable to tolerate success, they fear counseling may succeed. Family therapist James L. Framo reports that one husband, whose marriage was improving as a result of counseling, said to him one day: "I can't stand it. My wife is nice to me and even my car is working!"

Sometimes couples have never learned any other way to make contact with each other than by fighting: when the fighting stops they feel empty; they don't know what to do instead. Some people worry that their improved relationship can't last, and their anxiety paradoxically makes them want to put an end to the peace before it is ended for them—the old way may not have been so good but at least it was familiar. For others, as we have seen, blaming becomes a way of life; to take responsibility for their own feelings and actions is so foreign as to be uncomfortable. And still others dread change of any kind. They prefer the safety of what they have, no matter how grim it is, to the uncertainty of what might replace it.

For example, a childless couple in their thirties, both attractive and successful but terribly unhappy with each other, said they stayed together because the thought of being alone scared them.

HUSBAND: It's better to come home to a house with a light on, and
    fight, than to one that's dark and empty.
MARCIA LASSWELL: It sounds like you're saying you'd rather
    remain in a predictable hell than try to make or find a more
    rewarding way of life.
WIFE: At least we know what kind of hell it is . . . what kind of
    hell it will be tomorrow. That seems safer to me than not
    knowing anything about tomorrow at all.

For those who cannot, do not, will not, or need not turn to a
professional therapist, self-counseling provides a practical way to
minimize the flaws and maximize the satisfactions in a marriage.

At first blush, this may seem a startling proposition. Spouses,
heal thyselves?

Yet evidence is growing that self-counseling is not only feasible
but extremely effective. Instead of just talking about their marriage
on a theoretical level with a third person, husband and wife are
themselves engaged in the real work of changing for the better the
intimate context of their lives.

Whether self-counseling can work for you depends on you—on
the skill and will with which you apply it. Perhaps it may prove
more effective in some areas of difficulty than in others. It may be
the only tool you need, or it may serve to open a gateway to other
counseling methods. Obviously, self-counseling is not a cure-all.
Some conflicts may be too deep-seated or complex to be aided by
it. In many respects the value of marital self-counseling may be
compared to the value of a "family home guide" for medical problems. Both can help you to recognize and identify the early symptoms of distress. Both can suggest remedies, or at least ways to alleviate discomfort. Both can prescribe techniques to prevent new
difficulties and provide supportive after-care. But neither can be a
substitute for skilled professional advice and treatment where the
well-being or even life of the patient or the marriage is in immediate danger. Under "heart attack" or "acute appendicitis," for example, the book will describe the symptoms, outline emergency
measures, list what *not* to do, and instruct you to call a doctor at
once. It is clear that you are not to perform open-heart surgery or
remove an appendix in the living room. Similarly, some marital

problems can be dealt with by a couple themselves, while others clearly need the expertise of a trained therapist.

Unlike some other methods for instant self-improvement—open marriages, freer sex, no-holds-barred arguing—that have been promulgated in recent years, marital self-counseling is not meant to be a game or a gimmick. It is, rather, hard work. It can be demanding and emotionally draining. It can lead to occasional failure as well as to success, to sadness as well as to exultation. Those who use it must be prepared to deal with all of this, for there is no such thing as growth without some pain.

2

HOW TO ANALYZE
YOUR MARRIAGE

"What do you think your marriage will be like five years from now? Where do you think you will be as a couple?"

We often ask these questions of counseling clients. A few have answers, usually vague or impractical, naïve or overconfident. Yet however woolly-minded or ingenuous, these couples are making some attempt to anticipate the future. In most cases husband and wife look at each other blankly and then say something like, "God only knows."

These are not unintelligent couples. They look ahead and plan ahead in other areas of living. Quite often the only thing they leave to chance is the course of their marriage: where it is heading, where they would like it to go, and how they plan to steer it in the right direction. In many cases this default stems from not knowing where their marriage stands *now*. Yet if mutual concern and affection are one prerequisite for effective self-counseling, then another is marital self-knowledge. No therapist would presume to offer guidance without knowing the facts about the marriage he or she was treating. Self-counseling couples, similarly, need a clear idea of what is good, bad, or indifferent about their relationship.

This sort of analysis is missing from most marriages. There may be a spark of it in the latter half of the newlywed year. The first rosy flush of romantic idealism has by then begun to be shaded with the soberer tints of reality. Counselors find that not until couples reach this stage are some of them willing to examine the actualities of their marriage. Most couples, as we have seen, continue to sweep them under the rug for a much longer period. For them, questioning the state of their relationship is seen as a threat, a potentially dangerous lid-lifting of Pandora's box. Only when conflicts reach a crisis are they willing to look at the truths of their life together. And some couples can't or won't do it even then.

Human beings have always managed to find reasons to keep from facing up not only to their needs and problems, but also to their wants and wishes. We are just as disinclined to probe our satisfactions as our dissatisfactions. Marriage offers many such handy reasons. We're busy earning a living, raising the children, keeping the house, acquiring things, making friends, being active citizens. Who has time or energy for introspection? As a result, many of us are strangers to ourselves, our partners, and to our marriage. Yet any attempt to deal with marital problems—and certainly any hope to move toward solutions—must be grounded in some knowledge of the dynamics that are at work between the spouses.

Marriages are for the most part simplistically classified into "good" ones and "bad" ones. Few people can define a "good" marriage. Husbands and wives who say they are content can seldom spell out the exact reasons. Everyone, of course, knows what a "bad" marriage is. Unhappily wed couples can cite chapter and verse of what's wrong. But, then, we have all seen "good" marriages suddenly blow apart; conversely we have all seen marriages which by our standards were obviously "bad" continue to survive and even flourish.

What forces are at work underneath these surface labels of goodness and badness?

To begin with, there are some basic ideas that seem to hold true for most functioning marriages. As a first step in analyzing your marriage, answer each following "true/false" question and compare your response with those established by a consensus of family experts. There are no "scoring" instructions because this is not a quiz in the traditional sense. The point is to examine the accuracy of the ideas about marriage you bring to your own relationship:

1. The wife's role in marriage has changed more than the husband's in the last five years.
2. Marriages between persons of different religions have an unusually high divorce rate—as much as six times higher.

3. Love is the single most important factor in holding all marriages together.

4. Marriage tends to make a spouse's annoying personal habits more tolerable as the years go by.

5. Children of unhappy parents and broken homes are usually poor marital risks.

6. Sex is the cause of most marital troubles.

7. Any marriage that lasts for a number of years is bound to have some fairly serious and hostile fights.

8. Any time you see a wife-dominated marriage you know something is wrong somewhere in the relationship.

9. Most of the time, the source of a conflict is some minor occurrence that does not amount to much.

10. If two persons have accommodated to each other's ways, it is a sign their marriage is happy.

11. It is best to vent your feelings and get anything bothering you out when you feel like it rather than to wait any appreciable time.

12. If a couple agrees on most areas of their lives together before they have children, chances are they will also agree on child-rearing.

13. When you put your mind to it, there are virtually no marital problems you and your spouse can't solve by yourselves.

14. When you live with someone for a long time it's fairly easy to tell what he or she is thinking.

15. With the divorce rate so high, it is getting increasingly unusual for a couple to reach their fiftieth wedding anniversary.

16. Having children creates a positive influence on marital satisfaction.

17. Studies show that the partner who earns the most money makes most of the family's decisions.

18. If your spouse is not jealous of you sometimes, he or she obviously does not care much about your relationship.

19. The nature of conflicts over money in marriage changes as the amount of family income changes.

20. Marriages that have been in trouble for years usually have little or nothing left to build from when the couple finally realize they have reached a crisis.

All of these statements are false.

For generations, the stereotypes and folklore of marriage, the "common wisdom" of pseudo-experts, all gave credibility to those ideas. But though family sociology is far from an exact science, every recent study has shown that these beliefs and attitudes and judgments are wrong. Anyone who has been looking at his or her marriage in terms of these outmoded notions is making a serious mistake. (In subsequent chapters we will examine these marital clichés in more detail.)

Another error that some couples make is to try to analyze their relationship through unrealistic or even invidious comparisons. There's an old and rather cruel joke about the man who, when asked, "How's your wife?" heehawed back, "Compared to what?" Yet when a couple sets out to assess the quality of their marriage they always have to ask: "Compared to what?"

Compared to being single? Single and lonely? Single and popular, with a constant flow of dates? Looking back at "how it used to be before we were married" is one of the most common mistakes people make when judging the satisfactions or troubles in their marriage. Another is fantasizing what one's life might be like *now* if one were still single.

Compared to how things were in those first years when you were both relatively free of responsibilities? That is both unreasonable and immature, for who escapes (or would want indefinitely to escape) the responsibilites of adulthood or parenthood? A psychologist named Angus Campbell once said that "The best of all possible worlds is to be newly married and not have children." But despite the financial and emotional obligations children entail, most couples do choose eventually to have them. In so doing they forfeit any legitimate right to contrast post-parental marriage with that earlier one.

Compared to a friend's marriage, a relative's, a neighbor's? Because any couple puts the best face on the public image of their marriage, we assume everybody else's must be better than our own. The fact is we are completely ignorant of what other people's marriages are really like. Even if we knew the truth, copying another couple's pattern is a futile exercise. To use it as a measure is to use no measure at all.

Compared to artificial standards? Every so often society tries to tell us what we *ought* to seek or get from marriage. Over the decades the models change: social status, togetherness, the perfect housewife or the liberated woman, security or adventurousness, many children or no children. But each of these is still an arbitrary pattern that bears no relation to our individual needs.

Compared, finally, to some ideal concept of marriage? Even marital therapists do not agree on what that might be. The two criteria most generally used to describe successful marriages are *stability* and *happiness*. But both are flawed touchstones. A marriage may be stable—that is, capable of mere survival—because although the two persons in it hate each other they lack the courage to separate. As for happiness, that elusive quality depends on what a couple believe it to be. One couple's happiness may be another's apathy and still another's chaos. No one has invented a satisfactory way to measure how "happy" or "unhappy" a marriage is. No survey or test is conclusive. No one knows how accurate the answers are. No one even knows how relevant the questions may be. Moreover, in most instances the "happiness" scores are self-reported—there is no way to distinguish truth from wishful thinking. If counselors have learned anything over the years, it is that there are an infinite number of marital styles; and all of them may work for some couples some of the time. Clearly, the choice of yardsticks used to measure the quality of one's marriage is important. Moreover, it's quite likely that each spouse will be making those measurements from a different starting place, and thus disagreeing on results. A good example of this happened recently during a young couple's preliminary counseling interview:

MARCIA LASSWELL: How do you see your marriage, Sue?

WIFE: I think it's in a rut. Everything's scheduled, predictable, routine. I once heard a rut defined as a "grave with no end to it."

ML: That does sound pretty bad . . .

HUSBAND: I've heard Sue say that before. But I don't feel our life is that deadly. I think of it more as being in a groove.

ML: That's an interesting distinction, Dave. "In a groove" certainly sounds better than a "grave with no end."

H: A groove is comfortable, secure. I need to know what I can count on . . . what's going to happen next.

w: And I see it as confining and dull!

ML: So, what's a rut to you, Sue, is a groove to Dave. You each see the quality of your marriage differently. But at least we've established that you are both talking about the same problem, and that's something.

Since Dave and Sue arc not yet able to understand nor ready to accept each other's outlook, where do they go from here in assessing their relationship? A sensible next step is to search their own emotional centers more objectively. Each person is, after all, the world's leading expert on what he or she requires from life in order to be satisfied.

Thus, a sound technique for analyzing your marriage is to analyze your needs, your wants, and your expectations.

Satisfaction in and from marriage depends to a considerable degree on three basic factors:

- How much of what you *need* are you getting?
- How much of what you *want* are you receiving?
- How much of what you *expect* actually comes to pass?

It is not being selfish to focus this much attention on your needs, wants, and expectations. The health of a marriage depends on the extent to which they are met by each partner.

Let's talk first about needs. A need, by definition, is something you *have* to have. It is imperative, compelling. I may desperately need you to hold and talk to me every time I wake with anxiety at three in the morning. There is nothing "right" or "wrong," "sensible" or "ridiculous," about the fact of that need. Those questions arise only when it comes to discussing whether you really are obliged to go through marriage doing that.

All of us share basic physical needs: food, shelter, sex. But each of us has a host of personal emotional needs. To name just a few: acceptance by those who matter to us, caring and affection, having someone to share our good and bad fortune, having our self-image validated by others, being free to be our own person. Some of these needs may stay with us for a lifetime; others may diminish or disappear; still others may develop as we change and grow.

Counting on each other to meet these various needs is the basis for marital dependency. If you can meet all or most of your needs by yourself, or at least without your partner, there is a minimum of dependency. The more you *have* to have from each other, the greater the dependency. It may well be that some couples stay together precisely for this reason: they are so mutually dependent that they can't imagine living apart. If the other aspects of their marriage are satisfying, there is no problem. But it is easy to see how, under certain circumstances, such dependency could keep a couple bound in mutual misery.

Clearly, then, the amount of satisfaction you get from your marriage is determined in large part by how well you and your partner agree to meet certain of each other's needs. It also depends on the degree of opportunity and encouragement you get from each other to meet some of your *own* needs, such as the freedom to seek individual growth. (We'll discuss this further in Chapter 12 on "liberated" marriages.)

Yet even the most loving partner may not be aware of an important need you have. Or, though aware of it, may not comprehend its importance to you. Or, knowing its importance, may not be willing to meet it. Or, willing, may be unable to meet it. That's why self-analysis—finding out what your needs are, how well your partner meets them, or how much he or she frustrates you in meeting your own—can yield a significant assessment of your marriage.

Sue, the wife who thought of her married life as "a grave with no end," learned this in a subsequent counseling session:

WIFE: I can't live this kind of humdrum existence. Every day is just like the one before. Get the kids off to school, go to a job that's routine, come home, eat, watch TV, and go to bed. The big excitement of the week may be a movie, if I'm lucky.

HUSBAND: We go out to dinner sometimes; and you play bridge once a week while I baby-sit. . . . And we went camping just last month.

MARCIA LASSWELL: We've already discussed how differently you two view your marriage structure. For each of you to rehearse why it is bad or isn't so bad won't solve the problem.

H: Well, do you think Sue has it so bad?

ML: Dave, what I think is irrelevant since I'm not married to either of you. I can't judge what's enough variety for Sue, or how much would make you uncomfortable. What we have to do is find out what *Sue needs* and what *you need,* and if you can help each other, and if you can each satisfy some of those needs on your own. Other than your basic physical needs, what *do* you need, Sue?

W: Well, what comes to mind is some variety—some surprises. I wish Dave would not be so predictable.

ML: Let's not get into what you *wish* or *want* just yet. Let's stick to what you *have* to have. How much variety is essential and how much does Dave have to provide for you to continue to live with him?

At this point Sue had considerable difficulty giving up her attempts to blame Dave for her boredom and to focus on just what it was she had to have. Sue gradually began to realize that she was not sufficiently aware of the difference between her needs and her wants. Indeed, she sometimes confused the two completely. This put Dave in a difficult position. He not only had a different notion of the kinds of satisfactions their marriage should provide, but his wife wasn't even sure what it was she had to have to *be* satisfied.

Confusing needs with wants is a common failing. In analyzing yourself and your marriage, however, it is a perilous trap. It is essential for effective self-counseling to make a clear distinction between the two.

There's a tendency to think of needs as substantial, authentic, verifiable; and to consider wants as capricious and unrealistic. But just as some needs may be unrealistic yet nevertheless essential to the person who has them, so unrealistic wants may be equally urgent. To dismiss a want as "unrealistic" before you know what lies behind it is in itself unrealistic. Indeed, to learn to distinguish between realistic and unrealistic wants is a significant step in self-analysis. And since wants are usually more unmet in marriage than needs, it is important to know more about them.

When Sue says she wishes Dave were less predictable, she is actually saying she wants him to change so they can have a different kind of life together. This may be selfish or unreasonable on her part—and it is certainly unrealistic—but to deny that it is what she *wants* is not going to solve their difficulties. A person's wishes must be acknowledged as an integral part of the problem-solving approach to marital conflict. This holds true even when they are what might be called "negative" wants—perhaps the most irritating sort. Many people want something but cannot tell you what it is. They are "not happy the way things are" . . . "something is missing," but they cannot pin-point it. They can, however, talk at length about what they *don't* want. Psychologist Erik Erikson understood this when he developed the concept of "negative identity" to describe a stage we pass through on our way toward establishing a positive self-image. An adolescent, for example, who violently announces he doesn't want to be like his parents, or their generation, has a firm negative identity well before he has an alternative set of personal goals or values. So with Sue. She does not want Dave to be predictable. But she cannot be specific or positive about what she wants him to do:

MARCIA LASSWELL: What is "less predictable," Sue? Describe for me how you would like Dave to act.

WIFE: Just not—so—predictable. *You know!*

ML: No, I don't know. Do you, Dave?

HUSBAND: I guess she means I should be a surprise a minute, and dreaming up new things. Hell, what do you want, Sue?

W: See, that's the problem. He even wants me to tell him how to get out of his rut!

H: *I'm* not in a rut—*you're* the one complaining!

ML: You *are* the one complaining, Sue, and until we know what you want we won't know if the problem can be solved. It may turn out that Dave will see your point and that you both will agree your position is valid. But until you let us know more concretely how Dave can meet your wishes, we aren't going to know if he can or will do it.

This "negative want"—"I know how I don't want it to be but I don't know how I want it to be"—must be converted to a positive statement before new goals can be set or a relationship improved. Concretizing your wants—no matter how unrealistic, selfish, or unlikely-to-be-granted they may seem—is essential to a clear analysis of any areas of dissatisfaction in your marriage.

Even positive wants tend to be highly generalized and need to be pinned down with as much relevant detail as possible. A technique many counselors use to accomplish this is fantasy. This does not mean indulging in idle visions of castles in Spain, of a handsome stranger appearing to "take you away from all this." In a therapist's office fantasizing is "guided"—that is, focused on those aspects of marriage which are causing the dissatisfactions. Thus, when Sue complains that she is the one who always has to suggest going out, and that she has to plan social activities, the guided fantasy is used to help her pin-point what she wants:

MARCIA LASSWELL: Sue, let's imagine that it is Friday and you want to do something interesting on the weekend with Dave. But you don't want to suggest or plan it. Now, if you could have him behave any way you'd like when he comes home from work, how would your fantasy make it?

WIFE: Anything I want? Well, this would never happen . . .

ML: Don't worry about that. It's your fantasy, so you're writing the script. Anything can happen.

W: Okay. He'd come in the door, and he'd look pleased about something. He'd kiss me and say: "Let's go out to dinner." We would go to a place he's heard about that is good—nothing fancy, but good. He says he'll call the sitter while I get changed. So we go and it *is* good food and we laugh a lot (Sue's fantasy winds down) . . .

ML: Then what happens?

W: You mean I can have more?

ML: Let's do the whole weekend. Make it a dream come true for you.

Sue continued for nearly forty-five minutes while Dave listened with mixed reactions. He later reported that at different times he felt anger, sadness, hope, excitement, relief. He was surprised when Sue's fantasy weekend included sex more often than they usually had it; a walk in the park, which he also enjoys; going to a movie with their children; and a good amount of time alone so that he, too, could have his valued privacy. Dave's feelings of relief—and hope—grew out of his realization that Sue's fantasy wasn't as demanding of him as he had feared.

The following week it was Dave's turn to fantasize a weekend. His instructions were to disregard Sue's fantasy and to make his exactly the way *he* would like it. Dave had trouble imagining what he would want to do. Later therapy showed that this was a part of the couple's over-all problem. Dave not only liked his "groove," but his uninspired imagination kept him from thinking of ways to get out of it temporarily—even though he tried to do so as an "emotional gift" to Sue. Some of the activities Dave did fantasize included two which the couple had enjoyed in the past. However, both were ones Sue had originally suggested. Clearly, the familiar was more comfortable for Dave; he didn't *want* to be unpredictable. At this point the couple's problem was far from being solved, but at least in creating and listening to their fantasies both Sue and Dave knew more specifically what each wanted.

You can use guided fantasizing in both self-analysis and self-counseling. Actually, you probably already do so without realizing it. Daydreaming, conjuring up wish-fulfillments is often condemned as time-wasting escapism. Sometimes it *is* an escape from reality. But there's nothing wrong with that; done in moderation it is psychically beneficial. The average person seldom has exotic fantasies. Most of them—especially if they are centered or guided—are projections of reasonably realistic possibilities. As such, they provide a valuable way to get in touch with wishes we have repressed, with wants we are only dimly aware we have. When a guided fantasy is consciously recalled and discussed between husband and wife, it can be a valuable aid to marital problem-solving.

The third base on which marital satisfaction rests, along with needs and wants, is *expectations*. In the context of this chapter we define expectation not as mere hope, nor even anticipation; we use the word in the sense of *counting upon* something to be done, automatically *assuming* a certain event or reaction will—or will not—occur.

Everyone has a set of expectations for his or her own behavior, for a spouse's behavior, for marriage itself. They are a product of everything we have seen and heard and read, of how we were brought up, of our goals and dreams and values—and all, of course, strained through the filter of our unique psyche. Expectations range from the modest—"My spouse will always try to be considerate of my feelings"—to the monumental—"My wife will always be ready for sex," or "My husband will never complain about how I spend money." When expectations become too grandiose, too unrealistic to be fulfilled, a marriage heads toward trouble. Indeed, perhaps the main conflicts that arise in the first year or so of marriage result from one or both partners' expectations that the marriage in and of itself would produce instant bliss . . . that one's spouse would meet *all* of one's needs and wants (and expectations!).

We are conditioned to have many expectations of marriage. Surveys show, for example, that, for the most part, young men and young women both assume (wrongly) that "love" will overcome all problems. At the other end of the scale both sexes also tend to take it for granted (this time rightly) that husbands are permanently responsible for taking out the garbage. But these are exceptions to the unfortunate truth that most couples frequently do *not* share a uniform set of expectations. Moreover, there are other unfortunate truths. A person may not know about the other's expectations. Knowing, he or she may be unable to understand or accept them as realistic. Even if one *can* accept an expectation as valid, one may be incapable of meeting it.

Unfulfilled expectations are often at the core of marital disillusionment. It may result from the build-up of a series of minor expectations that are left dangling time and again; or from one huge disappointment. As with needs and wants, your approach to expectations must be examined if you are going to analyze your relationship effectively. It is not as difficult as you may think to discover how you and your partner deal with expectations. Answering and discussing the following questions will help you to get started.

Do you know what expectations you really have of your marriage and your partner? Most people do not—because they have never bothered to think consciously about them, or because they are unwilling to acknowledge them. Yet it is what we do not know and will not admit that causes trouble. Getting our expectations out in the open, to ourselves and to each other, sets up choices for action: 1) we can judge which ones are reasonable and which are not; 2) we can agree to try to satisfy the former and discard the latter; 3) we can decide to hang on to all of them and hope for the best; 4) we can change some of our expectations.

Do you know each other's expectations? If not, how can either of you possibly meet them? If the answer is yes—but the expectations have gone unmet—the way is opened for a discussion of the reasons why.

How unrealistic are your expectations? Not until they make a written or verbal list do some people become aware that their expectations are absurd, impracticable, unattainable. Can you admit that you have been expecting marriage to provide total happiness? All the money you want? Lots of freedom but also total security? Continuingly exciting sex? Privileges and perquisites without responsibilities?

Do you have an open-ended "expectation schedule" that makes it difficult for you ever to be satisfied? "I'll really be happy when I get a better job," a man says. He gets it. "I'll really be happy when I become a vice-president of the company." He does. "I'll really be happy when I make a million dollars." He makes it. "I'll really be happy when I can retire." He retires. "I'll really be happy when I find something interesting to do with my time—"

The fact is that this mythical but typical man will never permit himself to be happy because he always has another expectation waiting to be fulfilled. The syndrome, of course, is not limited to men. "I'll really be happy when we have a child," a woman says. A child is born. "I'll really be happy when we can move to a house in the country." They move. "I'll really be happy when Bobby's old enough to be in school all day." He goes. "I'll really be happy when—"

Are you sufficiently in touch with your expectations to know whether or not they are being met? The quickest way to get in touch is to pay attention to how often you feel angry, hurt, disgusted, or generally upset with your husband or wife. These emotions usually are clear signals that you expected something you didn't get—or got something you didn't expect. When you are aware of negative feelings ask yourself: What is it I expected just then? An illustration from a counseling session may help to crystallize this process for you:

MARCIA LASSWELL: How did the week go for the two of you?

WIFE (turns to husband): Well, why don't you tell her, Doug? You're the one who got so mad.

HUSBAND: We had a real blowup. I came home from work one night absolutely down. You know, I have this new sales job and I thought I was doing Okay at it. Well, the manager called me in and damn near chewed my head off. Said I'd better get on the ball, or else. . . . That was bad enough, but later the same afternoon we got a memo with higher sales quotas for every man. I mean, if I'm not selling enough to keep the boss happy now, how am I going to do it with the new quotas?

ML (as husband falls silent): Then what happened?

W: Then he came home!

H: Yeah . . . Well, I was going to stop on the way for a beer with two guys from the office. But I figured if I'm out of a job soon I'll need every penny I've got. Better not waste it on beer.

ML: In other words, Doug, you were feeling sorry for yourself . . . martyring yourself.

H (startled): I suppose you could say that. I didn't think of it that way. So I came home and told Carole the whole story— and she just sat there and looked at me. Looked at me rather coldly, too, I must say.

ML: It sounds as if you expected something else. Do you have certain expectations for how she should behave under such conditions?

H: No, I didn't expect her to behave any particular way.

ML: Then why did you get mad?

H: Who wouldn't get mad? I come home with these problems and my wife just *looks* at me? Not a word of sympathy? Not a word of encouragement? She always used to be so understanding when something went wrong for me, when I was depressed.

ML: Is that correct, Carole?

W: I was Old Faithful. Always in there pitching with "Isn't that awful!" or "How can they treat you that way?" or "Things will get better."

ML: And this time—?

w: This time I just couldn't take it any more. I love Doug, and I'm an understanding wife, I think. But Doug expects sympathy by the bucketful, and I've about run out of it. At least for little office hassles. I don't think Doug's job is in danger. I think the manager is just trying to light a fire under him, but that's part of sales work. I used to do it, too, so I know.

ML: Don't you think you owed Doug some expression of your feeling?

w: If he wants to *talk* about the situation, fine. If he just wants to cry on my shoulder and be patted, forget it.

ML (to Doug): It seems clear to me that you *did* expect Carole to go through the motions of being sympathetic. When she didn't, you got angry because your expectations were not met. More than that, when she looked at you "coldly" you got something you *didn't* expect.

h: Well, that was hitting below the belt, as bad as I felt.

ML: Doug, it isn't pleasant to have an expectation unmet. Especially when you are accustomed to having it met. But now we know what you did expect, and how Carole felt about it. Maybe we can talk about other things both of you expect— perhaps without realizing it—and which aren't being fulfilled.

(Unmet expectations are such a common source of stress in marriage—especially when you set them up deliberately—that we'll talk more about them in other chapters.)

THE LIFE-CYCLE OF MARRIAGE

When a baby starts saying "no" to everything . . . when a little girl experiments with mascara . . . when a teen-ager becomes rebellious—we say, calmly if possible, that "it's only a phase." It is accepted that children go through "stages" of life as they grow up, and we know each stage has its charms and its drawbacks, its idiosyncrasies and crises. We are also beginning to realize, through the findings of psychologists and sociologists, that adults go through stages too: the venturesome twenties, the career-building and family-building thirties, the "middle-age crises" of the forties and fifties, the adjustment to retirement and mortality of the later years. These adult "phases"—linked as they are to the external happenings in our lives—form the marital life-cycle. It provides a totally different but equally important perspective from which to analyze your marriage.

"How old are you? How long have you been married? When was your first child born? How old are your children now? Are your parents living? What work do you do? Is this your first marriage or a remarriage?" When a counselor asks these questions he or she is not going through routine motions, filling out a form for form's sake. The information is important because it indicates the developmental stage of your marital life-cycle, and because it provides potentially valuable insights into *why* certain problems exist. For different as every marriage is, similar tensions tend to arise at similar stages in most of them.

Sociological studies have proven this to be true time and again. Here are some examples:

- Parents of young children show a marked drop in the amount of time they spend conversing with each other, and a similar decline in social activities.
- Couple-interests and couple-activities fall off as a man or woman rises to more responsible job levels.
- Arguments over money tend to increase as a family's income increases.
- Sexual infidelity is more likely to occur when a man or woman reaches the late-middle years.
- All measurements of "marital happiness" begin to drop when a couple has children, and do not go up again until the last child leaves home.

None of these findings is particularly startling if you think about them logically. We mention them only to show that the life-cycle stage you and your spouse are in can have a substantial impact on the state of your marriage. (Moreover, there are short-term fluctuations *within* each stage. Each person goes through a complex rhythm of biological and psychological cycles—"ups" and "downs" which exaggerate the good and bad experiences of the day or week or month. All marriages have peaks, but they cannot be sustained; all marriages have troughs, but they pass. It's important not to let memory make the present unduly wonderful—or terrible—by contrast.)

And all of this holds true for all couples regardless of differences in economic or social status, occupation, education, personality. In other words, certain phases of marriage tend to create certain difficulties no matter how husband and wife feel about each other. However, not every couple will experience the same kinds of stresses at exactly the same stage. (That is especially true if your marital pattern is atypical: if, for instance, there is a considerable age difference between you and your partner; or if either of you has been previously married; or if you are childless.) But if you both wed in your early twenties (the national average for age at first marriage is twenty-one for women and twenty-three for men) and you are still wed to the same person, these sketches of marital life-cycle stages will provide a valid basis for analysis.

From twenty-two to twenty-eight: Enthusiasm for life and the desire to prove oneself as a capable person usually combine to help ward off disappointments. Couples are buoyed up by tomorrow's potentials and do not overly dwell on the past. Marital conflicts are most likely to center on in-laws, money management, outside friendships retained from one's single days, and the stresses of caring for young children. These problems are more likely to affect couples who have not successfully broken away from their parents, and who have not developed the emotional independence needed to live intimately with another person.

From twenty-nine to thirty-two: A particularly difficult transitional stage in the life-cycle of both partners. A woman, usually busy caring for her family, often feels "trapped." A man finds it is not so easy as he thought to support a growing family, but he is also "trapped" by the need to keep his job and struggle for advancement. The desire to escape these traps can often involve a husband or wife in an extra-marital affair. For both sexes thirty seems to be the age when one feels one has crossed the line between "youth" and "middle age." Since it is extremely hard to understand a spouse's emotional crises, husband and wife are apt to blame each other for their troubles. Children, too, contribute to the marital "distancing" that occurs at this stage, but childless couples experience it as well. Because this stage usually arrives about seven years or so after marriage it has acquired the folklore label of "the seven-year itch."

From thirty-three to thirty-nine: A more settled period. The children are growing, spouses are working to build financial security and family unity. A basically good marriage has by this time evolved methods of minimizing conflict and sharing responsibilities. However, tensions may begin to ferment over differences in values and goals. There may be jockeying for "power"—for control of family decisions. But both spouses are so busy with work, children, social, and community activities that these conflicts usually remain beneath the surface of the relationship. At this stage, too, spouses may feel lonely, alienated from each other. This may lead to an extra-marital affair—but more likely the "affair" will be with one's job or with the PTA.

From forty to forty-three: Another stressful transition period. The children are now teen-agers—busy with their own lives and often rebellious toward parents. Half of all women in this age group go to work, but few have emotionally rewarding jobs. Men begin to realize they have gone about as far as they will go in their careers. Both men and women must come to grips with "getting older"; it's natural to feel a growing desire to get more out of life, to make up for what they have "missed." Often the alienation process that began in the previous stage comes into the open and couples become emotional strangers. There is an urge to question old values, to start over. All in all, this can be an explosive stage when a person is apt to behave in unexpected ways. (A large age difference between spouses can ease the tensions since they will not be experiencing the same emotional crises at the same time.)

From forty-four to fifty-three: For those who survive the earlier upheaval this can be a calm and peaceful stage. With the children gone and on their own, couples move back toward each other. Marital satisfactions rise. Money pressures tend to lessen as tuition and mortgage payments draw to an end. But these years are not without their characteristic stresses. For some couples there is the beginning of concern about *their* aging parents. For others, the absence of children who held them together merely emphasizes the emptiness of the marital relationship. Women who never developed outside-the-home interests feel unneeded and depressed.

Menopause, the male climacteric, fears about aging—these combine to cause concern about sexual performance, or lead to a search for new and more "exciting" bed-partners.

From fifty-four to sixty-five: Called by many the "mellowing" stage. Husband and wife seek companionship and empathy from each other. Conflict arises most often from the failure of a spouse to provide this emotional support. Occasionally a couple who have stayed together to this stage *despite* a long series of unresolved conflicts may find their problems suddenly come to a head and can no longer be ignored or controlled.

Analyzing a marriage in terms of the life-cycle stage it has reached is one way to remind (or reassure) yourself that what you may think are unusual problems—or tensions unique to yourselves—are fairly commonplace. It can also serve to alert you to conflicts that may be out-of-phase. This "early warning" signal may help you to take them more seriously or to deal with them more promptly. The fundamental point is that marriage is a highly flexible institution. A satisfying relationship at one stage may become troubled at another—only to rebound still later. Continued satisfaction over a lifetime together requires a willingness to adjust to this flexibility—to be resilient enough to meet the marital cycle's changing demands and opportunities.

DESIGNS FOR MARITAL MODELS

Another way to assess why your marriage is giving or withholding satisfactions is to analyze it in terms of marital "styles." Few marriages, of course, fit neatly into any single type. But by familiarizing yourself with the variety of categories and classifications experts have identified, you may be able to find the one most similar to yours.

Some couples, for example, see their marriage in terms of sex-identity roles. These are largely tradition oriented relationships where the wife's "role" is to be homemaker and the husband's to be breadwinner. When most marriages followed this pattern, and when society reinforced it with approval, it offered a good deal of security and satisfaction. Today, as we know, many couples denounce this pattern as sexist, or as limiting to personal growth.

A person carrying out a role he or she no longer believes in is going to find this style of marriage unrewarding and in need of change.

Other types of marital models reflect the emotional make-up of the people in them. For instance, marriages have been classified as "task-oriented" versus "relationship-oriented." In the former, husbands and wives are primarily concerned with efficient performance of the chores of marriage: earning money, raising children, keeping house. In the latter, they are primarily concerned with exploring and improving the emotional links between them. It is more important, these couples say, to talk together than to scrub the kitchen floor; to take a holiday together than to save money for a new kitchen appliance. Perhaps the most elaborate and best-known typology of marriage was constructed several years ago by sociologists John F. Cuber and Peggy Haroff. They postulated five categories:

1. The "devitalized" marriage, a placid but half-alive match without enough emotional involvement on the part of either spouse to lead to conflict or to passion.

2. The "conflict-habituated" marriage, in which the couple fight constantly but seem to enjoy the battling (indeed, are hardly able to do without it).

3. The "passive-congenial" marriage, a comfortable relationship with few ups or downs. Each partner has many personal interests, and their marriage is largely a pleasant convenience.

4. The "total" marriage, characterized by constant togetherness and mutual interests. All experiences are supposed to be shared. The closeness of this marital unit makes for an intense—but dangerously fragile—relationship. A single conflict, perhaps due to the changing life-cycle, may shatter it. In addition, it limits individual growth.

5. The "vital" marriage, in which the partners are highly involved in each other's interests but are not locked into the restrictive imperatives of the "total" marriage. It has been described as a marriage in which reasonably well-adjusted people are willing to take the risks involved in revealing themselves meaningfully to each other.

Nine Significant Questions and Answers

As a final step in analyzing your marriage, here are nine questions that can bring out a number of significant but often-overlooked facets of your relationship. Each of you—*without consulting the other or discussing the questions together*—should write down your answers in as much detail as possible before going on to compare them with our observations.

1. If you could be doing anything you want, anywhere you want, with anyone you want, how would you like your life to be five years from now?
2. Do you make a distinction between loving someone and being *in* love with someone?
3. List five loving things you have done for your spouse in the past month.
4. List five things he or she has done for you in the past month for which you have felt appreciative.
5. What first attracted you to your wife/husband?
6. When you are separated for any length of time, do you write and telephone each other often?
7. When was the last time that the two of you went away for a weekend or longer together?
8. Are most of your friends in marriages that you consider to be satisfactory and stable?
9. Do you view life positively or negatively?

1. We've already mentioned how useful fantasy can be in revealing your real needs and wants. The theme of your fantasy answer may be a useful clue to the satisfaction you get—or do not get—from your marriage. If the "five-year plan" *includes* your partner, this is one of the best predictors that a relationship will continue to grow. Counselors believe that couples whose plans, real or fantasied, include each other retain the essential ingredient for marital success.

2. Every therapist has heard over and over, "I love him (or her) but I'm not *in* love." Just what this means is hard to put into

words. Obviously, some feeling is missing when a person says he or she is not "in" love. But research shows that each of us has our own definition of what love is. Some people think being "in" love is a vestige of adolescent romanticism that should yield with maturity to just plain "love." Others think it isn't possible to remain "in" love after the normal disappointments and conflicts of years of living together. (In Chapter 9 we'll take a more detailed look at what people mean by love, and have a questionnaire to help you find your approach to it.)

3./4.   If you cannot recall five loving acts performed by you or for you during the past month, you need to reassess the extent to which you really are thoughtful, considerate partners. One of the first "homework" assignments a marital therapist would give you is: Do at least one loving thing for your spouse every day.

5.   When a marriage is not going well, spouses often forget what first attracted them to each other. Obviously there was a time when you had common interests, shared common goals, did things together that you both enjoyed. Recalling them—perhaps even reviving some of them in actuality—often has a tonic effect. Most important is the realization that much of what originally drew you together is still there to be used constructively.

6.   Couples who communicate well are seldom willing to let physical separation stop them from exchanging news or feelings. Some people even make notes during the day of things they want to remember to put in a letter, to mention in a phone conversation. Couples who have difficulty communicating are likely to take advantage of separation to retreat further into their private shells.

7.   If it is very long since you went on a trip, you may be unwittingly *avoiding* the prospect of being alone together. Or you may have to face the fact that your tastes in holidays are so different as to be mutually incompatible, and perhaps you *should* consider separate vacations. You may be overly child-centered—or you may simply be using concern for the children as an excuse not to be alone with your spouse.

8.   Having friends whose marriages are in trouble can often affect your own. Perhaps you are concentrating on what's wrong in your relationship because so many people around you are doing the same thing. Perhaps you would secretly like to "be free" and the example of a friend's divorce becomes alluring. Conversely,

couples who have good and flourishing marriages can serve as models for working out problems of adjustment. In a way, it's like playing tennis: If you want to improve your game you play with someone whose technique and skills are better than yours, not someone whose game is worse.

9. A pessimistic view of life wastes energy. Worse, it often leads to what sociologists call "self-fulfilling prophecies." That means that if you constantly *see* yourself as unhappy or disappointed, you are more likely to set up conditions that will actually *make* you more unhappy and disappointed. If you look for injustices you are more likely to find them. If you expect to have an argument, you probably will. Realistic optimism works in reverse. A change in this kind of perspective can make the same marriage look quite different.

Knowing—within all these general limits—what kind of marriage you *have* can be a starting point for thinking about what kind of a marriage you *want*. No one of the patterns we've outlined is considered "ideal." None is a guarantee of marital happiness or marital success. What is important is to find a style of marriage that works for you. It is equally important to learn whether the style you have does *not* work for you—and, if so, how to go about learning why it doesn't and how you can change it. The rest of this book is designed to help you achieve those two goals.

3

HOW YOU CAN DO
WHAT A COUNSELOR DOES—I
Identifying the Problem

When a couple visits a marriage counselor for the first time there is one question the clients are virtually sure to ask. We've heard the scenario play itself out the same way in hundreds of initial interviews. The wife and husband, once over the hurdle of being in a counselor's office at all, plunge into a recital of what they believe is wrong in the marriage—complete with hand-picked examples of real or alleged marital misconduct. Then, as if their responsibilities were over, the clients sit back, fix the counselor with a hopeful gaze, and ask The Question: "What should we do now?"

Even though a counselor knows The Question is on its way— that it is natural for a troubled person to want to be told some magic words, given some magic recipe that will solve the problem —it always means the client must be told: There is no magic. For while a counselor is often compared to a doctor, dealing in sick marriages rather than sick bodies, the parallel is false. A doctor gives advice and prescribes remedies. With rare exceptions, a counselor can do neither.

This comes as a surprise to most people who seek help. Their single biggest misconception about the process of marital therapy is that the counselor will tell them what to do. But professional counselors have always been aware that their primary function is quite different—indeed, much harder.

In the words of Emily H. Mudd, one of America's pioneering marital therapists, a counselor's task is to help a person or a couple "come to grips with their own problems so they can work them out themselves." One part of this job is to help a person begin to look at his or her marriage in a realistic and analytical way. Once this is accomplished, the counselor's function is to serve the client as a sounding board, a reflecting mirror, a catalyst—always making it clear that it is the spouses themselves who do the real therapeutic work of restoring marital harmony. Put another way, a counselor may be described as an objective observer who absorbs a picture of your marriage and then shows you how to view it from a new and more constructive perspective.

Marriage itself has been defined in many ways. Perhaps one of the most appropriate definitions (a bit cynical, perhaps, yet sympathetically understanding) was suggested by a colleague, Gerhard Neubeck, when he called it "the last stronghold of amateurism." Indeed, despite the spread of so-called "family-life" courses in high schools and colleges, most of us enter married life almost totally uneducated in its dynamics and untrained in the various delicate skills that make those dynamics work. We are but sketchily forewarned of marriage's subtle pitfalls; we are even less forearmed to avoid or to cope with them. Less specific knowledge is required to get a marriage license than to get a driver's license. It's hard to imagine taking on such an important commitment with so little preparation.

If this is so, it may seem paradoxical to suggest that amateurs should then embark on the process of self-counseling.

Yet everything that professionals have learned about making marriage work better incontrovertibly indicates that *the best marriage counseling is, in effect, self-counseling.* Consider, for example, these statements by two former presidents of the American Association of Marriage and Family Counselors:

> There is still considerable doubt whether . . . the interventional processes of counseling or therapy are effective at all as compared to the individual's effort in his or her own behalf. (*Gerhard Neubeck,* Professor of Family Social Science, University of Minnesota)

> The counselor's job is not to tell John or Mary what to do, but to help them find their own solutions. Only a solution that comes from them—out of their own thinking and feeling—is any use. (*David Mace,* Behavioral

Science Center, Bowman Gray Medical School, Winston-Salem, North Carolina)

Why is this so?

We think of husband and wife, traditionally, as being "joined" in matrimony. But apart from the legalities of the matter, that is largely a figure of speech. Marriage is a union, yes. But it is a union (especially nowadays) of individuals each with his and her own background, ideas, attitudes, needs, goals, dreams. The result is not so much a "joining"—with its implication of smoothly meshing separate personalities into one unit—as a "relationship"—with *its* implication of two diverse people trying to work out methods of bridging the differences that exist inherently between them. When we think of marriage this way we can better understand the original concept behind the word "therapy." While many tend to think of it as referring to deep psychological or psychiatric probing, the term actually derives from the Greek word *therapon*. As usual, the Greeks not only had a word for it but the definition is more significant than we realize. "Therapon" means "a comrade in a common struggle."

Certainly no struggle is more common than marriage, and no comrade closer than a wife or husband. Thus for spouses to work together on their relationship . . . to self-counsel . . . to be each other's therapist seems both logical and fitting. It is also likely to be highly effective when the necessary skills are mastered. Clearly, there are times and circumstances where the training and objectivity of a professional counselor are necessary to get useful results. Self-counseling may be impossible when a conflict has reached a crisis stage; when hostility is so deep-seated that any attempt to break through it is instantly turned away; or when a problem is so emotionally overwhelming that it paralyzes one's capacity for action.

For example, we know of a case involving a young husband who struggled for six years to try to save his marriage. He was helplessly in love (and for once this trite phrase seems to have been unfortunately true) with his strikingly beautiful but totally irresponsible and promiscuous wife. She had countless and blatant affairs. She would disappear for a night, a week, even several weeks. Each time she came back home she promised it would never happen again, and each time her husband forgave her. He covered up her escapades with family and friends. He made good the large debts she ran up. He tried to conceal from their young son the wife's disinterest in being a mother, and to compensate for it. But only a saint's tolerance does not reach the point of no return. After the umpteenth tearful reconciliation and promises to change, the wife began still another affair. At that, the man finally went to a counselor. After several sessions (in some of which the wife also took part) the husband began to be able to accept emotionally the realities he had always known but had refused to admit until the counselor spelled them out: that the woman he loved had serious problems, and that the only way to save himself and his son was either for her to get immediate psychotherapy or for him to end the marriage.

The tensions and conflicts most couples experience are far less traumatic. Moreover, the overwhelming majority are reality-connected rather than the result of psychic disturbances in one or the other partner. They grow not so much from internal crises as from external clashes; not so much from major breakdowns as from comparatively minor flaws. (Sometimes, of course, these can grow into major problems.)

Until relatively recent times most counselors ignored the fact that marital problems can stem from superficial conflicts. They tended to follow the lead of psychotherapists who believed it was vital to develop a client's insight into his unconscious, to make him or her find and confront hidden or repressed reasons for troubling behavior. But we agree with the current opinion that a person, or a couple, may waste time trying to understand *why* there is a problem. That time can be productively used to develop ways by which the problem—whatever its origins—can be overcome or eliminated. This does not mean that "understanding why" is not useful or sometimes even necessary. But it is at best a slow process and sometimes an impossible one.

Who knows why we do some of the things we do? Psycho-analysts may see patients several times a week for years to determine *why*. Most marriages in trouble can't wait this long! We know people who have been in therapy for years—working on a problem of spousal hostility, for instance—and week after week the probing goes on: Why does the husband hate his mother (which, let's say, has been diagnosed as the real cause behind his hostility to his wife)? Yet this endless poking about in his emotional underground seldom helps to change his actual behavior. A good many of that man's problems may indeed have their origin in his relationship with his mother. But the chances are far more likely that most of the tensions that disrupt that marriage arise out of the interplay between the spouses.

Indeed, some couples subconsciously use the old-fashioned "psychoanalytic" approach as a way of avoiding action or change. "As long as you're *discussing* things," the devil's advocate inside us cunningly suggests, "you don't actually have to *do* anything." Of course, there must be talk—to clarify the problems, to sort out attitudes, to plan action. But all the talk in the world will accomplish little if there is not also an effort to change behavior. Sometimes a marital therapist has to keep reminding a couple that action is what counts, that talking about a problem is easier than doing something about it. The following case from our files shows how one couple was afflicted with this tendency. They were at odds over a proposed visit by the wife's parents.

MARCIA LASSWELL: After our discussion last week, Helen, what did you and Joe do about your folks' plans to visit you?

WIFE: Nothing, really. I don't want them to come unless Joe will be nice to them. He won't promise that, so I haven't answered their letter yet. I don't know what they must be thinking.

HUSBAND: I don't like your parents. We've been through this a hundred times. Shall I go over the reasons again?

ML: Please don't. That doesn't help to solve the problem.

W: But *why* don't you like them? I mean the *real* reason underneath all your excuses. I think you're reacting to your own childhood—you don't like parents, mine *or* yours.

H: I *like* my parents! I just don't like *yours*.

W: I really think Joe has an authority problem. Can't we work on this?

ML: Helen, we've been over your diagnosis of the situation several times already. We could do it one more time but I think your conclusion would be the same—Joe's feelings run very deep. The real issue right now seems to me not to be to change

Joe's feelings nor your parents' behavior, but to work out a way you can relate to your parents as Joe's wife.

H: I think you've got a hang-up about staying tied to your parents, Helen. You need to grow up. Why don't we talk about *her* hang-up?

ML: Unless my memory fails me, I remember this topic came up before too. Helen thinks you've got a hang-up and you think Helen has a hang-up. But blaming each other does not help to reach an agreement on when and where Helen will be able to relate to her parents as a married woman.

W: I have to let them know soon. But I feel that if we could get at Joe's problem, things would work out.

ML: You could be right, Helen, but my estimate is that it would take several months to clear up these issues. If, in fact, they exist as you see them. Can your parents understand not hearing from you for several months?

W: No, I guess that would be bad. I'd like to work out a way to see them that Joe would be satisfied with.

ML: Joe, could you list, in order, your preferences for Helen's contacts with her parents? Would you start by preferring that she *never* see them?

H: Of course not. (Pausing to think) I'd probably like it if *she* went to see *them* . . . maybe twice a year.

ML: Then what would be your second preference? And third?

H: Well, maybe they could visit her when I'm away on a business trip. Or just don't get me involved or expect me to see much of them.

ML: You are giving us several options now, Joe. You're smiling, Helen. What's going on with you?

W: I never thought you'd give in that much, Joe.

ML: You haven't heard yet how much you're going to give in exchange, so better hold off on the smile. We're trying to solve a problem and you both will have to give a lot. Let's get on with a plan to handle your differences.

This case history shows one aspect of self-counseling in action: the counselor functioning as a helper and leader to keep the couple on the track of identifying a key problem in their relationship and figuring out a way to deal with it. But what about the great number of couples who, as we have seen, do not have ready access to a trained therapist? What about the couples who would prefer to explore and improve their relationship privately?

We believe that most husbands and wives can learn the fundamental techniques that counselors use to make marriages work better. We believe that most husbands and wives can then learn how to apply these techniques effectively to the needs of their own marriage. We believe that to a considerable extent you can do for yourself what a counselor would help you to do.

How You Can Do What a Counselor Does
Four Basic Keys

There are several basic keys to the principles of self-counseling. In this chapter, we shall talk about the four keys you can use in *diagnosing* or identifying marital problems. In the next chapter we shall discuss the keys that will show you how to begin dealing with those problems. In a sense, both of these chapters will provide you with a set of theories and techniques that form a basis for effective self-counseling. How these theories and techniques may be applied in greater depth and detail to various specific conflict situations will be explained in subsequent chapters.

The First Key: When a couple work with a counselor, the nature of that relationship automatically creates what is called a "therapeutic environment." With a special place—the counselor's office, usually—and a fixed time—the regularly scheduled counseling hour—to talk about their situation, a couple tend to be mentally and emotionally prepared to do so. Moreover, since they are paying for the counselor's time they don't want to waste any of it by getting into pointless or peripheral discussions (once they have learned how to avoid this pitfall). Some clients arrive with notes they have made to remind them about developments that occurred during the previous week, or questions they want to raise. Others "prepare" for the session by going over what they want to talk about while driving to their appointment, or they review what took place during the session while they drive back home. All of these elements contribute significantly to the degree of continuity and intensity that a couple can bring to the counseling experience.

A self-counseling couple can create a similar "therapeutic environment" for themselves by setting a special time and place for their own discussions and by sticking to them. They need to allow enough time for a thorough discussion; they need to prepare for it; and afterward they need to evaluate what was said. Uninterrupted privacy is also necessary.

This seems obvious enough, but it is amazing how many couples do not or cannot carry this out. They try to settle arguments at the dinner table with the children present; they get involved in debates at bedtime when both are exhausted. They raise issues of great importance just as one or the other is rushing off to work, or minutes before guests are expected. Most people seem unaware of the important role *timing* and *privacy* have in the resolution of problems. Self-counseling requires an emotional atmosphere conducive to calm discussion and careful thought, with enough time available to pursue a topic to a reasonable end, and with enough privacy to speak with total frankness. A couple experimenting with self-counseling should set up their own "appointment schedule." And they should choose a specific place—a room with doors that can be closed; their car; or if necessary, a secluded bench in the park. We have even recommended to couples that they rent a motel room for an afternoon, or borrow a friend's apartment while no one is at home. The telephone should be taken off the hook and the doorbell disconnected or ignored.

The Second Key: Most counselors set aside some time during the initial interview to take a client's personal and marital "history." This includes biographical data, family background, previous marital and sexual experiences. Some counselors like to have highly detailed information; others feel that only the essential facts are useful. We believe competent counseling of any kind depends on getting the facts that may have a bearing on the problem—and that it's not very likely a therapist can tell which facts *do* bear on it unless he or she has all of them. Rarely does a therapist make a mistake because of knowing too much. The reverse happens often.

Getting all the facts can be time-consuming when a crisis is at hand and one needs answers in a hurry. That's why couples who

keep their communication open, who know each other well, have a
head start on couples who are more like strangers to each other. In
regular marital therapy, couples are encouraged to begin the process of getting to know one another on their own between sessions.
One couple got this "homework assignment" from their therapist: spend one hour a week (not very much time, really) *getting
acquainted*. This couple had been wed nearly twenty years, but
had focused so much on their parenting functions that they called
each other "Mother" and "Dad." They never really had talked to
each other about personal thoughts and feelings. The "homework"
enabled them to learn many new things about each other that shed
light on their problems. In this instance the counselor was also trying to save precious counseling hours which might otherwise have
been spent trying to achieve this openness.

You can do this kind of homework on your own. Many couples live together for years discussing only such "important" things
as what time dinner will be and whether to get braces for the children's teeth. Set aside some quiet time on a regular and frequent
schedule to talk together about your deeper thoughts, your feelings, your dreams.

It is important for a self-counseling couple to explore each
other's life stories. This may seem an unnecessary step. After all,
you already know each other's history. But do you? Do you really
understand what makes your spouse act, or feel, or react in certain
ways? How often have you said to your husband or wife, in some
surprise, "I never knew that about you!" Or, "I had no idea you
would feel that way!" Even things partners *think* they know about
how the other feels may be far off base. A lot of "mind reading"
goes on in most marriages. What your partner doesn't tell you is
often guessed at, and then *acted* upon as if it were the truth. This
must have been part of what the famous analyst Alfred Adler had
in mind when he coined the term "fictional finalism." We often
make up information for which we have no background, he said,
and then we act upon it in a final way that makes it seem like truth
instead of fiction. The following case from our files illustrates this:

HUSBAND: What I don't understand is why you always interpret
  what I do in the worst possible light, Vickie. You *never* give
  me the benefit of a doubt.

MARCIA LASSWELL: We've talked before about how you tend to keep things to yourself, Jeff. When you don't tell Vickie what's going on with you, she has to make up her own story so she'll have something to go on.

H: Why does she always make up the worst possible story and get mad at me for it?

WIFE: I *don't* do that. You don't realize when I make up "good" stories because I don't get mad then.

ML: And when you make up good stories are you sometimes loving and supporting?

W: Of course. If I figure it out one way, I get mad or hurt; another way and I'm loving.

H: But when you get mad or hurt you've usually figured it out all wrong.

ML: You know how to fix that now, Jeff. The more correct information Vickie has to go on, the more accurate her conclusions will be. If you want her version to match yours, don't leave so much to her imagination.

Getting to know each other well depends a great deal on how much of yourself you are both willing to reveal. Most of us are not mind readers, and to understand complex human behavior you need to give each other the benefit of as much information as possible. This is especially true nowadays when Americans increasingly marry across all sorts of boundaries: religious, economic, social, geographical, ethnic. This makes getting to know each other a lot more complicated than it was when married couples usually grew up in similar environments. For most couples today, the divergence in their backgrounds is still not extreme—not an "either . . . or" matter. This is because people who feel strongly about a belief or a custom are usually too rigid in their viewpoints, or too hemmed in by their heritage, to become seriously involved with someone from a vastly different background. But there are still enough differences to complicate matters. Different "labels" (Catholic, Republican, etc.) don't necessarily mean people are really different, of course. A husband and wife in an interfaith marriage, for instance, may agree completely about spiritual values and moral systems. Or they may both be so *dis*interested in religion that the labels of faith they are tagged with are meaningless so far as causing tensions between them are concerned.

What is important is that both partners should know as much as possible about each other's backgrounds, about the way they grew up, about the lifestyles of their parents. There is a good deal of truth to the notion that how we act as wives or husbands—and how we expect our spouses to act—stems from the attitudes and behavior of our own parents. Take, for instance, a couple who argued continually about how they should divide household responsibilities. The husband's mother had always waited on her family like a servant. The wife's mother had worked outside the home and her father had willingly shared many chores. The young couple, as a result, continually traded accusations—"slave driver" . . . "lazy" . . . "male chauvinist" . . . "woman's libber."

It is amazing how the circumstances of one's background—even trivial or long-forgotten events—can years later haunt a marriage. A woman who had several more serious problems in her marriage seemed most upset by the fact that her husband failed to appreciate her skills as a gourmet cook. "He enjoys food," she told the counselor, "and I go to a lot of trouble making special dishes for him. But when I serve him chicken in a special cream sauce, or lobster bisque with just the right amount of sherry in it, he complains that I never give him meat loaf or potato soup. I am *sick* of hearing about the potato soup his mother used to make!"

She may have been sick of hearing about it, but it was certainly important for her to know about it. The husband had been brought up in a home where simple, earthy food was not only an economic necessity but a sign of love. Meat loaf and potato soup epitomized his mother's concern for her family's financial and emotional well-being. Later in life the husband came to appreciate more subtle and elegant dishes—but at a deeper emotional level he resented them as a "put-down" of his family. When the counselor suggested this might be a reason for his attitude, the man's response was vigorous, "That's it!" he said. "I couldn't explain it to my wife . . . but whenever she serves those fancy meals I get this feeling that she's saying, 'See, your parents couldn't afford to give you this . . . your mother couldn't cook a dish like this.'"

To begin to uncover some of these hidden troublemakers the

way a counselor does, therefore, you should use an early self-counseling session to begin the exchange with each other of all that you can think of about your backgrounds. This means more than just the facts. It means sharing that wealth of significant emotional material that is wrapped up in your dreams, goals, hopes, fears; in things you are proud of or ashamed of but in either event affect you as an adult and as a marital partner.

Here again it is important not only to speak honestly but to listen attentively and with respect to those qualities that make your partner unique. If you can do so without feeling self-conscious (or without making your partner self-conscious), you may want to make notes for future study and reference, or even tape-record your discussion. At first, your choice of what information to share will depend upon how much you already know or think you know about each other. You may want to begin by checking out for accuracy what you *think* you know. Then you may want to volunteer current thoughts or feelings, or stories from your past—maybe even something you've shared before but would like to talk about further. Each of you may have questions that will take these conversations deeper. Counselors often find it helpful to initiate such topics as:

- "Tell me about how you spent holidays when you were growing up."
- "What do you know about how your father and his father got along?" (Or mother/mother; mother/father; father/mother).
- "What are your favorite (or worst) memories about your mother?" (father)
- "If you could do anything you want this summer, what would you do?"
- "What do you really feel about your body image?"
- "If you could live it over again, what would you change about your life up to now?"

Questions should be asked in the spirit of caring and understanding, never to put your partner on the spot. The purpose is to get closer—not to drive between you a wedge of defensiveness. The same is true of what you tell—these are not meant to be "dumping" sessions where you hurt or depress each other. They are meant to give your partner new insight into some of your behavior and your goals.

The Third Key: A therapist tries to make both spouses see—and acknowledge—that a marital problem really does exist; and to realize exactly how—and how much—each contributes to it. Here is how a session with a client couple achieved those goals:

MARCIA LASSWELL: You both seem to be saying you don't have any problems. Yet you tell me you are here because you're unhappy. You are going to have to be more explicit before I can help you, I'm afraid.

WIFE: It's just that I feel depressed about us. We don't fight like lots of our friends do . . . but we don't enjoy each other, either.

HUSBAND: I find that I don't really want to come home from work. I look for excuses to stay late, or I volunteer to do the out-of-town jobs. Evenings at home are tense.

ML: Sometimes the best way to pin-point a problem is to focus on how you would like things to be.

W: But how?

ML: First, we need to know how each of you would define a pleasant evening together. How do you see it? Second, what is each of you willing to do to make this happen. One of your problems, as I see it, is that each of you is waiting for the other to do something first. Someone has to break the pattern. How about you, Phil?

H: Okay, I'll start with my version of how I'd like things to be. I'm not sure how you're going to like this, Sandy, but maybe I won't like your version either.

Phil described how he would like Sandy to behave toward him on a typical evening at home and how he would like to react. Sandy, in turn, gave her version of a happy evening together. Their ideas were not as far apart as they thought. The second step—volunteering what each would do to facilitate such a relationship—took much longer to work out. Finally, they were able to agree that their major problem was "waiting each other out" so as not to be the first to make a positive move. Once they saw how futile this was they could move ahead more co-operatively.

The third significant key to effective self-counseling, then, is for a couple to work through to the point where both can agree that a real problem does face them; that each one is at least partially contributing to it; and that each must take some action to help solve it. Here is a practical example of how a couple can accomplish this for themselves:

HUSBAND: I feel you've been distant all weekend. What's wrong?

WIFE: Nothing. I'm tired, I guess.

H: Maybe . . . but it seems like something more than that. If you're upset, I'd rather hear about it than have this uneasy feeling of waiting for an explosion.

W: There's no use talking about it. It's the same thing I'm always upset about. Talking doesn't change anything. You don't listen or do anything different.

H: Oh . . . I guess you mean my blowing up at the kids Friday night?

W: Yes. You have a way of ruining what starts out to be a nice family time nearly every week. I'm getting to the point where I think you don't even like the children.

H: You know how they get on my nerves when I'm tired and they start bickering. I'm not always like that; just when I'm tired.

W: You're tired most of the time. You work too hard. When we try to get you to relax you're like a bear with the kids. They're getting to dread Friday nights.

H: Maybe I ought to cut down, find some time to unwind. But you could do something that would help: don't insist on having family night on Fridays. That's the worst night you could pick.

W: You never mentioned that before. Sure, we could do it another night . . . if you'd try to be civil. I get so mad at you. But nothing I've said before made any difference.

H: When you yell at me I just clam up. This time it was different. I guess we should remember to talk these things over when we're both in the right frame of mind. I know there's a problem and I'm willing to work on it if you're willing to let me off the hook on Friday nights.

This couple not only waited to talk about their conflict until tempers were down and they were relaxed, but they both acknowledged that *they*—not just one of them—had a problem. It may sound overly simplistic to say both persons must *acknowledge* that a conflict exists, or that a relationship can be improved. After all, don't we *know* when something is wrong or missing in a marriage? Not necessarily. Time and again counselors hear couples go through this typical exchange:

WIFE: What I really can't stand is the way my husband ———. It's gotten to the point where ———.

HUSBAND (honestly surprised): I never knew that! Why didn't you tell me you felt that way?

W: Tell you? I've told you a million times. You never listen.

She may be right. Perhaps he doesn't listen. Or perhaps he listens but does not *hear*. There is a vast difference between the two. For example, a woman says that to please her husband, who had been complaining about the pile of magazines and old clothes that cluttered their attic, she arranged to have it all carted away. "I was telling him about it one evening and he kept nodding and saying uh-huh and oh, yes. I was a little miffed that he wasn't more pleased. Then, a couple of days later, he said, 'Are you ever going to do anything about that junk in the attic?' I was furious. He hadn't heard one word I said!"

Listening, in marriage, involves more than merely registering sounds and acknowledging them with "uh-huh" or grunts. It means paying attention to what is said. More important, it means interpreting what you hear and responding to it appropriately. *Most* important, it means seeking out the unspoken messages that often lie beneath the words. Counselors call this "listening for *process*." You can learn to do this, too, by heightening your sensitivity to the emotional nuances underneath the surface phrases. For instance:

HUSBAND: The weather is certainly beautiful this weekend. I suppose I ought to take advantage of it and take down the storm windows and put up the screens . . .

He lets the end of the sentence hang in the air, waiting for his wife's response. Does he want her to tell him to forget the chore and enjoy the day? Or does he want her to encourage him to get the job over with?

Depending on how good (or concerned) a listener she is, she may make one of several responses:

- "That would be nice . . . the house is like an oven these days."
- "It's up to you, whenever you feel like doing it."
- "You'd rather play tennis, wouldn't you? Well, if the windows stay up another week we'll manage."
- "It's a rotten job, but I know it has to be done. Why don't I help you, and we'll get it over with?"

The simple act of attentive and intuitive listening can be one of the most basic skills in effective self-counseling.

If poor listening habits help to prevent a person from recognizing the presence of a problem, the opposite—poor verbalizing of the situation—is often equally to blame. In this case, whoever *is* aware of a difficulty in the marriage does not clearly communicate the facts or the feelings. Sometimes a person is simply unable to put the problem—a sexual one, perhaps—into words. Sometimes a person is hesitant or afraid to raise an issue directly. But vague allusions, deep sighs and stricken looks seldom produce results.

When one partner is unwilling to complain or reluctant to force an issue, the other can hardly be held responsible if tensions build. All too often the dissatisfied spouse swallows resentment and withdraws into silence, or makes up excuses for what the other says or does. How often do we say, "Oh, she's just going through a phase." Or, "If I keep my mouth shut and wait, he'll get over it." But usually the "phase" doesn't end . . . he doesn't "get over" whatever it is. And the unfaced, unadmitted problem intensifies.

In some cases it seems to take an emotional earthquake, a clash of massive proportions, to get a person to admit that something is wrong. A problem may exist for years, yet one partner goes along denying it, or seemingly oblivious to it, until the other is forced to a desperate gesture as a cry for attention and help. Every marriage counselor has had the experience of seeing a couple for the first time with one of the spouses virtually in a state of shock—stunned because the other has taken a dramatic step that makes it impossible to keep on denying that a problem exists. One husband refused to admit there was trouble brewing in his marriage until the day he returned from a business trip to find that his wife had left home with their children, their car, and their joint savings account. There was a succinct note stuck under the saltcellar on the kitchen table: "We have gone, and if you don't know why, you should."

Leaving home, starting an affair, confessing to an affair, going on a spending binge, asking for a divorce, having a "nervous breakdown"—all are desperation moves consciously or subconsciously designed to make a spouse admit there's trouble in the marriage. When the first shock wears off a therapist can only hope the realization hasn't come too late. Sometimes so much damage has been done that no repairs are possible. Not only has one partner failed to listen; the other has failed to get the message across in a reasonable way. The dramatic gesture is often too late—and too hurtful—to be converted into the beginnings of a constructive approach. It's a poor substitute for learning how to talk about marital conflict.

The Fourth Key: A popular television quiz show once was built around the idea of having panelists ask questions designed to distinguish an actual expert or celebrity from two impostors. The mystery guests, all well briefed, gave occasionally conflicting but remarkably reasonable answers. And when the master of ceremonies asked, "Will the *real* —— please stand up?" the denouement was almost always a surprise.

A marriage counselor faces the same challenge: to listen, to probe, to evaluate, to judge, and finally to identify—among the mass of red herrings, false trails, and minor truths—the *real* problem his clients have. For what couples *report* as their problem is frequently merely a symptom of it, the visible tip of the hidden conflict. Sometimes the symptom is a valid clue; sometimes it is a disguised one; and sometimes it is a misleading signpost unconsciously chosen to point deliberately away from the basic conflict—which may be too unpleasant or threatening to confront. It is the counselor's task to help a couple find the truth.

Those who intend to self-counsel must also identify the "real" problem that underlies their surface complaints. Successful self-counseling begins at this critical point. Many couples who enter counseling think they already know what their difficulty is. Those who go to therapists may start the first meeting by saying something like, "Our problem is sex," or, "The big thing we disagree about is how to discipline our kids." Studies show that these "presenting problems," as counselors term them, fall into half a dozen conventional areas: money, sexual incompatibility, child-raising, the uses of leisure time, in-law relationships, the division or sharing of household and family responsibilities. Nearly half of the couples say they want help for conflicts over children. A third report they "never do things together." Sex is a frequently named villain; 30 per cent of couples in an initial interview pin the blame for their trouble on an unsatisfactory sex life and/or one partner's infidelity. (The total adds up to more than 100 per cent since many couples offer more than one "presenting problem.")

It is possible that what a couple sees as the problem in their relationship will turn out to be the real one. But experience proves this is most unlikely. The basic conflicts that create stress are not so easily identifiable. They do not come equipped with handy labels. They are rarely mentioned in surveys of "marital problems." Nor do they come readily to mind when the question is asked: "What do you think is wrong between you?"

Consider the case of a couple who came into the office a few months ago and announced that everything was fine in their marriage except that they argued a great deal about their two children. With considerable asperity (suspiciously more than might be expected in an otherwise "fine marriage"), Mrs. K. launched upon a series of complaints. Her husband, she said, took virtually no interest in the youngsters. He refused to spend time with them on weekends; he rarely would help them with homework; he almost never went to meet their teachers. In rebuttal, Mr. K. announced that he did indeed love and care about his children, but that he worked hard to provide for the family and he considered child care in all its aspects his wife's responsibility. Besides, he said, he had no intention of becoming either the children's "pal" or their disciplinarian.

MARCIA LASSWELL (to husband): What was it like in your family when you were growing up?

HUSBAND: My mother took complete charge of the children and my father worked to support us.

WIFE: But your mother didn't have to work outside to make ends meet either.

H (angrily): You don't *have* to work. I make a decent living. You just want to get out of the house.

W: We couldn't live on *your* salary. You don't buy the groceries or pay the bills so you don't even know what it costs to live. I *do* have to work.

ML: Mrs. K., do you like your job?

W: Not particularly. I'd rather stay home and enjoy my children than go to an office every day. But I have no choice.

ML: Because if you preferred to work, it would be a different matter from your feelings about *having* to help support the family. It seems to me you both have angry feelings about matters that may be separate from the parenting issue.

H: I still say she doesn't have to work. She does it to have money of her own she doesn't have to account for.

ML: You two obviously don't agree on the need for two incomes, and I'm in no position yet to tell who is right. So I'll assume you both are reporting how you see it—no exaggerations to make your own version sound more convincing—and that our problem is to find out why you are so angry with each other.

W: I'm angry over how he neglects the children. That's what we came to talk about.

ML: And we will, eventually. But the anger seems to permeate other areas of your marriage, as well. It's easy for children to become the focus of it. I know they are a real concern to you, and we won't lose sight of that, I promise.

H (speaking directly to wife): She's right. I feel angry toward you a lot about the way you put me down. There's plenty of tension between us that has nothing to do with the kids. You don't like the kind of father I am . . . and you are just as negative about me as a husband.

W: You want to get into all that? All right, I admit it!

For Mr. and Mrs. K. "fighting about the children" was a symptom of their repressed anger at each other. The tension resulting from her feeling unappreciated and his feeling put down was coloring their whole relationship. Releasing this tension was a needed first step in dealing with their conflicts over parenting. In much the same way other "presenting" problems also often camouflage basic marital tensions. For example, Mrs. R. spent her entire first session castigating her husband for his carelessness with money:

WIFE: We're never going to get the living room furnished because Jim spends so much money on his boat. He can't say "no" to anything he wants for it, but when we need new furniture there's never enough money.

MARCIA LASSWELL: Do you and Jim ever discuss your finances except when you argue over what he spends?

W: He says he makes the money and he has a right to buy what he wants. I suppose I could run up a bill at the furniture store, but he'd be furious.

ML: What do you feel when he says that?

W: It makes me angry . . . and I feel helpless to do anything about it since I don't earn money. I guess I feel he doesn't care about my feelings, that he's selfish.

ML: Money, as you know, is a symbol of many things—love, security, power. When you say Jim is selfish and you feel he doesn't care about your feelings, I sense a bigger problem between you than just living room furniture. Are there other areas where you believe he doesn't care about your feelings?

W: I would say my feelings count very little with him in general. He always has the last word on everything, and he says if I don't like it I can always leave . . . or sometimes *he* threatens to leave.

ML: And what happens then?

W: Well, I've got three children and I got married right out of high school. I couldn't support myself and the children, so I don't see that I have much choice but to let him have his way.

You don't have to be a trained counselor to read between the lines of these complaints. It wasn't money or furniture that was troubling Mrs. R. She was feeling insecure, unloved, and vulnerable. She was feeling angry and powerless. Obviously, a professional counselor is trained to translate "presenting" problems into the real ones that must be dealt with if a marriage is to prosper.

Can self-counseling couples learn to do this for themselves with any reasonable expectations of success? Can you learn how to dig beneath the surface signs of trouble and identify their true source? Can you learn how to peel away the layers of symptoms until you reach the core conflict?

Any good problem-solving course will emphasize that if you don't pin-point the real problem you can waste precious time coming up with a solution to the wrong one. Then, when things don't improve after this effort, it is easy to become discouraged, to give up. Another bonus that results from an accurate diagnosis of the problem is that many times the very process of isolating it produces a solution. Here are some steps you can follow to isolate your basic problem as a marital therapist would:

• Listen for themes behind your statements (such as the K.'s anger or Mrs. R.'s vulnerability). Learn to recognize the themes that come up frequently between you. Perhaps it will be anger—consistently present whether you are discussing children, money, or sex. Is your relationship characterized by apathy, anxiety, lack of trust, lack of respect? If your conversations are riddled with anxiety and lack of trust, for instance, it may not matter *what* they are about because it is the underlying theme in your relationship that needs to be changed.

• Problems seldom arise in clear-cut forms; often there appear to be several intertwined issues. You have to use *logical analysis* to peel away the layers—going from the general statement to the particular, from the obvious to the not so obvious. Since you are a part of the problem yourself and you may be upset about it, you can expect this step to be difficult. It's not easy to be logical and objective when you are emotionally involved. One advantage the therapist has is his or her lack of emotional involvement. But you can train yourself to do this too, much as you learn any skill. Probably the easiest way to ensure objectivity is to write down your version of the problem. Be as specific as you can. Give evidence for each statement you make. Do this as if you were preparing for a school debate: Get the facts you need and check them out for accuracy. Try to approach your diagnosis with an open mind. The most foolish thing you can do is to "stack" the issue—using only the facts that support your preconceived ideas.

So much for theory. Let's see how you can apply this symptom-peeling process in self-counseling practice:

Ted and Susan Hathaway realized their frequent arguments about their lack of common interests were symptomatic of a deeper problem in their marriage. They were determined to cut through the surface complaints and try to find out what really was causing them to grow apart. They set aside every Tuesday evening after their children were in bed as their self-counseling hour. Ted unplugged the telephone jack to guarantee them uninterrupted time, and he and his wife settled themselves in facing chairs.

TED: I get very upset when we fight the way we did this weekend.

SUSAN: So do I. But when you accepted that invitation to the Parkers' I got furious. I mean, they're so dull!

TED: Most people wouldn't agree. Ev Parker probably knows more about state politics than anyone I know.

SUSAN: But that's just it. That's all he knows. And it's dull to talk about politics all night.

TED: Not for me. I'm very interested in it. And besides, as a lawyer I can benefit a great deal from being at the Parkers'. They have some very influential people at those parties.

SUSAN: But I never know what to say to them. The women all talk about the trips they've taken and the designer clothes they've just bought. I feel completely out of it.

TED: Not all the women are that way. Some of the wives are right in there with their opinions. Mary Carter and Jill Knox will be there, and they're lawyers working on antitrust cases.

SUSAN: Well, I *certainly* wouldn't know what to say to them. And you abandon me to them while you talk politics.

TED: I don't feel I should have to be responsible for you socially. You need to do some reading or take some courses so you'd know how to hold your own in a group like that.

SUSAN: But I'm not interested in politics.

TED: You're not interested in very much that I'm interested in. My whole life is law—and politics is where I'm headed. If you reject these, it's like a rejection of me.

SUSAN: I don't see how you can say I'm rejecting you or law. I worked for five years to put you through law school! Now my life is my home and children, and I feel you're abandoning us for a new life I can't be part of.

TED: Ironic, isn't it? You feel abandoned and I feel rejected.

Ted and Susan rather quickly have discovered the themes beneath the surface of their argument over Ev Parker's party. They were able to accept these feelings and then move to the second phase of diagnosing their problem—to make their feelings more specific and their reactions more objective. Now Susan needed to say what would make her feel less abandoned. Ted found that just complaining about rejection didn't solve anything; he needed to explain to Susan what behavior of hers would help him to change his feelings.

SUSAN: I don't want us to grow apart. I realize we can't have all the same interests, but I know I'd feel better if you took more interest in the children. You eat, breathe, and sleep law and politics. What I hear you telling me is that if I don't do the same, I'm rejecting you as a person. That's not true. It's just that *I'm* a person, too, and I have other things I'm interested in.

TED: I can understand that. But *you're* giving me the same message. If I don't share *your* interests, then *I'm* abandoning *you*.

SUSAN: Okay. So we both need our private interests and we have to respect each other's right to them. But we need to involve ourselves a little in each *other's* interests, too. I probably wouldn't mind Ev Parker's parties so much if I thought you'd go to a PTA meeting sometime. I'd be willing to take a course or two in history or politics if you'd go with me to a parent training class.

TED: Susan, those things aren't intellectually stimulating. It doesn't take any brains to go to a PTA meeting!

SUSAN: If PTA is *my interest,* are you saying I don't have any brains?

TED: I'm saying you aren't using the brains you've got.

SUSAN: I don't agree. But if you think you are ahead of me, and growing faster than I am, then I'm afraid we really are losing touch.

TED: I guess I really do feel that way. I'm afraid of it, too.

SUSAN: Maybe we don't agree on what "growing" is. Maybe what
we should do is think about what *I* could do that would make
you feel I am growing. And then think about ways you could
be more involved with our family that would interest you.

Ted and Susan didn't resolve their problem on this particular
Tuesday evening. But in one hour of self-counseling they came a
long way from thinking that their disagreement was over a party at
Ev Parker's.

Here is another example of how a couple can probe beneath
their apparent differences and arrive at the core of their problem:

Charles and Carol Williams typify a relationship increasingly
common in these days of divorce and remarriage. Carol is
Charles's second wife. When they married eleven years ago, he
was a vigorous fifty-two and she was thirty-six. But the sixteen-
year age difference did not seem so wide a gap as it does now,
when he is almost sixty-four and she is only forty-seven. Moreover, Charles's children from his first marriage are in their late
twenties and completely on their own, while the couple's own ten-
year-old is still a financial and physical responsibility. Until a year
ago the Williamses had an excellent marriage. But in recent
months they have been increasingly at odds with each other. They
seem to argue about almost everything: money, their daughter,
where to live, what to do on vacations, how to plan for the future.
Both Charles and Carol sense that there is some fundamental
reason why they disagree over so many seemingly disparate
decisions.

CAROL: No way do I want to buy that property up north—it's isolated. What would I do there? Besides, the schools aren't any
good for Laurie, and all her friends are here.
CHARLES: Look, I'm retiring next year, remember? We don't need
this big house—can't afford it, in fact, on my retirement pay.
I've *had* it with the city and the smog. The air is clear up
there, and there's fishing and hunting—and you could paint.
CAROL: *You're* ready to retire. *I'm not.* I'll paint pictures when I'm
sixty-five. What's happened to you? I never thought I'd see
the day you turned into a "back-to-nature" person.
CHARLES: I'm in a different place, Carol, from where I was a few

years ago. Do you realize that if I live to my normal life ex-
pectancy I'll be dead in ten years? I think I have a right to
my last years of peace.

CAROL: You sound like you're dead already. I want some excitement and stimulation in my life—the theater, lectures, my
friends in the city.

CHARLES: When we were married, sixteen years' difference didn't
matter much. But it sure does now, doesn't it?

CAROL: I guess that *is* the problem. You're at a slowing-down
point, and I feel that I'm just gaining the freedom to do a few
things after ten years of being tied down with Laurie. I can
understand how you feel, Charles, but I don't want to have
my life changed by *your* feelings. So, what do we do?

CHARLES: As I see it, we've got four possibilities: one, you win;
two, I win; three, we get a divorce; four, we compromise.
What do you say we try for a compromise?

In self-counseling (as in counseling), the clearest possible statement of the essence of a marital conflict is the firmest basis for
successful diagnosis. Charles and Carol got quickly to the core factor in their many disagreements even though their problem was
not going to be an easy one to resolve. The more complex the
problem, however, the greater the need for clarity. And the more
important to spend as much time as necessary to achieve it.

4

HOW YOU CAN DO
WHAT A COUNSELOR DOES—II

Working Out the Problem

A kindergarten teacher tells this story about the time she decided to have a class Halloween party. Each child brought a pumpkin to school, and the teacher helped to cut off the pumpkin tops, scoop out the insides, and carve the remains into funny/scary faces. All the youngsters were delighted with their jack-o'-lanterns except one little boy who grew more and more silent as the candles were lit inside the shells.

"Don't you like your pumpkin face, Billy?" the teacher asked.

Billy nodded. "Yes, but you want to know the sad part? First, you have to kill it."

Like Billy, many men and women think that in order to bring about desired changes in a marriage something in it has to be sacrificed. They believe that treating a marital conflict always requires violent marital surgery. The facts are quite the contrary.

Most problems are likely to be solved by a planned sequence of moderate changes designed to result in new ways of behavior. Sometimes what appears to be a small—even insignificant—change can be the start of a cycle of progress. Couples in counseling discover that a systematic series of seemingly minor but positive steps can lead to major advances in working out their difficulties.

For example, Beth and Dan Harris had reached the point, after eleven years of marriage, where they argued bitterly about almost every major decision they had to make. When the counselor suggested they learn how to settle an *un*important difference of opinion first, they objected.

WIFE: What's the point of spending time on the way Dan leaves the bathroom every morning when we have really big problems to talk about?

MARCIA LASSWELL: I agree, the condition of the bathroom is a relatively insignificant issue. But if you practice working out small differences first, you can move on with those same techniques to the larger ones. It's like learning to play the piano—you have to learn the scales and chords before you tackle the concertos.

HUSBAND: You're saying that if we can't talk about a minor point without fighting, we don't have much hope of tackling the major ones.

ML: Yes, because big issues are complex and involve deeper feelings. I know it doesn't seem like much to talk about your bathroom, but you will be learning a *process*—a way of working out a problem—that you can use later on the other issues.

W: We have to take this a step at a time?

ML: Yes. You can't undo eleven years in one day.

With practice and sincerity, a couple can learn how to use this and other self-counseling techniques to make changes in their behavior that can improve their marriage. A good way to see how the method works—and to discover how much progress you can make on your own—is to experiment with it. Choose a specific "trouble area" in your marriage. Discuss what bothers you about it. Say how you would like to see matters improved. Don't begin with a major problem or one that is loaded with emotional overtones, such as sex or in-laws. Rather, start with an issue that though minor continues to annoy you.

For instance, if you argue a lot over how you spend weekends, you might choose to explore ways of changing your behavior to make them more restful, or livelier. If you are bugged by the clutter and confusion of the morning "rush hour," when everyone in the family is trying to leave on time for work or school, you might want to talk about how you would like to see that routine changed. Every couple can isolate a minor irritant to serve as a guinea-pig topic. If even those suggested so far seem too emotional for comfort, try something safer: priorities for home improvements, or whether to send the children to summer camp. Here is how one young couple applied the technique:

For Karen and Joe, five to seven in the evening is an aggravating time. Joe, a trouble shooter for a data processing company, puts in a grinding day. He must placate customers, solve electronic foul-ups, and fight traffic on a long drive home. The couple have three children, aged two, six, and eight. Three afternoons a week Karen has a sitter while she takes courses toward a college degree. Both Joe and Karen are tired and tense when they get home. The five-to-seven time should be a "decompression" period, but instead it is usually hectic and punctuated by squabbles. The couple get so irritated that dinnertime is often spoiled, and sometimes the emotional fallout lasts until bedtime and affects their sex life. Karen and Joe decided to do something about the situation by frankly but calmly telling each other exactly how they felt and what they would like to see changed:

JOE: I feel like I'm walking into enemy territory when I come home. The kids are screaming, you're cranky. I don't even get a welcome. You're always at the sink or the stove. Sometimes I wonder if you care whether I come home or not.

KAREN: Of course I care, but I don't have time to make a big production out of it. The children are tired, and I'm tired. I'm in the kitchen because I know you don't like to wait long for dinner. I need you to pitch in and help.

JOE: I need *some* time to unwind. I'd like a chance at least to take off my tie and wash up. But if I go upstairs for five minutes you start yelling at me.

KAREN: You think it's only five minutes, but it's a lot longer than that. The children want to be with you, you know.

JOE: And I want to be with them. But I can't start playing with them the instant I walk in.

Their complaints aired, the couple move on to the next step— trying to work out a different way to deal with the problem.

JOE: All right, we agree on what bugs us. Now, how do we change things?

KAREN: Well, how would *you* like things to be?

JOE: I'd like to walk in and have you stop stirring the pot or shouting at the kids for maybe thirty seconds. I'd like you to kiss me, to be glad to see me.

KAREN: I'd like that, too . . . and for you to be glad to see *me*.

JOE: Then I'd like ten minutes to go upstairs and get myself together without any pressure to rush back to help you, or to be with the kids. How does that sound to you?

KAREN: Well, I could survive for another ten minutes if I knew that then you'd ask what you could do to help. Sometimes I might like it if you'd hold the baby, or take all the children outside to play. Also, it would make things easier if we didn't have to eat right away.

JOE: I thought *you* wanted to eat promptly. I don't care that much. You say the children get cranky if they wait too long. Maybe it would be better if the kids didn't eat with us?

KAREN: It's a lot of extra trouble to feed them separately. And they'd miss being with you. The older ones aren't really the problem. I think the baby cries because he can't sit through the whole meal.

JOE: Why don't we play it by ear? Let's feed him till he starts fussing and then I'll put him in the playpen. Would that be okay?

KAREN: We can try it. If that doesn't help we'll think of something else. Anything will be an improvement.

This may not seem much of a problem, nor that Karen and Joe made much progress toward solving it. But in counseling terms, they did. They were able to talk openly about each other's behavior, to suggest directions for changing it, and to agree on new ways of responding to each other's needs. All that is far from a minor accomplishment. Moreover, by agreeing on new approaches Joe and Karen achieved several significant gains:

• They felt better about themselves and each other.

• They made a start at heading off the emotional erosion that was undermining their marriage.

• By proving they could deal with a minor problem, they got the reinforcement to tackle larger ones.

• They learned that behavior *can* be changed. That alone gives them an excellent prognosis for further self-counseling success.

This is frequently nothing short of a revelation to spouses who are convinced the husband or wife is "hopeless" when it comes to changing. Indeed, if counselors let themselves be influenced by the defeatist feelings couples sometimes have about each other we would all soon quit the profession. But counselors know, out of training and experience, that every person can change. And on occasion, change dramatically. The desire and effort to change are the ingredients of what sometimes seems to be a minor miracle.

If Karen and Joe had gone to a professional counselor they would most likely have started to work on a similar small-scale issue; specific improvements in trivial areas are the building blocks of major problem-solving. Often the easing of a minor conflict can lead to improving a couple's total relationship. For example:

WIFE: I get angry with Art when we're around his parents. He always takes their side.

MARCIA LASSWELL: Can you give me an instance so I can be clear about what happens?

W: Well, this last visit, his mother and I got into a thing over whether the children could go with her for an ice cream cone when they hadn't eaten their dinner.

ML: And you sided with your mother, Art?

HUSBAND: It seemed a shame to put a damper on the kids' time with their grandmother. They don't see my parents often. I felt Shirley could ease up this once.

W: This *once!* You always take her side, whether it's over the kids or anything else.

ML: And how do you feel about his mother when Art sides with her?

W: I feel she gloats! Her precious son chose her over me.

ML: Do you like her at times like this?

W: I hate her! And I've tried to like her, believe me. I know she doesn't like me much, either. I've tried to get her to accept me, but the whole thing is hopeless. She's not about to change.

ML: Does Art's mother treat you differently from the way your own mother does?

W: My mother died when I was seven and I had two stepmothers—

both witches. When Art and I got married, I really thought
I've got a mother at last. But only her son and grandchildren
count with her.

ML: Sounds like you feel left out, Shirley . . . almost like a rejected
child. Your anger may mask a lot of disappointment.

H: I never knew you felt that way, Shirley. I think my parents *like*
you. But you want more than that, don't you?

W: I've never thought of it this way before. When I see how they
feel about you, I think I feel jealous.

ML: It's almost sibling rivalry, isn't it? It hurts not to be a favored
child. It makes the child angry. Maybe if you're not so angry
with them they will show their love more.

H: We *are* a pretty clannish family. And I never realized how
much you needed to be part of us.

Art spoke to his parents about Shirley's needs. Shirley made an
honest effort to control her anger. Soon both reported that the
family visits were growing progressively more comfortable for everyone. There are many techniques for bringing about such
behavioral change. We will see in the following chapters how they
work in specific areas of marital tension. The balance of this chapter will outline *basic* methods for stimulating change and show you
how you can adapt them for use in self-counseling.

*A counselor attempts at the outset to establish rapport with the
client.* In self-counseling, rapport between the couple is even more
essential since there is no "third person" to act as intermediary.
Without some willingness to understand each other's feelings, a
couple cannot effectively share their problems or confide their
thoughts.

Rapport means to establish an open approach to each other.
This is often an important factor in itself. Several studies show
that successful therapists have one main thing in common: They
quickly create an atmosphere of warmth and genuine interest with
the client. In self-counseling it is just as essential that you show
each other this consideration and caring. Only when you feel your
partner is genuinely trying to understand you will you feel free to
open up your feelings and motives. If he or she frequently inter-

rupts with "That's ridiculous" or "You shouldn't feel that way," no rapport can develop.

To increase rapport during self-counseling one person should wait attentively until the other is finished talking. The listener may then ask questions for clarification. Don't interrupt. Obviously, when emotions are running high these steps will be difficult, if not impossible. So we recommend that self-counseling be postponed until feelings have had time to calm down. We have already mentioned the importance of having uninterrupted time to discuss problems; it's worth re-emphasizing as a factor in building rapport.

A counselor tries to reduce hostility between spouses. Unexpressed anger is an oppressive emotional weight. We've said, "Get your emotions under control before you undertake self-counseling." But what do you do with your hostility?

In recent years it's become popular to encourage husbands and wives to vent their anger openly—to give free rein to irritations, resentments, even hatreds. The advocates of this technique believe that "honest combat" and "uninhibited leveling" are the best way to get marital discord out in the open. This theory is based on the classic idea of "catharsis"—ridding oneself of negative emotions by expressing and experiencing them. Bottled-up animosity only grows more intense. If angry feelings are ventilated, however, inner tensions and hostility will lessen. With the emotional atmosphere cleared, the theory holds, a couple can begin to deal with the real issues.

But does "letting it all hang out" really help? Can a husband and wife then calmly proceed to deal with their differences? Some couples seem to be able to do this but we think most cannot—and many other counseling experts agree. Indeed, the dangers of aggressive leveling, and its counterproductiveness in counseling, were illustrated by a couple who for several months had poured out their complaints in counseling sessions with no holds barred. But later, when they continued to do it at home without a "referee" to intercede, the battling got out of control. "We'd make vicious remarks without feeling the least bit apologetic or guilty," said the husband. "After all, we'd been told this was all right, even healthy." But their anger only seemed to grow, and soon verbal attacks turned into physical ones:

WIFE: Once I said something particularly hurtful, and to my astonishment Chris grabbed my arm and twisted it violently.

HUSBAND: Adrienne cried out in pain, and I let go right away. I was frightened by what happened, and I apologized.

W: For days afterward we were terribly polite to each other. But, you know, it was like the first small break in a high-pressure line.

MARCIA LASSWELL: And then what happened?

W: A few days later we had another go-round and Chris took me by the shoulders and shook me till my head rattled. So I threw a pot at him.

H: It just missed my head. Then the worst happened. I slapped Adrienne without even being aware I was doing it.

ML: One attack makes it easier for others to happen, doesn't it?

W (nodding): We just stood there, shaking. I thought, *My God, what's happening to us? . . . What kind of marriage is this?*

ML: You know now how easy it is to lose control. And you know that kind of behavior doesn't solve problems but creates more serious ones. Your anger and hostility will still arise from time to time. But let's see if we can't find more constructive ways to handle these feelings.

What steps *can* a couple counseling themselves take to reduce hostility? Here are some suggestions:

Indirect release—When you feel furious with your spouse, try the technique a woman we know uses in her own marriage. She goes out to the garage, sits in her car, pretends her husband is next to her, and then says to "him" every horrible thing she can think of. "When I go back into the house," she reports, "I'm always able to discuss our differences much more reasonably." This is a harmless and useful way of venting hostility.

Use a mental "safety catch"—When you feel your temper rising, pause and ask yourself *why* you are getting so angry. Do this literally. Say to yourself (or aloud): "Why am I mad? What is really going on here?" Quite often the effort to analyze the cause of your feeling will be calming in itself. Or it will indicate how or why your anger is misplaced. Of course, you have a right to feel angry and to express that feeling. Repressing or failing to admit your anger is not going to help matters. It is essential that you learn to recognize when you are angry. Many people cannot do that. They deny. anger while clenched fists, gritted teeth, and stony silence give them away. Afterward, they report feeling "tired," or they have a headache or a crying spell. Before you have a self-counseling session you should come to grips with your anger and get it under control. *Controlled anger* can then be discussed with your partner this way: "I was in a rage when you said that. I had to go out in the yard and pull weeds—every weed was *you*—until I got it under control. I'm still angry but not in a rage."

A counselor tries to reorient a person's attitudes toward a problem situation. For instance, a counselor may try to get a client to be more objective about a stressful situation he or she blames solely on the spouse. A wife or husband may be encouraged to look at old hang-ups from new perspectives. If a person has been "spoiling for a fight," reorientation might involve deliberately avoiding conflict; if one has been running away from confrontations, perhaps it is time to face up to them. The point is that if what you have been doing hasn't worked, a new approach is needed. For example, many couples begin to discuss their problems by detailing their complaints. This is sometimes a necessary step (although the complaints are already familiar) but there comes a point when no forward movement is being made. A switch from complaining to describing how you wish life could be is one way to break out of the stalemate. Karen and Joe, the young parents, did just that when Karen asked: "How would you like things to be [when you come home]?" Another technique (to be discussed in detail later) is role-playing—where you switch roles to see how it feels to be in your partner's shoes. It's surprising how much understanding you can gain if you force yourself out of the old patterns. Here are some techniques for doing that:

You can be each other's "co-therapist"—In formal counseling, the therapist may from time to time suggest that one spouse or the other function as a "co-therapist" in a particular area of conflict. For instance, a couple in their late forties had a problem with sex. The husband—seemingly disinterested in sex and occasionally impotent—was made to feel even more distressed by his wife's complaints. Since she had a vested interest in his sexual performance she agreed to "help him with his problem." (Of course, it was *her* problem, too, but the therapist decided they could make more progress by enlisting her aid.) The husband's impotence was partly due to his *fear* of being impotent—the classic vicious circle. His wife's demands for sex only increased his fears and failures. In addition, the man was trying to bury his anxieties in work and alcohol. As a co-therapist, the wife was told to substitute a neck and back rub for the several drinks her husband usually had before going to bed. She was also asked to limit her sexual demands until he was more rested and confident. The woman was able to do these things because she now saw herself as part of the therapy program rather than as a "neglected" wife.

Here is an example of how the "co-therapist" device can work for a couple with a money conflict. Mr. L. earned a good income as a master plumber but the family was always short of money. Mr. and Mrs. L. tried to stick with a budget but it always seemed to get sabotaged. For instance, when Mrs. L. bought new living room draperies the "only ones" she liked cost $800—more than twice what the couple could afford. Another time money was so tight the L.'s had to cut their food expenses, yet the wife chose that moment to buy a blender, an electric coffee-maker, and a sandwich toaster for $175. In a third incident, Mrs. L. bought a set of expensive matched luggage for a one-week trip to visit her family. When the couple finally went to a counselor for help with their "money problem," it did not take long to uncover their real difficulty:

MARCIA LASSWELL: Can you tell me why you bought new luggage for such a short trip?

WIFE: We needed it. We hadn't bought any since we got married.

HUSBAND: We didn't need anything that expensive.

W: What would my folks think if we showed up with those old suitcases?

ML: Is it necessary to impress your parents?

H: She always has to impress everybody. Those appliances and the drapes . . . that was to show the neighbors.

W: I want people to see we have good things, that we're worth something.

ML: And you believe that having nice things will make people think highly of you?

W: Well, I never looked at it that way, but—I suppose so.

It was clear that the way Mrs. L. spent money was closely tied to the poor image she had of herself. Without "nice things" to bolster her ego she had little self-esteem. When her husband reacted to her buying sprees by getting angry or "punishing" her in some way, the cycle was back at its starting point. The counselor explained this to Mr. L., and suggested he "join in the therapy" and help to build his wife's self-esteem in other ways, such as praising her for the good qualities she did have. As Mrs. L. came to feel better about herself as a person, she had less need to spend money for "show."

In working out problems in self-counseling it's often useful for one partner to adopt this "therapeutic attitude," to ask "What can I do to help?" For example, a couple had agreed to stop criticizing each other in public and the wife wondered whether she could really break the habit.

HUSBAND: You can if you want to. Just think before you speak.

WIFE: You make it sound so easy, but *you* can't quit smoking. This could be just as hard for me.

H: Okay, would it help if I gave you a signal when I hear you putting me down?

W: That might work. If you said, "I think I'll quit smoking," I'd get the hint.

H: Very funny. But all right, you come up with something I can do or say, and I'll think of a signal for you. If we help each other, maybe we *can* kick the habit.

You can work on changing attitudes by giving yourself "marital homework." Many counselors give clients between-sessions homework. They ask them to practice new ways of acting toward each other, new ways of dealing with conflicts. Self-counseling homework can include:

Constructive arguing—This is different from the "aggressive leveling" we talked about earlier. Here are some guidelines to prevent frank talk from becoming rancorous:

Don't argue in ways you know your spouse can't stand. Some persons are comfortable with a good deal of screaming; others are dismayed by it; still others are shattered by the *absence* of a spouse's reaction. We know a couple who once drove two hundred miles in total silence after the husband refused, for the *previous* one hundred miles, to say one word in response to his wife's complaints about their sex life. At the end of the trip she got out of the car, called her lawyer, and told him to start getting her a divorce.

Learn to recognize and avoid "displacement" in disputes. The patterns should be familiar—i.e., the man who quarrels with his wife because he can't with his boss. But displacement often shows up in subtler ways. Take the man who comes home after a rough day to find that his two children have each asked a friend to stay for dinner. The father explodes in a nasty scene which ends with the embarrassed children eating alone, the mother not eating at all, and the man going out to the nearest hamburger stand. Is he truly that upset at having to eat with children when he was looking forward to a relaxing dinner? Is he irritated at having to feed extra people when groceries are expensive? Or is he angry because he subconsciously senses that his wife uses the children as a buffer to avoid being alone with him? Making a scene and walking away won't help the couple to focus on their real problem. But they might have handled it with this self-counseling technique:

WIFE: What did you expect when you came home?

HUSBAND: I don't know. I do know I was tired and nobody seemed to give a damn. It looked like the whole Little League team was there making noise.

W: Yes. I *know* what you didn't like. But I'm interested in how you wanted things to be.

H: Quiet, peaceful, you paying some attention to me. The kids have you all day.

W (flaring up): They do not! They just got there. (She regains her calm with some effort.) You know, this isn't easy to do. Well, are you saying you want some kind of special reception when you get home?

H: No, just a little recognition that I'm there . . . a little appreciation for how hard I work.

W: You don't feel appreciated?

H: Not really. I feel taken for granted . . . you know, the guy who pays the bills to feed all the kids in the neighborhood.

W: It's hard not to defend myself right now, but I guess a real counselor would try to find out more about *your* feelings. If that's how you *do* feel, let's try to figure out some way I can help you that won't upset me, too.

Hard as it was, the wife stuck to her homework. She fought down her natural desire to defend herself. She resisted the temptation to expand the argument. It is important in self-counseling not to dredge up old grudges, make threats, be sarcastic, or zero in on the other person's weaknesses. Some other "no-no's" are:

- Don't generalize—"You always . . ." and "You never . . ."
- Don't downgrade—"Your problems aren't important . . ." "You're just spoiled . . ."
- Don't dramatize by shifting from a specific point to a test of power and caring—"You'd see it my way if you really loved me . . ."
- Don't offer unsolicited advice—"You wouldn't have these problems if you would only . . ."

Another kind of homework is to emphasize marital "positives" rather than negatives. Spouses tend to retreat into the "need to blame" when a marriage is in trouble. Yet it is more useful to concentrate on what you have going *for* you than on what is dividing you. Some time ago a couple came for the last-ditch counseling California law provides for when a marital dissolution case is filed. They scarcely spoke to each other, and pain filled the room, but the counselor made an effort to shift their focus to happier times:

MARCIA LASSWELL: What do you remember about the day you were married—August 30, 1962, wasn't it?

WIFE: That's right. What do you want to know?

ML: How did you feel when you walked down the aisle and saw Bill standing there?

W: Scared. Excited. I really thought I was in love.

ML: What did you love about Bill?

W: Everything—he was so thoughtful and kind and he loved me.

ML: Why did you love Edie, Bill?

HUSBAND: Well, she was so bright and pretty—and sexy.

ML: And have you both changed so totally?

H: I don't think I've changed.

W: And I don't either.

ML: But somehow your perceptions of each other must have been altered if you have lost sight of the reasons you married in the first place. You've focused so long on the bad that you've lost sight of the good.

As the couple talked it was clear that the antagonism between them was gradually draining away as they remembered happier days together. When they left they were thoughtful. A few days later they called to ask if they could return. On their own, they had continued to talk about the pluses in their marriage, and they felt there were enough to warrant trying to work things out.

Concentrating on positives is not quite so easy as it may sound. For one thing, couples usually think in terms of "problems." For another, spouses tend to take each other's good qualities for granted. They grow accustomed to strengths and virtues, yet become quicker to notice failings and weaknesses.

Yet where this "positive" approach has been tested, it has proved valuable. Some years ago Carl T. Clarke, a psychologist-counselor, asked small groups of husbands and wives to talk—some for the first time in their married lives—about why they loved and felt loved. "We discovered," one wife said later, "that our feelings for each other were far deeper than we had imagined." A husband said: "Until I actually listed all the things I like about Helene, I had no idea how many there are or how important they are to me." Couples also saw each other's *behavior* in a clearer light. A husband said how touched he was when he realized his wife had spent half a day looking for a special yarn to make a birthday sweater for him. He had accepted the sweater almost perfunctorily; but knowing the care and thought that went into it revealed something significant about the kind of marriage he had. Another man told his wife he got up ten minutes earlier than necessary every day to squeeze fresh orange juice for her because "it's one small way I can show I love you." She looked at him in surprise: "I thought you felt put upon, doing that . . . I didn't know you wanted to."

What are some "homework assignments" that can help to reveal the positives in your own marriage? Here are several suggestions:

• Make a *written* list of things you and your spouse have in common. Because differences create tensions we are too keenly aware of them; similarities are overlooked. A "sharing list" can provide insight into the way you mesh.

• Make a point of noticing—and remarking upon—whatever your spouse does well. A wife may be a poor cook but a superb hostess; a husband may be useless at home repairs but marvelous with his children. Honest compliments, especially when they indicate you have noticed a comparatively minor effort, are an excellent way to emphasize positives. One wife used this technique to encourage her husband, who was immersed in business matters, to be more thoughtful about her needs. "I knew complaining would only make things worse," she said. "I decided to praise him. Finally—after I reminded him five times!—he remembered to bring home a book I'd asked for. I thanked him as if he had given me a diamond necklace. He looked puzzled, but I could see he was pleased. I did this sort of thing a few times until he began to *want* to think about me because he enjoyed being appreciated."

• Take joint inventory of your marital resources. Each marriage, no matter what its problems, has something special in its favor. The very act of *sharing* these often-unrecognized assets can provide a new viewpoint on one's marriage. An interesting side effect of group marital therapy is that when a couple hears the problems of others they often realize their own aren't so bad.

• Role-switching is useful "homework" for finding new ways to approach old problems. An open mind is essential for self-counseling. We must accept the idea that no matter how *we* see a situation, the other person's actions are based on how he or she sees it. Shutting our eyes to this reality accomplishes nothing. Yet obviously it's hard to be objective when you are personally, emotionally involved. It takes an effort of will plus a large portion of *good*will. One way to cultivate objectivity is to switch roles with your partner temporarily—to take his or her side, voice his or her arguments, imagine his or her feelings.

Suppose a wife wants to give a large dinner party and her husband objects. He wants a smaller group of guests. Both have perfectly good reasons for their positions. She points out how long it has been since they entertained, how many people they "owe" socially, how much easier it is to give one big party than several smaller ones. He counters by ticking off the cost, the fact that some of the people they would invite don't get along with others, the problem of fitting a large group into their modest apartment. If this couple merely go on repeating their reasons, chances are that in twenty minutes they will be locked into positions from which no gracious retreat is possible.

Suppose, on the other hand, they switch roles. The wife must now give all the reasons *against* having a large party, and the husband must argue in *favor* of it. If done with reasonable sincerity, each will understand the other's attitude better. They may find a way to compromise . . . they may convince themselves the other person is right . . . or they may decide not to have a dinner party of any kind! Role reversal of this kind is "as if" behavior— like an actor's "becoming" the character he portrays. It can be fun . . . or it can be emotionally draining . . . but it is bound to shake up any one-track minds.

A counselor acts as a mirror to a marriage, reflecting it to the couple so they can see it from a new perspective. In self-counseling, one excellent way to do the same thing is to use a tape recorder. For a long time now emphasis on "communication" in marriage has been on the need for spouses to talk honestly with each other. But it often seems that some people talk too much and listen too little—either to their partners or themselves. Many of us are not truly aware of the emotional meaning of words. A simple "What would you like for dinner tomorrow?" may show a woman's wish to please her husband. But *"What* would you like *tomorrow?"* (with a sigh) may mean she could use some menu suggestions. And "What would *you* like tomorrow?" (with heavy irony) can mean she's had enough criticism of her meals.

Since we don't listen carefully, a tape recording of marital conversation can be revealing. Counselors often tape sessions so clients can hear intonations, interruptions, "mind reading," and the like. A counselor may ask a couple to switch on a tape recorder when they fight at home, so he or she can hear what really happens.

Try this exercise. Record your breakfast, dinner, and bedtime conversations for one week. You will quickly get used to the idea of a live microphone in the room after a day or two; instead of being self-conscious about it you will ignore—or even forget it.

When you play the tapes back you will be truly *listening* to yourselves for the first time. You will hear emotion where you could have sworn none existed. You will hear yourself saying things that you would otherwise deny ever having said. You will hear the nasty tone of a remark you were sure at the time was spoken "in fun." You will find a whole new light shed on "I didn't say *that*." "Oh, yes, you did" . . . "Why didn't you tell me that?" "I did!" controversies. You can't argue with a recording that shows with enlightening (and sometimes frightening) accuracy a living segment of married life.

Use the tape recorder as a "silent observer" in a self-counseling session. In addition to providing a factual record, the tape will show significant communication patterns. Where do you both go off the track? When do you get defensive? Argue? Fall silent? What do you hear in each other's voice you never noticed before? To hear yourselves is a powerful, illuminating, sometimes painful, but always useful experience.

Finally, a counselor encourages a couple to act on what they have learned—to set new goals, to make new plans, to change their ways of behaving. Self-counseling couples can do the same thing. The simplest yet most efficient technique is the "contract"—a mutual agreement, verbal or written, that promises a certain kind of changed behavior. It may cover a specific area such as household tasks, or be complex enough to cover many areas in a marriage. It is not meant to limit or to freeze a situation, but to free a couple from unpredictable vagueness. We saw how Joe and Karen used the contract technique to deal with their dinnertime conflict. Now we'll see how it can be used to find a solution to a more difficult problem.

Paula and Gene were married ten years when they agreed she should resume her career as a reading specialist in a child guidance clinic. Soon she was also consulting for the local school and lecturing at the community college. Meanwhile, Gene's engineering firm was thinking about promoting him to a management position. The couple had worked out many problems in their dual-career marriage, but the one on the horizon troubled Paula.

PAULA: Gene, I'm worried about something and I need to talk to you. You said you think the company's going to move you up to management. Is this what you want?

GENE: I'm pretty sure. More scope to the job, more interesting work—more money, too.

PAULA: I'm all for that. But I've worked hard to get my own career off the ground. If your new job means moving to another city . . . well, I don't want to have to start all over again in a new place.

GENE: I can understand that. I guess I just assumed we'd pack up and go the way we always did.

PAULA: I think we have to look at this carefully . . . weigh all the options so we know where we stand. For instance, suppose *I* wanted to move for a better job and you didn't?

GENE: Well, one, I'd say okay if I could get as good a job in the new town. Two, we could live apart for a while. Three, I might go along but I'd get to make the choice next time it came up.

PAULA: Let's list all the pros and cons for all those possibilities and think about them.

They had much to consider. Paula could probably get another job but she would have to begin at the bottom again. They certainly wouldn't like living apart, yet if the distance wasn't too great, it might be a temporary solution. Gene's job had forced three moves already, and normally Paula would feel she had the right to make the decision this time. But since Paula hadn't given up a career in those previous moves, she didn't think it was fair now to press her opinion on Gene. The couple had to find a compromise both could live with comfortably.

What kind of agreement would you and your spouse come to if you were role-playing Paula and Gene's problem? There are any number of possible compromises. And there is no one *correct* solution. It is the *process* of reaching a contract both persons can accept that is important.

Couples who use these techniques with intelligence and perseverance can make self-counseling succeed. But they must be prepared to work hard at it over a sustained time. (The same is true for couples in traditional counseling. Indeed, it takes effort to make a marriage function in the first place.) We recently suggested self-counseling to a couple who had survived seven years of an alternately lacerating and rewarding relationship. They were concerned about their ability to forget past hurts.

"Can we wipe out of our minds all the grievances . . . the angers . . . the humiliations?" the couple asked.

"Can you," they were asked in response, "go on forever punishing each other for what happened five years ago, or one year ago, or last month?"

Most of us don't think that dilemma through. While we may tell ourselves we want "revenge," we really do *not* want the endproduct of revenge—which is the destruction of the relationship. What we do want, in most cases, is the selfish satisfaction of having "gotten back" at the other person. We block out the fact that, in marriage, revenge creates a backlash that harms oneself as well.

How does one deal with past hurts? How do you keep them from affecting the here and now? Basically, you have to recognize the difference between forgetting and forgiving, and make it part of your self-counseling discipline. You may never forget what has happened between you. But forgiving means to put it behind you emotionally. In that sense, to forgive is necessary if you are to move forward together.

There are other stumbling blocks to overcome in self-counseling:

Expecting too much progress, too soon. It is foolhardy to look for quick or major changes. When they don't take place, one is tempted to give up the whole process. Instead, that is the time to ask yourself some questions. For example: Have you accurately identified the problem? Is your timing wrong? Have you lowered hostility so you can work together? Have you done your marital homework? Are you asking too much of each other?

Failure to stop "blaming." Instead of seeking solutions, are you going along with self-counseling in the hope it will change your partner but let *you* stay the way you are?

Distorting facts and feelings. Therapists talk about the three ways to perceive a marriage—the husband's, the wife's, and a combination of the two based on new understandings. The third version seldom resembles the first two.

The fear of change. Some people prefer to stay in a "living hell" rather than risk the unknown. No matter how awful, its predictability makes it comfortable. But dealing with conflict and improving a marriage mean rocking the boat at least a little. Growth —though sometimes painful—is part of the process. Self-counseling does require the courage to plan and carry out changes.

Using self-counseling for one-shot answers to specific problems. Marital conflicts do not usually exist in emotion-tight compartments. Plugging one leak may only increase the pressure elsewhere. Moreover, marriage itself is not an inflexible state. Circumstances, roles—even spouses—change. As Americans increasingly divorce and remarry, it's unlikely that what worked for Problem X with Spouse 1 will also work with Spouse 2. The techniques of self-counseling, however, will be useful repeatedly.

Couples need to learn more than how to patch up a disagreement here, repair a breakdown there. They need to acquire basic skills for coping with a whole range of marital stress. The French author André Maurois observed that "happy marriage is an edifice that must be rebuilt daily." Self-counseling can make that constant renewal possible.

5

"IS THERE ANYTHING LOWER THAN ZERO?"

Dealing with Differences

Some time ago a friend arrived for a weekend visit at the country home of a well-known marriage counselor. It had been a long and tiring trip, and the guest was looking forward to a glass of wine, a good dinner and some relaxing talk around the fireplace. But when the counselor enthusiastically suggested that they take a brisk hike around a nearby lake his friend did not know how to decline politely. Then the counselor turned to his wife, a research sociologist:

"How would you like to join us in a walk around the lake?" he said jovially.

Without hesitation—and equally jovially—she replied: "Is there anything lower than zero?"

"Ah, well," said the counselor. "If that's how you feel, why don't we all just skip it."

The guest, though glad for the reprieve, was puzzled. "What went on there?" he asked.

The explanation was simple. The couple—both trained in research techniques—had adopted for their own use the "zero-to-ten" scale on which subjects of social surveys and personality tests are often asked to rank their responses to questions. Normally, zero represents total disinterest, unenthusiasm, or displeasure; ten signifies total enthusiasm, enjoyment, agreement. When the counselor or his wife had to express a preference, make a choice, or indicate their attitude about something to one another—whether it be taking a lakeside walk or making love—they often conveyed their feeling via a rating on the scale.

By answering with numbers the couple gave each other an immediate and clear-cut idea of their feelings. They had neatly eliminated, for the most part, those endless and self-defeating discussions most of us go through: *I will if you want to . . . No, I will if you want to . . . But do you really mind? . . . Not if your heart is set on it . . . Well, maybe we shouldn't . . . I don't care, it's up to you.*

When these exchanges are over neither spouse knows for sure how the other truly feels. And more often than not both end up disappointed. Consider, for example, the man who asked his wife if she wanted to join him on an out-of-town business trip during which he was going to have a make-or-break interview with a client.

"If you'd like me to," she said.

"Well, would you enjoy it?"

"Oh, yes. . . . But I might be in the way . . . and I have lots I can do here while you're gone."

"All right," the man said after a moment's silence, "I'll go alone."

Actually, the husband very much wanted his wife to accompany him. He needed her emotional support. She wanted very much to be with him, to give support. But she wasn't sure he meant the invitation, so she decided to give him a face-saving "out." He assumed she was turning him down. She assumed he was turning her down. A couple who both yearned to express mutual love and need ended up believing each had been rejected by the other.

To convey honest feelings openly is for many men and women one of marriage's most difficult obligations. Essentially, most people assume that too much frankness may lead to conflict. It is this potential that alarms them. For when we express true feelings we always run the risk of showing—or finding—that they differ from our spouse's feelings. To have to acknowledge that this is so can be frightening. Yet differences of opinion in marriage are normal. They arise out of the value systems each partner has developed over the years. Value systems are complex, often emotionally loaded, and structured to result in behavior that seems comfortable and "right" to the individual. But one partner's ease is another's discomfort; one's "right" the other's "wrong." What characterizes a successful marriage is how a couple learns to deal with these differences.

Sociological studies show that a main characteristic of "dysfunctional" families—those with the severest conflicts, with recurrent crises, with the least ability to solve their problems—is an extremely low tolerance for differences of attitude or opinion within the family. Any sort of disagreement, no matter how minor, tends to be emotionally threatening to a troubled or anxious person. To a lesser degree, *everyone* gets upset when differences occur. "We just don't agree about anything." That's a statement one hears regularly from couples in counseling. They say it in a tone of voice suitable to confessions of enormous guilt or personal failure. They believe that one or both of them are somehow at fault. But, as we pointed out in discussing the concept of "no-fault" marriage, no blame necessarily attaches to either partner.

Why *should* they agree on everything?

Why should they ever have *expected* they would?

Each of us is unique. We all differ from one another genetically, physiologically, psychologically, socially, culturally. It would be impossible if out of this welter of differences we did not vary in our attitudes and feelings, our preferences and prejudices. Indeed, what could be more unlikely than two people who *always* think alike, react alike, want the same thing at the same time?

Most couples fail to realize that marital tensions do not arise so much out of the differences between partners as out of their inability to deal with them: to face them, express them openly, find ways to accept or to bridge them. The point is not *whether* you and your husband or wife have divergent attitudes or disparate values. Of course you do. The point is whether you are able to explore, understand, and respect each other's value systems. Learning how to be comfortable with differences is a vital step in self-counseling.

THE ROOTS OF DIFFERENCE

Some of the patterns by which we shape and run our lives grow out of biological basics. We can no more be held accountable for them than for the color of our eyes. Take, for example, the rhythm of the internal time clock by which our body works. Scientists know that humans are subject to the influence of many periodic "cycles"—light and dark, seasonal changes, moon phases, electromagnetic ebbs and flows in the atmosphere. They do not yet fully understand exactly *how* these cycles modify behavior, but it is agreed that they have significant effects. Differences in a couple's internal clocks can be one source of trouble in marriage.

We're all familiar with the "morning" person. He or she bounces cheerily out of bed at 6 A.M., is filled with energy to face the day's activities, begins to slow down in the afternoon, and has trouble staying awake much past mid-evening. The "night" person seldom begins to function adequately before noon, picks up speed as the day passes, and is still going strong long after midnight. What can happen when a "morning" person and a "night" person marry was illustrated recently by a couple who sought counseling for—they said—a sexual problem. Questioning unearthed the fact that the husband was ready to retire at ten o'clock. He wanted his wife to go to bed at that hour, too, even though she was wide awake and in the midst of her most energetic and productive hours. Otherwise, he said, there was virtually no opportunity for any sex life.

HUSBAND: By the time Alice is ready to turn in, I'm asleep. And in the morning I'm out of bed long before she's even half-awake.

MARCIA LASSWELL: I can see that if your internal clocks are that much out of sync, it must be difficult to arrange a mutually agreeable time for sex. Outside of arguing about it, have you made any efforts to reach some sort of compromise?

WIFE: Well, I'm just not ready for sex in the morning, so I volunteered to go to bed early some nights so we can make love.

ML: And that hasn't worked?

W: The problem is that he doesn't like it when I get up again. He wants me to stay in bed. But I'm not sleepy then.

ML: It seems to me that you have more than a sexual problem. What's really going on here, Curt, is that you'd like Alice to change her sleeping habits to match yours.

H (reluctantly): When you put it that way, I suppose . . . well

. . . yes. It doesn't make sense to stay up till two in the morning and then be bleary for half the next day!

ML (to husband): You really do believe that early-to-bed and early-to-rise is the best pattern, don't you?

H: It *is*. Everyone knows that. If you can't get up early in the morning to greet the day, something's wrong in your life.

ML: Curt, where did you find your "golden tablets"?

H: *What* "golden tablets"?

ML: The ones that give you the *truth*. You sound so positive that this is absolutely right for everyone.

H: Well, that part *is* true about greeting the day, isn't it?

ML: About half the people in the world will disagree with you, I expect. You know, much of how early you can cheerfully "greet the day" depends on when you went to bed. You have a value about when to go to sleep that comes from your own internal time clock. Every person's peak energy hours seem to be determined largely by this biological fact.

H: Then how do we work this out?

ML: First, you have to *accept* your difference. It is just *there*. No one is creating it on purpose . . . it is neither your fault nor Alice's. Then you identify and isolate the problems that grow out of the difference and try to figure out ways to deal with them—as we've started to do in your case.

It was not easy for this husband to accept the fact that his wife's different energy pattern was biologically based. He would have preferred to think she was being stubborn or selfish, for then he would be able to blame her for their conflict rather than have to work toward a compromise. Yet when the shoe was on the other foot he saw differences more clearly. In a subsequent counseling session with this same couple, the wife brought out a complaint of her own: She usually stuck to a task around the house until it was finished, while her husband took frequent "breaks" from the job on hand.

WIFE: It really gripes me when you sit down for a beer or read the paper while there's still so much left to do.

HUSBAND: I invite you to sit down, too, don't I?

W: I *can't* sit down until the work is done—if I did, it wouldn't get done!

MARCIA LASSWELL: Are you saying that Curt doesn't do his share?

W: No. It just makes me mad to go on working while he's sitting there.

ML: Why do you stop when you know it upsets Alice so much?

H: I'm tired—that's why! When I work I give it all I've got. I do the maximum in the minimum amount of time. She's more the slow and steady type.

ML: Who actually does the most work?

H & W (Looking at each other for confirmation and replying almost simultaneously): It's pretty even.

ML: So, you each do your share in your own way. Why isn't that okay?

Personality differences between spouses pose more complex problems. To begin with, one of you is male and one female. Although it is increasingly clear that Freud's dictum that "anatomy is destiny" is no longer valid, and although the women's movement has made remarkable headway in eliminating invidious distinctions between the sexes—nevertheless boys and girls are still socialized quite differently in their early years. The so-called "masculine" and "feminine" traits are learned early in life. The typical boy, for instance, is encouraged to "act like a man." This usually means holding in such emotions as hurt and fear. When this boy grows up to become a husband, the way he handles negative feelings may puzzle his wife—who as a girl was allowed to cry when she was distressed or afraid. Not long ago a couple who were not making much progress in their counseling began to wonder out loud whether getting divorced would be more painful to them than staying in an unhappy marriage. The conversation soon turned to the different ways in which husband and wife reacted to the idea of separating:

HUSBAND: The thing that bothers me is that a divorce will make the children so sad.

WIFE: And what bothers me is that you don't speak of your own sadness—just theirs.

H: Isn't it perfectly understandable to worry about the kids?

w: But you don't say how *you* feel.

MARCIA LASSWELL (to husband): How do you feel about the children's sadness?

H (slowly): I'm concerned about them.

ML (persistently): But how does your concern *feel?* Stay with what's going on inside you emotionally as you get in touch with what your concern causes *you* to feel.

H (fighting an obvious lump in his throat, which he attempts to clear): I feel sad . . . I don't want to break up my home . . . I really like being married.

w (gently): Why was that so hard to say? I tell you every day how sad I feel.

ML (to wife): But *he* is not *you*. What *he* feels comes out in a different way. This isn't a new problem—you've told me you always had trouble getting him to talk your language, emotionally.

w: Yes, I know. I've never really learned that his feelings are under there some place even if he doesn't talk about them easily.

H: It makes me just as uncomfortable when you *cry*, you know, as I think you are when I don't.

These two people had been trying to make each other over emotionally for fifteen years. Neither had really accepted the personality differences that caused them to react in opposite ways emotionally. They had proceeded all that time on the theory that "if it's different, it's wrong." Many of their problems stemmed from this incapacity to *let* the other *be* different.

Another source of divergent values between spouses is rooted in the family backgrounds each brings to the marriage. Every person carries through life the attitudes and standards imprinted on him or her by the culture in which he or she grew up. The values of parents, siblings, teachers, friends, the environment and experiences of childhood—all contribute to this pattern. It is, in effect, an internalized "rulebook" for the way we behave and think, and for the way we view others' ideas and actions. Some of us continue to follow those "rules"; some of us rebel and follow a diametrically opposite path. Either way, we are respounding to their influence.

Even the order in which one is born into a family—only or oldest child, middle child, youngest child—has a major effect on personality development. Experts in "birth order" tell us that this positioning affects our adult outlook on life in many ways. Only and oldest children tend to grow up to be conscientious, competitive, and controlling, but at the same time emotionally secure. Middle children, overshadowed by both older and younger siblings, carry with them a special need for attention. At the same time, they have learned to be self-reliant, tactful, able to get along with all sorts of people in a quiet and undemanding way. Youngest children, usually overindulged and babied beyond their time, are likely to go right on as adults craving affection and being dependent, always yearning for the love and attention they got in their early years. Obviously these differences are apt to give rise in marriage to conflicting—or at least diverging—attitudes and needs.

These heritages from what sociologists call one's "family of origin" did not always cause so much trouble. A generation or two ago most Americans married within their own social and economic strata, within their own religion, indeed for the most part within their own community. Thus, one's background and view of life were likely to be quite similar to that of one's spouse. This is, of course, no longer true. As a result, counselors are seeing an increasing number of couples whose inherent differences are complicated and intensified by the dissimilarities in their backgrounds. For example:

• A couple came to the brink of divorce because she was accustomed to having a full-fledged Sunday dinner after church, and he was used to a large, late-morning brunch and a light supper. Their battles over this ruined virtually every weekend.

• A man whose parents came to the United States from southern Italy, and who was raised in a traditionally male-dominated home, accepted the idea of his wife's taking a job—but he forbade her to have lunch with any male co-worker. "As far as he's concerned," the woman said, "it's equivalent to infidelity."

• A man who grew up in a home where serviceability—in furnishings, clothes, cars—was more important than style or showiness married a woman whose parents insisted on the "right" things even if it meant having fewer of them. For years he forced his way of life on his wife despite her increasing complaints. Their crisis came when, no longer able to contain her yearnings for the lifestyle she remembered, she threatened to leave her husband.

The clash of background influence appears most clearly, perhaps, in disagreements over the management of family finances—no matter whether the total income is large or small. Ideas about which spouse should handle the money, which should make financial decisions, how income should be apportioned between spending and saving—these are more often than not formed by what one's parents did. Like it or not, *their* approach to money exerts enormous influence on your financial values, goals, and attitudes. When a money decision must be made, the voice of a parent still echoes across time saying, "This is how to do it." (As we noted earlier, a person may follow that voice, or go 180 degrees in the other direction—but it is that voice to which we still respond.) The following excerpt from a case file shows vividly how husbands and wives not only continue to replay "family of origin" recordings, but how they use them against each other:

HUSBAND: I can't see this baloney about having six months' income in a savings account. Why save for a sailboat when I can get it now and pay it off while I enjoy it? Mary acts like my job is going to fold tomorrow and we'll starve to death. My parents always told me: "We work hard, so we deserve to have what we want."

WIFE: But we have so many bills already. You act as if using a charge card isn't really spending money. It *is*—plus the extra we pay for all that interest.

MARCIA LASSWELL: Just out of curiosity, Mary, did your parents buy things on credit?

W: My parents were divorced when I was ten and my brother was twelve. My mother went to work in a department store and my dad sent what little support he could. We *never* bought on credit because we couldn't afford the extra charges. And it scares me to death not to have a savings account . . . I remember times, when I was a kid, when any emergency expense became a disaster.

ML: Bob, was there enough money when you were growing up?

H: Yes, but we weren't rich. We just enjoyed our money. We always bought top quality because it would last longer.

W: That's another problem. I usually buy the least expensive item and even if I have to replace it sooner, it adds up to less than what Bob will pay.

ML: You'd make a good accountant, Mary. You've learned some practical approaches to money. But do you suppose you're more frugal than you *need* to be, now, because you believe Bob spends too much?

W (after a moment's thought): No, I don't think so. I really feel we'd be bankrupt if I didn't hold the line. I have to save to make up for Bob's spending.

H (emphatically): And we'd live like paupers but die with a bankful of money if Mary had her way!

ML: Do you suppose your spending patterns, Bob, are a reaction to Mary's thriftiness—maybe even *more* extravagant than they ordinarily would be?

H: I have to admit that sometimes I do it to try to loosen her up a bit.

ML: So, what it comes down to is that you, Mary, may be extra-thrifty to make up for Bob's spending; and you, Bob, are extravagant to "loosen up" Mary. It's not unusual for two people with opposing views to react by exaggerating their positions. But doubling your efforts to compensate for what you see as shortcomings in each other's values is only driving you further apart. You're not convincing each other. You're only becoming more antagonistic.

W: So, what's the answer? I just give in to him?

H: Or me to her?

ML: Nobody has to "give in," as you put it. What you must do is work out a philosophy about money that you both can live with. But it has to be *your* philosophy—not your parents'. What worked for them isn't important any more. What counts is what will work for both of you.

Fortunately, most couples *do* hold many values in common. Otherwise they would never have been attracted to each other in the first place. One of the strongest factors in choosing a mate, sociologists tell us, are shared goals and attitudes. What often occurs to confuse this, however, is that a couple dazzled by the glow of romance see similarities where none actually exist. Many studies show that a person tends to "idealize" the image of the one he or she loves . . . to gloss over faults, to deny differences or to ignore them in the foolish expectation that they will disappear—i.e., that the other person will change—after marriage. (The latter, of course, seldom, if ever, happens.) Moreover, a person in love makes every effort to please; so, quite often, he or she *pretends* to agree with—or even temporarily adopts—the other's values.

The upshot: a variety of later conflicts which are directly traceable to the inaccurate picture we have of the man or woman we marry. Inaccurate either because of pretense or idealization. Indeed, it is not surprising for a spouse to accuse the other of changing his or her values once the wedding takes place. As one distressed young woman wailed: "The minute it was legal, he changed. We were still on our honeymoon and Bill said, 'Okay, the fun and games are over. Now you have to do your duty as a good wife.' I was absolutely flabbergasted! Here was this thoughtful, solicitous guy who couldn't do enough for me, suddenly telling me how I had to change—and *right now!* His ideas of a good wife were totally different from what he had soft-soaped me with for six months."

Differences are also part of the initial affinity between people. Similarities can be powerful magnets that help draw a man and woman together, but there is also some truth to the saying that "opposites attract"—at least early in a relationship. A marriage therapist will often ask a couple in one of their first counseling sessions, "What attracted you to each other?" It is not unusual to get such replies as: "She was outgoing and easy to talk to. I am rather quiet and I always have been drawn to extroverts." "He is so sensible and practical and I'm the spontaneous type. I could always count on him to keep things in focus." "He's an outdoor man. I never was any good at those things even though I always wanted to be."

And Mary and Bob, the couple with opposite values about money, might well have answered the question this way:

Mary: "Bob really knew how to have a good time. He took me to the nicest places and he was always generous. I grew up poor, and there were so many things I could never afford that it was a whole new way of life to me."

Bob: "Mary was appreciative; she never expected me to spend a lot of money on her the way other girls did. So it made me feel good to give her things she'd never had. And when I gave her something she took good care of it, put it to good use. She was sensible and practical, and I liked that."

HOW TO DEAL WITH DIFFERENCES

Most couples feel defeated by their differences. Quite often a counselor's hardest task is to make them realize how wrong this attitude is. We begin—as you can for yourself—by emphasizing that it is natural for each partner to have his or her own value system . . . that it is *not* a sign of basic discord or of deliberate antagonism. We try—as you can—to develop a common-sense approach in a couple: to distinguish surface differences from deeper discord; to be aware that differences are not as critical as the intensity of the accompanying emotions makes them seem; to be aware when disagreements are subconsciously being used to aggravate a problem that has no real relation to those disagreements—as when a couple, say, attack each other's child-raising methods to vent anger over a sexual conflict.

But common sense, awareness, insight, are difficult to develop. This is especially true when couples are concentrating on what separates them rather than on what can join them. As a result, counselors frequently use various "action" techniques to help couples deal with differences in practical ways. We've adapted half a dozen techniques that are suitable and effective in self-counseling.

The zero-to-ten rating scale. By asking "Is there anything lower than zero?" the wife in our earlier story conveyed a highly negative view of a walk around the lake. Her husband's enthusiasm for the project was then promptly re-evaluated in the light of her feelings. Almost any specific situation can be dealt with in this fashion, thus short-circuiting much misunderstanding and disappointment, many resigned silences or martyr-like compliances.

When you use the rating scale, however, you must be absolutely honest. (We'll say more about marital honesty in a moment.)

Announcing a number need not be the arbitrary end of the matter. For when both of you have indicated numerically where you stand, negotiations can begin. For example, sometimes an exploration of why your partner voted as he or she did can actually change your vote. To learn that the party you are too tired to attend is in honor of long-time neighbors who are moving away might change your mind about going. To discover that your husband doesn't want to go to the museum on a Saturday afternoon because he is not feeling well may make you stop pressing the issue; you might even decide to go alone and let him take a nap in a quiet house.

The zero-to-ten technique is of particular help to husbands and wives who tend to "hold back" on how they really feel when a decision is to be made. There are many reasons for being reluctant to announce bluntly where you stand. You may wish to avoid an argument, or to encourage a special interest your spouse has just taken up but which you do not share, or simply to please the other person. But sometimes you say something you don't really mean because you're not sure of your feelings, or because the reasons behind them are vague. For example, if you're asked whether you want to go to the movies and you answer, "I'm about five on that," it could mean "I can take it or leave it, it really doesn't matter"; or, "I'm ambivalent—part of it sounds good and part I don't like." (When "yes" or "no" is the answer to "Do you want to go to the movies?" a lot of information may be omitted. And merely saying, "I don't care," can mean, so far as your partner is concerned, anything from a passionate "yes" to a violent "no.") By answering "five" you are not only quantifying your feelings but also opening up a reasoned discussion. For example, perhaps the idea of a movie sounds good but you have already spent a lot of money on entertainment that week. Rather than say "yes" or "no" in that case, it is easier to hedge with "I'll go if *you* want to." But that doesn't get anybody anywhere. How much better to say, "I'm five. Actually, I'm eight on seeing the picture but I'm two on spending that much money before payday."

Not all differences can be reduced to a simple scale. Some are too complex to quantify. It would be hard to pick a number for

"Do you want to buy a house?" or, "How do you feel about having a baby?" Perhaps a few rare couples might be able to reduce these topics to numbers. But a woman who votes three on having a baby when her husband votes nine obviously has some serious talking to do with him.

Get your "hidden agenda" out in the open. One partner or the other often has secret motives that influence his or her thinking. The other person is seldom aware of the existence of this "hidden agenda." Nor does the *real* reason behind the decisions ever become known. A typical example came up recently in counseling:

WIFE: My husband hates to eat out but once in a while, just to be nice, he'll suggest it. I feel I *have* to go even if I don't want to. This happened just last week. I was too tired to get dressed up so I said let's go to a neighborhood coffee shop. Since I hadn't wanted to go out in the first place, and since the food was just so-so, I didn't feel it was really "going out." Then, last Saturday I suggested we go out to eat. He looked at me as if I was crazy. "I just took you out on Tuesday," he said. I said, "You call that going out?" And he got furious.

What happened? Both spouses had gone out when neither wanted to. The wife broke that important rule: *Never say what you do not mean.* When two people are trying to understand each other, giving reliable information is essential. Having a "hidden agenda" makes this difficult, if not impossible. If the message you give or get is not an honest one, then the best-intentioned behavior can be far off the mark. The husband took his wife out to eat because she said she wanted to go. He acted in good faith. But the act was based on unreliable data. To have it come out well would have been most unlikely. If the couple had used the zero-to-ten technique things might have gone something like this:

HUSBAND: You look tired. Would you rather eat out than cook tonight?
WIFE: I *am* bushed. But to tell you the truth, I'm only two about going out.

H: Well, you know I am *always* about zero, so that suits me fine. What *would* you like to do about dinner?

W: Could you pick up some Chinese food on your way home?

H: I'm about three on Chinese food, but I'd rate pizza about ten.

W: Okay, I can come up with a seven on pizza myself.

Develop the art of "viewpoint-meshing." There are few situations in life where there is one—and only one—*absolutely right way* to think or feel or act. Even diametrically opposed attitudes can both be perfectly reasonable in certain circumstances. Indeed, there are probably several approaches that would work equally well. The trick is to mesh them so that you maximize their combined strengths and minimize their weaknesses.

The first step in this process is to realize that there are no "golden tablets" engraved with "the truth." Each of you has an equal right to your opinion. If you want your partner to respect your viewpoint, you must respect his or hers in return. To deny your partner's right to have individual differences is to deny his or her integrity and intelligence—to deny personhood. But to accept a difference is not the same as to approve of it. You don't have to like something just because it exists. If, for instance, you planned to take the family on a picnic and wake up to find that it's raining you will not be pleased by the weather. But you are certainly not going to deny that it *is* raining. You are disappointed, but you accept the situation.

The work of viewpoint-meshing begins with this acceptance. So long as you refuse to acknowledge the possible validity of another's ideas you cannot begin to merge the differences between you. (And merging differences—or meshing viewpoints—is more than mere compromise. The latter attempts to find a neutral middle ground between two positions; the former attempts to take the best of both and combine them into a single perspective.)

It is not easy to sit across from someone with whom you strongly differ and try to find the points on which you can agree. If face-to-face confrontation is difficult at first, you can experiment with an approach derived from the techniques of Socratic dialogue. The Greek philosopher Socrates traditionally conducted his discourses to his students by asking questions and answering them himself. You can adapt this as a way to try meshing viewpoints in certain situations. For example, a husband and wife differ strongly about when their ten-year-old daughter should go to bed. The wife wants her to go to her room promptly at eight each night; the husband says, "let her stay up till she's sleepy." Rather than argue with her husband, the woman asks a series of questions of herself, and answers them:

Q: Why do I want her to go to bed early?
A: So she'll get enough rest and be alert when she goes to school.

Q: Any other reasons?
A: It's not good for her health to stay up late.

Q: Anything else?
A: Well, to be honest, I'd like some peace and quiet in the house so I can have some relaxed time for myself.

Q: That's all?
A: I need time to be alone with my husband. We never have a chance to talk when the child's around.

Q: Those are all valid reasons. Must they lead to a squabble?
A: My husband would think I was being selfish.

Q: Can I work this out with the child rather than with him, so that both our views can be meshed?
A: If I look at it that way, maybe I can. Suppose I made a bargain with my daughter that she can go to bed when *she* wants to if she promises to play quietly in her room and to get up promptly in the mornings.

Q: Would that satisfy everyone?
A: If it works.

Q: How can I know if it will work?
A: Give it a try, I guess.

Recognize when you are parroting parental attitudes. This involves learning enough about yourself to know which attitudes are truly your own and which are the subconscious remains of childhood experiences. You might even establish a "code word" that would automatically alert you—and your spouse—whenever you realize either of you are falling back into those early patterns. In Gilbert and Sullivan's comic operetta *Ruddigore,* for instance, a daft maiden who is subject to spells of delirium manages to snap out of them when someone says "Basingstoke!" Perhaps you could accomplish your purpose with a brisk "Family of origin!"

Learn how to meet the "empathy challenge." To merge differences one must understand a partner's point of view. You may ultimately become convinced his or her ideas have some merit. The kind of understanding we are talking about is called "empathy"—the ability to put yourself in another person's shoes long enough to conceive *how* he or she can see things as they do. No one is born with empathy. But anyone who is truly interested in or concerned about another person can learn to develop it.

Being empathetic is not difficult when the behavior you are attempting to understand is close to what you might do in a similar situation. "I can understand why he feels that way" usually means that his feelings are close to what yours might be if faced with the same circumstances. But empathy is harder to achieve when the other's way of reacting is out of your range of possibilities, or when it challenges a value you consider to be a "truth." Even marital therapists, for whom empathy is a necessary skill, have their share of difficulty when a basic value of theirs is challenged. But counseling is a learned art, and each time the empathy challenge is met the therapist grows a bit. A man and woman who expect to remain married to each other can well envision the creation of their life together as an art, too. Each time they truly understand each other, they also grow a bit.

Most couples in marital therapy have to be helped to develop the skills of empathy. One learning technique you can adapt for self-counseling is, as we mentioned previously, *reverse role-playing:* assuming your spouse's role in marriage long enough to get a "gut feeling" of what it is like. For example, if you believe you have been short-changed by the way household chores have been divided between the two of you, trading those tasks for a week may provide new insights into each other's situation. A husband felt his wife was an extravagant food-shopper; she complained that he didn't spend enough time on the lawn and shrubbery to keep them neat. They did each other's job for two weeks. "It's remarkable how our perspectives changed," the wife said. "He found out how much it costs to eat these days, and I discovered how much time it takes to do the yard *my* way."

Increased mutual understanding may not solve any problems by itself. But it does lay the groundwork for discussing them more sympathetically. A husband who must run the house and care for the children while his wife is ill develops a new appreciation for her burdens. A wife who goes back to work begins to empathize with the job stresses her husband complains about.

Another kind of role-reversal technique that can help to develop empathy is switching positions on issues about which you disagree —taking and defending the opposite point of view. Debaters often do this when they speak for a proposition they are emotionally opposed to, or in favor of one they disapprove. This is effective because it is impossible to voice the other person's opinion without gaining some new insight into his or her feelings. Even if your partner writes a "script" for you to read (this is one variation of the technique), acting it out with conviction still produces a new dimension of understanding. Or you can combine the zero-to-ten scale with position-switching. If you vote "eight" and your spouse votes "two" on going to a party, try putting forth each other's reasons and see if that narrows the difference between you.

Be honest with each other—but be clear about what you each mean by honesty. Truth-telling in marriage is a key factor in dealing with differences. We have pointed out how important it is never to say anything you don't really mean. But "honesty" means different things to different people. Some insist on absolute truth; some accept half-truths, or little white lies, or discreet silences. Even if a couple agrees on a definition of honesty, a partner may not always speak or act in a way consistent with that definition.

There may sometimes be an overriding reason for *not* being honest. It may reflect consideration for a spouse's feelings: "When I know my husband had a hard day at the store, I don't think he needs to hear about my little problems. So I say my day has been 'fine' even if it hasn't." Or the reason may be to protect yourself (or someone else) from the consequences of telling the truth: "Our son took the car against my husband's orders and drove it into a neighbor's fence. He didn't damage the car, and he's going to pay for the fence repair out of his own money. So I didn't see any reason to make trouble by telling my husband about it."

Yet, are you always sure of your motives? Do you know when "consideration for a spouse's feelings" is actually a camouflage for your reluctance to be frank? It is important to be honest with *yourself* about why you are saying something that is not true, or that you do not mean. Withholding information, or providing inaccurate information, may occasionally be wise or necessary. But the decision to do so should be a conscious one on your part.

One marital counselor recommends what he calls "measured honesty" between spouses. This involves asking yourself three questions before you volunteer any information: Is it true? Is it necessary that the other person know it? Is this the right time to talk about it?

If the information is not true, why are you passing it on? What is the purpose of responding to a spouse's suggestion by saying, "I don't mind," or "It's okay with me," if, in fact, you *do* mind and it is *not* okay? Some people agree to a plan they secretly dislike and grouse about it later. A grumbling husband who says, "I didn't want to go in the first place but I could see you had your mind set on it," is not being fair or helpful to the wife who took him at his original word. The wife who regularly "fakes" orgasm to please her husband is not solving their sexual problem, but preventing it from being solved.

If the other person doesn't need to be told something, why volunteer the information? There are purists who believe that deliberately leaving truth unspoken is as dishonest as telling a falsehood. But carrying a definition of honesty to this extreme means that many private thoughts, anxieties, dreams, fantasies—all would have to be shared. Who among us really tells all? Who among us really wants to know all? Indeed, total frankness may sometimes be more destructive than helpful. It is always sensible to ask yourself: *What is behind my words? Why am I asking this question? Do I really want to hear the answer?* A woman who repeatedly asked her husband if he thought she was overweight finally learned this lesson. Out of consideration for her feelings he had been evading the truth with statements such as: "Well, there's just a little more of you to love," or, "You're such a good cook, I've put on a few extra pounds myself." One day he gave her the answer she did not want to hear. It hurt badly. Why then did she go on asking the question? Surely not to get a truthful answer. Being honest with each other is more than giving truthful answers—it is asking honest questions based on an open agenda. And even if a fact or feeling *is* true, and it *is* necessary for the other person to know about it, measured honesty requires that you choose an appropriate time to communicate it—when you are relaxed and have privacy.

Measuring honesty so that it does not hurt or offend your partner is an acceptable technique when you are volunteering information. A trickier question is what to do when you are *asked* for information you have some doubts about giving. "What did you do all day?" may be a wholly innocent question. On the other hand it could be a leading question designed to get confirmation or denial of something on the questioner's "hidden agenda." Not long ago a couple in counseling raised just such an issue.

The husband, a jealous and controlling person, had seen his wife's car parked outside an expensive restaurant one noontime. That evening he "casually" asked, "Where did you eat today?" Actually, she had lunched with an attractive man who worked in her office. For two reasons—irrational guilt feelings, and to avoid a scene with her jealous spouse—she said, "I just grabbed a sandwich in a delicatessen." Instantly the trap snapped. The husband said he'd seen her car, accused her of being involved with a man, and cornered her into defiance. There was a violent scene, and both spouses told the counselor how distressed they were at the way they had handled the situation.

MARCIA LASSWELL: Let me suggest another way you might have handled it. For instance, Toni, when John asks where you had lunch and you really don't want to tell him, you have a right to know what's behind his question—what his "hidden agenda" is, if any.

WIFE: You mean I should say, "Why do you want to know?"

ML: You could ask that, I suppose, but it sounds more like an attack than a question. What was your first reaction to John's question?

W: I thought I must have been acting odd, or that he was psychic.

ML: Then could you have said, "John, that's the one part of my day that I don't want to discuss. Is there some special reason it's so important to you?"

W: (dubiously): What would you have done then, John? Would you accept my saying I didn't want to discuss something you asked about?

HUSBAND: Probably not. I would really have been suspicious then.

ML: But you were *already* suspicious. How would being more suspicious have changed your behavior?

H: I guess I would have gotten even madder.

ML: What answer would have made you feel okay, John?

H: Oh, I suppose if she'd said she was with a girl friend.

ML: Then you really *didn't* want to hear the truth? I think you were convinced she wasn't with a girl friend or you would simply have said you saw her car. Why hide what you knew if you weren't trying to corner her?

H: If I said, "I saw your car there," she'd have a better chance to cover up.

ML: Isn't that an admission that you were setting a trap? Now, the question is whether or not you wanted a confession? Did you want to hear that what you suspected—that she was out with an attractive man—was true?

H: No, not really.

ML: Then why did you ask? Asking questions to force Toni into revealing what you don't want to hear makes no sense.

H: Now I'm confused. What *should* I have done?

ML: Knowing that your jealousy is a problem, the honest thing would have been to have made a statement: "I saw your car at lunch time today." Toni, then, would have had a wide range of things she could have said that were true. What *would* you have said, Toni?

W: If John had given me his entire "hidden agenda," I would have told him that I like this man as a friend but that John has no need to be jealous. I only see the man once a month, and I just enjoy talking with him.

ML: Those are all true statements? Nothing there you don't mean?

W: It's all true. He *is* a very attractive man but I love John and I don't want to do anything to jeopardize our marriage.

ML: When either of you wants information from the other, you have an obligation to say why. Nobody has a right to "mind-probe" without identifying his or her purpose.

Anthropologist Ruth Benedict often wrote about the "co-operative energy" that flows like an electric current through a harmonious group. Similarly, two people working together can achieve more than either could individually using the same amount of time and effort. This effect is called "synergy"—the enrichment, the added strength, the extra hidden ingredient that occurs when a couple complement each other by bridging their differences.

Indeed, the differences are almost as important as the similarities so far as the synergic reaction is concerned. A traveler in a foreign country who fears or fights the differences in its culture does not enjoy his trip nearly so much as the traveler who accepts, respects, and even enjoys those differences. Much the same is true in marriage. If two people are exactly alike (which, of course, no two people are but which some couples seem determined to become), they limit the potential that synergy provides. For differences add not only interest but also strength when both husband and wife have learned how to deal with them.

6

WHY "WINNING" DOESN'T WORK

• A woman in her early forties discovers that her husband is having a series of brief affairs with several younger women in his office. She is reluctant to force the issue for fear that a confrontation will break up their marriage. Yet she is determined that he won't get away with his philandering. Bitterly, she tells herself she is not about to "take this lying down"—a classic Freudian translation of her subconscious attempt to retaliate by refusing to sleep with her husband. For the next few months she "suffers" violent tension headaches almost every evening that "prevent" her from making love. She sees this as a victory in their undeclared sexual war. But by depriving her husband of sex at home, she gives him the excuse to seek more of it outside. As in the topsy-turvy Orwellian world of 1984, winning is losing.

• A man who married while still in college has to drop out in his junior year when his bride unexpectedly gets pregnant. He gives up his dream of going to law school and takes a dead-end job to support his family. He secretly blames his wife for the "accident." Resentful, he turns their life into a minor hell with constant criticism of everything his wife does no matter how much she tries to please him. After a year of this she offers to give him a divorce. He refuses. "Then will you go with me to a marriage counselor?" she asks. He agrees reluctantly but then does all he can to sabotage the process: fails to show up for appointments, stays silent through entire sessions, breaks promises to change his behavior. It is clear to the counselor that the man *subconsciously* does not want matters to improve. Any solution to the emotional impasse he has created would undercut the self-destructive revenge he "wins" each day. So the couple remain locked in a mutually miserable marriage. Again, winning is losing.

• Another couple continually pick fights with each other to prove who's "boss" in the household. The incessant quarreling makes their ten-year-old daughter tense and insecure; at school she becomes a troublemaker and an under-achiever. The parents in their neurotic need to "win" arguments at home, do not see that they are making their child the loser—and consequently they lose, too.

Like the Petri dishes of a high-school biology class, marriage provides fertile ground in which the germs of conflict can flourish. Simply by sharing space and time together spouses limit each other's freedom of choice and action in a score of ways every day. Out of these limitations, conflicts arise. The conflicts may be deep-seated and convoluted in their complexity, like the ones we have just described. Or they may be small struggles of wills over which movie to see, or whether to eat out or at home. Yet every conflict —big or little, long term or quickly over, fundamental or superficial —involves some emotional separation between husband and wife. *How* they approach that gulf is a key factor in whether it will widen or be made more bridgeable. Indeed, how well a marriage works depends in large part on how well a couple learn to handle their disagreements.

Some couples habitually fall into the trap of dealing with conflict on a win-or-lose basis. They do not seem to realize that this is the least effective, most alienating method they can use. The idea of "winning" a marital conflict is an illusion. In virtually every instance one person's "victory" eventually turns into both spouses' ultimate loss. Winning simply doesn't work.

It has taken many decades for society to recognize this truth in its approach to that climactic marital conflict—divorce. Only recently have we recognized that by forcing husbands and wives to confront each other in divorce court as legal adversaries—where one must "win" and the other "lose"—in order for a decree to be granted, we create a sink of ill will that spills over not only on the spouses but on their children as well. Fortunately, the concept of no-fault divorce has begun to do away with the labels of winner and loser in that arena. Perhaps the principles of no-fault marriage can in a similar fashion gradually help to eliminate the win-lose approach within matrimony.

How can a self-counseling couple go about discovering whether they seek to "win" marital conflicts rather than to *solve* them?

First, by learning to identify the techniques that can be used— consciously or unconsciously—to gain victory in a conflict. These are often well camouflaged. But there are certain clues that help to spot a person who has to "win."

Second, by learning why people behave this way—by coming to grips with the subtle motivations that lie behind one's need to be a winner. To such persons, being "right" not only seems to be extremely satisfying but actually essential to their sense of well-being.

Third, by learning constructive methods for settling differences, couples can break out of "win-lose" behavior patterns. Marital therapists teach couples to substitute problem-solving processes for their battle tactics. The couple start with small problems and practice until they can make the substitution easily. In self-counseling, learning how to solve problems step by step may seem to be a slow process, but it is surely worth the effort.

Techniques—How Some Spouses Fight to Win

Do You Ever Use Extreme or Irrational Tactics to Gain Your Point? Not long ago, at a dinner party at a friend's home, we were talking about arguing in marriage with a brisk, petite woman in her late twenties. She insisted that she and her husband always talked out a disagreement until they reached a mutually satisfactory decision. "But surely," we said, "one of you must have to yield to the other sometimes? What happens then?"

"Well, if it looks like I'm the one who's going to have to give in," the wife said brightly, "I get hysterical. Oh, not actually out of control, you know," she went on, "just hysterical *enough*. Say that I want to go to the movies and he doesn't. If we finally 'decide' not to go—and I *really* want to go—I let myself get hysterical . . . and we go."

Another time a husband confided that more than once he had surreptitiously let the air out of a tire or removed the distributor cap from the car to avoid going to a party he didn't want to attend. He said he used to chuckle at his cleverness until it struck him that his wife was always so disappointed that she withdrew into a depressed silence that sometimes lasted several days.

Are You Willing to Hurt Your Spouse in Order to "Win"? Some husbands or wives will use any handy emotional equivalent of the street-brawler's tactics: gouging a partner's self-esteem, jamming a knee into pride. Strictly speaking, this is not so much a way of winning an argument as it is of having the last word—of recouping one's position after the issue in conflict has already been lost.

For example, a recently married couple were planning their first important dinner party. Michele wanted it to be perfect—less to impress her guests than to make her husband proud of her. She took a half-day off from work to clean their small apartment, polish the wedding-present silver, arrange the candles and centerpiece of flowers on the dining table. No gourmet cook, Michele had planned a simple meal. But there was one thing she made superbly well—a graham-cracker chocolate cream cake. When Michele told Larry she was going to serve that for dessert, he warned her against trying it: "It needs a lot of time to come out right, and you're going to be rushed anyway. If anything goes wrong you'll have no dessert at all to serve." When Michele insisted, Larry shrugged. "I think you're crazy, hon. Keep it simple. *Buy* a cake."

Everything took longer than Michele expected on the afternoon of the dinner. She was late getting the cake out of the oven to cool. She waited as long as she could, until just before the guests arrived; but even so when she unmolded the cake the layers split apart. Larry heard her wail, strode into the kitchen, and took one look at the fragments on the counter. At that moment, Larry could have said any number of comforting words, made a variety of supportive gestures. He could have offered simple sympathy: *That's a shame, you worked so hard.* Or he could have just held Michele close for a moment until she calmed down. Better yet, he could have stepped into the breach with a helpful suggestion: *Don't worry—we'll cut the cake into sections and put some ice cream over them. It'll be fine.* Instead, Larry took advantage of the opportunity to prove to Michele that he had, indeed, been right all along. What Larry actually said was: "Didn't I tell you it was dumb to try to make that cake? *Now* what are you going to do for dessert?" In effect Larry was saying, *See, I win after all!*

Michele knew she had misjudged her time; she certainly didn't need Larry to keep pushing the point. She realized that her feelings didn't matter at all to her husband in his moment of "victory." "I came within an inch of throwing the whole mess in his face," she said later. "If it weren't for our guests, I would have!" The couple scarcely spoke to each other for days—a rather high emotional cost for a failed cake. One of the hazards of moving in for the "kill," as Larry did, is that there isn't always company coming to keep the other person from retaliating. If Michele had come back fighting, the couple might have started a cycle of conflict that could have escalated dangerously.

Do You Store Up Grudges and Use Them to "Blackmail" a Spouse into Surrender? Few techniques are so effective at winning marital arguments (or so destructive over the long term) as hoarding old emotional hurts, carefully nurturing them, and producing them at a climactic moment. For example, a middle-aged salesman, harried and tired-looking, came to the counselor's office with a common complaint: "My wife gives me no peace," he said. "No matter what I do for her, no matter how much I try to please her, she keeps nagging and hassling me. She always has to have the last word about everything."

After three counseling sessions with both spouses, the hidden source of the woman's behavior was revealed. Several years earlier her husband had been sexually unfaithful. It happened only once— a meaningless encounter during a business trip. The man, conscience-stricken and remorseful, told his wife about the incident soon after he returned home. Ostensibly he had confessed in order to be honest—"to make a clean breast of it and put it behind us," he explained. But the counselor was aware that confession also served, subconsciously, to help the man get rid of his guilt. In any event, the husband asked forgiveness and the wife "forgave" him.

Indeed, she said, she had never so much as mentioned the matter again.

But did she really forgive? As her behavior clearly showed, the woman was still angry. "Never mentioning" the infidelity was her subtle way of continuing to use it to punish him, to be an argument-clinching weapon. Obviously it remained the unspoken wrong he had done that permitted her, now, to torment him. Not until the couple's fifth counseling session was there a breakthrough of insight:

HUSBAND (to wife): But *why* do you keep hounding me? You have no reason to complain. I do everything you want.

WIFE: That's beside the point.

MARCIA LASSWELL: Then what *is* the point?

W (with a rush of anger, after a long silence): I want you to suffer as much as I have suffered! Do you think I can forget what you did . . . with that woman?

H: My God, if you wanted to get back at me for that . . . well, it would have been better if you'd had an affair yourself . . . had your revenge and gotten it over with.

W: That's what I should have done . . . that's what I ought to do.

ML: You mean if you could even the score, you wouldn't be angry any more?

W: I'm not sure. I think being angry has almost become a habit with me.

ML: And you use the one act of infidelity as a hook to hang your anger on? As a "hold" on your husband?

W: Do you suppose that *is* what I'm doing?

ML: It's worth thinking about. If you evened the score, you would lose that advantage. You couldn't excuse your anger as revenge any more.

W (slowly): I see what you mean . . . I think. I wouldn't feel I had the right to blame him any more.

Clinging to this sort of emotional advantage to gain an endless revenge is an extreme form of the desire to "win" at any cost. This woman had been as miserable as her husband all those years. Her attitude was self-defeating because it prevented the couple from *ever* finding a way out of their emotional impasse. In effect, she was postponing (or refusing to explore) any other way of ending their conflict lest she lose her main weapon—a weapon virtually guaranteed to inflict an endless series of defeats on her husband.

Some people have a strong need for this kind of revenge and may intentionally stockpile hurts to use them for that purpose. But most of the time this is not so much a deliberate act as it is an unconscious habit. A habit is something we do without thinking. To stop, we must bring the habit to the conscious level . . . become aware of what we are doing. Marital therapists are skilled at helping clients do this, of course. In self-counseling you will have to do it for each other. Once you are aware of your behavior you make a conscious decision to change it. And if you decide *against* acting out habitual behavior often enough, the habit can be broken. Stockpiling grudges is an extremely unhealthy emotional habit. The quicker one can break it—by burying past injuries or healing them once and for all—the sooner a couple can get on with the business of living.

Do You Deliberately—or Unwittingly—Manipulate the Art of Compromise So That It Becomes a Maneuver to Avoid "Losing" an Argument? Or to Store Up "Brownie Points" for Your Credit in Future Conflicts? Some "winners" see any compromise—giving even an inch—as losing. As a result, when they know a compromise is inevitable they deliberately set their demands considerably beyond what they really want. Then they appear to give in—but only to where they wanted to be in the first place. It's the kind of negotiating that goes on in labor contract bargaining, or in political horse-trading. But while it may be effective there—perhaps because *both* sides do it and both sides know it is going on—it can be a trap for couples who are trying to learn to reach honest compromises.

When a compromise is *un*wittingly manipulated, both partners really *think* they are co-operating but they are actually dealing with each other via "hidden agendas." One or both spouses may have preconceived limits beyond which they will not go—a secret decision to give in only so much or only on certain points. Others may feel that any compromise *must* be exactly fifty-fifty. Others may see ninety-ten as a reasonable compromise—if they receive the ninety. An especially destructive kind of "hidden agenda" is the

unspoken threat: "If you push me too far, I'll quit co-operating altogether." Greta, a striking-looking woman in her early thirties, is
married to a man fifteen years her senior. He is settling in to middle age. His hair is graying and there is a noticeable bulge around
his middle. Although he is a capable and tough executive, he
doesn't even *try* to "manage" Greta. She is strong-willed—a
"winner"—and marriage counseling seems to Gordon the only
way he can ever hope to learn how to break his "losing" streak
with her.

HUSBAND: One of the messages I get from Greta is that she feels if
    she can't have things her way she would just as soon live
    alone.
WIFE: I don't *ever* say that.
H: No, you don't say *that*. On the other hand, sometimes you say,
    "Who needs this?" and you walk out of the room.
MARCIA LASSWELL: And does that end the negotiations?
H: Yes, I always give in at that point.
ML: Gordon, let's try to see what you fear would happen if you
    didn't give in. What if you followed Greta out of the room
    and insisted that she compromise?
H: I guess I'm really afraid she'd say, "I'm leaving." Greta has a
    good job, plenty of friends . . . she could get along very well
    without me. She's young, attractive. Dozens of guys would be
    waiting in line.
ML: So, you're careful never to push her beyond a certain point?
    (Gordon nods) That's a powerful weapon you have, Greta, if
    Gordon's feeling is correct. Is it? Have you ever thought life
    would be simpler or better if you lived alone?
W: Yes, I often think that. But I never threaten Gordon with it.
ML: Well, he says he's threatened by it. And he *behaves* as
    if he's threatened by it. Evidently, you don't have to *say* it.
    If it's in the back of your mind, Greta, and Gordon senses
    that, it can stop compromise when he questions what you
    want to do.

There are other techniques for maneuvering to win. One is demanding a pay-off for a series of past favors: "I've typed all your
reports. It seems the least you could do is let me have my way

on . . ." (whatever it is—usually unrelated to the favors done). Another is to be tolerant about mistakes your partner makes and then demand to win the next argument because you have been "so patient." For example: "I've put up with a lot from you lately. I didn't even mention [listing the mistakes one by one] and now you surely aren't going to fight with me about this."

MOTIVATIONS—WHY SOME SPOUSES FIGHT TO WIN

Is "Winning" Necessary to Maintain Your Self-esteem, to Buttress an Image of Yourself as a Dominant and Strong Person? Almost every psychological study shows that having a good opinion of one's self—a positive self-image—is an essential ingredient for successful living. But some people attempt to build that kind of self-esteem on a shaky foundation. Essentially insecure and self-doubting, they create a false image to impress outsiders and subconsciously to deceive themselves as well. Thus to lose an argument, to yield on an issue, to give in or to give up—all threaten the idealized counterfeit version of their personality. The hot-shot businessman who runs a tight ship at the office—who has a reputation for making decisions and making them *stick*—for knowing when he is right and bulling his opinions through the opposition—may have trouble accepting the idea of having his decisions questioned at home, or even of having to reason them out with his wife. If he is honestly a take-charge person, then expecting agreement from others is natural to his temperament. His business success has come from being in control.

But sometimes authoritativeness is a compensation for repressed feelings of inferiority or insecurity. Then any crack in the facade—having to defer to a spouse, say—is a threat to the synthetic character that has been constructed. Tom Morgan was a quiet, self-effacing man who worked in a government office for twenty years. He was married to a lively woman who generally managed to have things pretty much her way. Morgan attempted to compensate for his feelings of inferiority by insisting that he could always sense other people's moods—especially his wife's. "I can read her like a book . . . she walks in the door and I know what she's thinking," he said. Quite often he would ask her, out of the blue: "What's the matter?" This never failed to irritate her. She'd say, "Nothing!" He'd say, "Of course there is. I can tell you're angry. Now, what's upset you?" Louder this time she would reply, "I'm *not angry*."

"Come on . . . I can tell . . . why are you angry?"

"I AM NOT ANGRY!"

By this time the woman was, indeed, furious, and her husband would point out how "right" he was: "Just listen to your voice. Of course, you're angry." He had "won." She really *was* angry now. They both had lost.

Is Winning Necessary Because You Tend to Confuse Wants with Needs? If you think you *need* something—a new car, more attention, more frequent sex, some new clothes—then clearly you are going to be more demanding, more self-righteous about getting it than if you merely *want* it. The trouble is, many of us cannot clearly differentiate wants from needs, and the confusion often leads to a fight to win one's point. A *need*, as we have said, is an essential, indispensable requirement. No one but you can make the final decision about what it is *you* truly need. But partners often try to do this for each other, and conflicts occur when one cannot see the other's need as a need. However, if you want your partner to respect your decisions about what is indispensable in *your* life, you must be able to make the distinction clearly. Remember the boy who cried "Wolf!" and don't cry "need" unless you mean it.

Do Certain Issues That in Themselves Are Minor or Unimportant Subconsciously Have Great Symbolic Significance for You? A family counselor tells of a couple who feuded for a month as a result of an argument that began over three cents. She wanted to send a letter to their son at summer camp by air mail; he insisted that it should go by regular mail. Another couple managed to ruin what had been planned as a romantic evening to celebrate their wedding anniversary when he wanted to take her out for dinner and she wanted to prepare a memorable meal at home.

When conflicts erupt over such seeming trifles, couples should make an effort to learn what the arguments are *really* about. A husband who creates a scene over an extra three cents' postage on a letter to his son may be telling his wife, for instance, that he is angry and hurt because he feels she lavishes more love on the child than she does on him. A woman who would rather cook than dine out on her anniversary may be trying to win praise for her willingness to economize, or for her skills as a homemaker.

Sometimes the symbolic significance of a disagreement may be rooted in the emotional loyalties—or antipathies—a person still feels toward his parents, or toward the way they dealt with aspects of family life. One couple, for example, fought bitterly over the question of how large an allowance their fifteen-year-old daughter should get. In the counselor's office, the father explained . . .

HUSBAND: I believe if you are going to give children an allowance at all, it should be big enough to cover everything they need— clothes, lunches, movies, cosmetics, all that.

MARCIA LASSWELL: That is a valid approach to the allowance question, Mr. Todd. Child psychologists recommend it, along with other plans. But I gather you, Mrs. Todd, have a different idea.

WIFE: I don't care *what* child psychologists say, I think giving a fifteen-year-old that much money is ridiculous. To tell you the truth, I don't believe in allowances at all. If children are going to learn the value of money, they have to earn it the way I did—not have it handed to them.

H: You only feel that way because *you* never had an allowance as a kid. But we aren't *your parents*.

ML: Even though you may not care what child psychologists say, Mrs. Todd, I must tell you that they agree with you, too. Both of you have good plans for teaching your daughter how to manage money. But it seems to me each of you is "replaying" the way your parents handled money decisions.

H: Well, having an allowance didn't stop me from being responsible about money.

ML: And your parents' system helped you to be responsible about it, too, Mrs. Todd?

W: Yes. I think it was important to my whole philosophy.

ML: So, your daughter's allowance has a lot of symbolic meaning to you both. You each have a loyalty to a plan that worked for you. What we need to do is see if we can reach a compromise plan for your daughter. The answer doesn't have to be either of the two we've talked about so far.

Do You Need to "Lose" a Marital Conflict? Just as there are men and women whose self-image requires them to be "winners," there are people who find it emotionally necessary to be "losers." They see conflict—in any form, for no matter how valid a reason—as a threat to their marriage. They prefer the bittersweet taste of martyrdom to the heady wine of triumph.

Many of us are taught as children that it is "bad" to feel angry at someone we love—or someone we are *supposed* to love. We learn to repress anger, to give in without too much of a fuss; to avoid conflicts that might create antagonism. Or, if we do stand up for what we think is right, we feel guilty later for having done so. Much the same emotional syndrome can occur in marriage. The man or woman raised to believe that family conflict is "evil," or that fighting with a spouse will provoke him or her to withdraw love, finds a neurotic safety in losing. Or in never taking a stand in the first place.

Are You a Marital "Scorekeeper"? Every couple is normally linked together in what family sociologists call the process of "reciprocity" or "exchange." That is, each spouse undertakes certain obligations and expects in return certain privileges or rewards. This may involve a division of roles: husband as breadwinner and wife as homemaker; or, if she works to augment family income he reciprocates by sharing household tasks. It may involve a division of labor: he mows the lawn while she cares for the garden. But marital scorekeeping goes beyond these normal patterns of exchange. Subconsciously fearful lest one partner get more than he or she gives—i.e., "wins" more often than "loses"—scorekeepers make sure they come out "even." Their concern is to keep the marital scales in balance.

Lise is a scorekeeper. For three months she has kept up a battle with her husband Arne because she feels he has not properly "repaid" her birthday gift to him. Lise spent several weeks before Arne's birthday in an effort to find out what gift would please him most. She steered conversations casually to that topic, made him window-shop with her to see what caught his eye, sounded out Arne's best friend. What Arne, a camera enthusiast, seemed most interested in was a special lens for close-up photography. Lise questioned the camera-store clerk for an hour before deciding exactly which lens to buy. Naturally, Arne was delighted with his present.

When it was Lise's birthday not long afterward Arne gave her an exotic negligee. It was expensive and flattering, but Lise could only compare the effort she had put into choosing Arne's gift with what she thought was his routine, last-minute choice. To Lise the moral was clear: *He doesn't care as much about me as I do about him.* Hurt that she had not been "properly" repaid, Lise turned her resentment into accusations and, finally, open conflict.

How does a marital scorekeeper get that way? Our society is largely based on the principles of exchange, of course. And though we may not be aware of it, so to a considerable degree are our emotional relationships. Children, for example, soon learn that "exchange" is a key tactic for dealing with parents. ("If you eat your spinach," bargains Mommy, "you can ride the merry-go-round when we go to the park." Or Daddy offers dollar bills for every A on the report card.) Our relationship with our siblings tends to reinforce the scorekeeping attitude. One woman still remembers that when she and her sister were teen-agers and took turns doing the dinner dishes, "I was terribly upset if there were more dishes on my night than on hers . . . I actually counted them!"

Since marital accounts seldom balance out neatly, a scorekeeping mate is bound to build up an unrealistic sense of injustice. When conflicts result, that spouse is not going to be satisfied unless he or she "wins" at least as often as he or she "loses."

To measure a person's tendency to scorekeep, Bernard I. Murstein, a psychology professor at the University of Connecticut, devised what he calls an "Exchange-orientation Scale." The following questionnaire is based on that scale. To test your scorekeeping quotient, circle the number which you believe most accurately represents your response to each question:

SA = Strongly Agree ("Definitely yes")
MA = Mildly Agree ("I believe so")
U = Undecided
MD = Mildly Disagree ("Probably not")
SD = Strongly Disagree ("Definitely not")

	SA	MA	U	MD	SD
1. If my spouse feels entitled to an evening out with friends of either sex, then I am entitled to an evening out with friends of either sex.	1	2	3	4	5
2. If my spouse needs help to carry out his or her responsibilities, I resent it because I don't ask for help with mine.	1	2	3	4	5
3. I feel it is only money that I earn that I can spend as I choose.	1	2	3	4	5
4. I feel uncomfortable if someone does me a favor and I can't repay it promptly.	1	2	3	4	5
5. If I feel injured in some way by my spouse, I find it hard to forgive even when he or she apologizes.	1	2	3	4	5
6. I believe I do more than my share to make our marriage work.	1	2	3	4	5
7. My spouse's caring for me seems to exert a kind of control or power over me.	1	2	3	4	5
8. It bothers me if my spouse is praised for something he or she never did, or did by accident.	1	2	3	4	5
9. Though I work hard for our family in many ways, I must confess I am taken for granted more than I ought to be.	1	2	3	4	5
10. I wish my spouse would show more gratitude or acknowledgment when I do something nice for him or her, or say something nice.	1	2	3	4	5

SCORE: Between 10 and 30 points, you may be a high-exchange
scorekeeping personality.
Between 30 and 40, you are a borderline scorekeeper.
Over 40, you are not exchange-oriented.

How to Stop Fighting to "Win"
Constructive Approaches to Conflict

1.   Learn what your most frequent or most intense arguments are really about. Do you become involved in conflicts over symbolic issues? If so, cut through the surface disagreements and try to work out the emotional meanings they have for you.

2.   Do not equate "losing" a dispute with a loss of self-esteem. Realize that you are the same person, with the same assets and good qualities, that you were before the issue was joined.

3.   Try to differentiate realistically between your wants and your needs. What one spouse *wants* at a given time may be irrelevant in terms of the *needs* of the other, or of the marriage as a unit. There may be moments, too, when your needs are not as important as your partner's.

4.   Keep in mind that marriage is a co-operative enterprise, not a competitive one. The goal is *not* to settle which of you is right or wrong. The goal is to reach a solution both of you can live with—a compromise that will make life together more pleasant. Many couples tend to view disputes as what sociologists call "zero-sum" contests, in which one person's victory inevitably means the other's loss. Chess—with one winner, one loser—is a zero-sum game. Charades, however, is a non-zero-sum game. For even if one person guesses what is being pantomimed, that does not make the person who acted out the charade a "loser." Indeed, the point of the game is for *both* persons to succeed: one to feel he or she has done a good job of acting, the other to feel he or she has done a good job of decoding. Most marital conflicts are essentially non-zero-sum in content; few transactions in marriage need to result in "victory" or "defeat." No matter whose view prevails, neither partner is likely to come out a total "loser." It is only when you don't co-operate that both of you lose.

5. ˙ Learn the art of effective and honest compromise. How can you tell when a compromise meets that definition? For example, when both parties are more or less (but not necessarily entirely) satisfied with the result. Or, when it is a compromise that both persons can reasonably stick to rather than a compromise that

leads one or the other to seek delays or modifications. A compromise that works—even if it is not an ideal answer to a conflict—is better than the most brilliant solution that one partner is apt to sabotage.

There are two kinds of compromise. One is the meeting-in-the-middle-ground: being reconciled to buying a medium-priced car rather than either the expensive sports car or the economy compact; or agreeing to sex three times a week when one partner would like to have it every day and the other prefers it once a week. A second type of compromise involves trading: A doing what B wishes in one area of marriage in return for B doing what A wishes in another area. Counselors call this a *quid pro quo* negotiation—a "this" for a "that." It's important that each partner take an active part in the bargaining, since it will produce a fair trade only if both persons believe they are getting a "good deal":

HUSBAND: My wife drives me crazy when she uses my tools and never puts them back.

MARCIA LASSWELL: Are you aware that you do this, Meg?

WIFE: I suppose I do. But I can think of lots of things Dick does that annoy *me*.

ML: Perhaps the two of you can negotiate a trade. Meg, what would you like Dick to stop doing in return for your agreeing to put away his tools?

W: It would be great if he'd clean up the sink and shower every time he's through using them.

ML: That sounds like a fair trade. What do you think, Dick?

H (after a long silence): Nope . . . it's not worth it. I'd rather put away the tools than do that.

ML: Okay, Meg, let's run down a list of the other things you'd be willing to trade for until Dick hears one he thinks is a fair exchange.

This may sound like the old "you-scrub-my-back-I'll-scrub-yours" routine. And perhaps it is. But since both persons come out ahead, what difference does it make?

6. Try humor as a way of mood-changing. A husband reports that his wife has a habit of writing little notes and reminders to

him which she characteristically signs, "Love, Wife." "One night," the man said, "we had a big argument. We went to bed still angry. The next morning I found a note beside my coffee cup. It was a serious comment on our dispute, but it was signed 'Distant Relative'. It made me laugh just enough to see how foolish our disagreement was. The joke didn't actually *solve* anything, but it did open the way for us to start talking together again."

7. Don't turn disagreements into crises. The mildest difference of opinion can rapidly develop into full-scale conflict if you overdramatize it, or use it as a way of reopening more basic controversies. For example, if you are arguing about where to go on a Saturday evening, keep the discussion to that specific point. Do not suddenly rake up serious differences about money, say, by accusing your spouse of being unwilling to spend a few extra dollars on the evening's amusement. Don't inflate the significance of a minor disagreement by setting deadlines, rigid conditions, or impossible-to-accept alternatives: "All right, I'll go. But at 10 P.M. sharp I intend to leave, no matter what." Dramatizing creates a "must win" situation for each spouse because, suddenly, power seems to be at stake.

8. Avoid setting up *or* falling into power traps. Certain phrases —"Give me an example" or "Prove it!"—are rarely used by a person who knows he or she is *losing* an argument. Those are statements made by a person who is ready to move in for the kill. Here is another power-trap sequence:

"Be specific."

"Well, I can't think of an example at the moment."

"Ha! Just as I thought . . ."

Or if an example *is* given, it often moves the argument away from its real point to what may be an irrelevant or petty side issue. People who need to win seem unable to resist taking (as well as dangling) this kind of verbal bait. Once in the impossible position of having to "prove" a feeling, however, they almost always lose.

Ultimately, the basic reason that "winning" does not work is that it reduces marriage to a power struggle. The alternative to power is love. Thus when power becomes the prevailing force in a marriage, love must be diminished. There can be no peaceful co-existence between the two. We can develop our capacity for one or for the other—but not for both at the same time. When couples deal with marital conflict they have a choice. They can opt for power and seek to "win." Or they can opt for love and seek to reach accord.

7

IN EACH OTHER WE TRUST

Not long ago a group of couples got into a discussion of what they thought was the most important element in a good marriage. There were many candidates. Love, of course, was mentioned; so was commitment . . . honesty . . . concern . . . reliability . . . selflessness. It seemed impossible to settle on any single factor until one woman said, "Aren't we all talking about the same thing? Aren't all of those qualities different aspects of *trust?*"

Trust is the basic glue that holds two people together in any long-term relationship. We tend to think of trust as something that is respected—or broken—mainly in dramatic situations involving emotion-charged areas such as sex or money. Yet trust is a constant presence in the ordinary routines of marriage. At the simplest level, a husband and wife trust each other dozens of times every day. It is assumed without question, for instance, that he (or she) will be home for dinner in the evening, or that one spouse will look out for the children while the other is at work. They take it for granted that neither will open the other's mail, eavesdrop on the other's phone calls, go through the other's purse or wallet.

But in taking trust for granted at these levels many couples overlook the fact that trustworthiness is a far more complicated matter. If you are not clear about exactly what you and your spouse mean by "trust," there is a real possibility for serious misunderstandings. One couple—rather unusual counseling clients—discovered this recently. Like many couples about to be married, Paul and Rebecca were taking part in a series of "premarital" counseling sessions. They, however, had each been married before. They

wanted to make sure that this time they would be prepared to recognize and handle any problems that might create future trouble.
They had been talking with the therapist about the kind of wedding ceremony they wanted:

REBECCA: We intend to have a rather conventional service. We
    want the bond between us founded on spiritual principles.
PAUL: But we're changing some of the traditional wording. Instead
    of "love, honor, and obey," we've agreed to say "love, re-
    spect, and trust."
MARCIA LASSWELL: Knowing you two, I can understand how you
    feel about leaving out the word "obey." Honor and respect
    seem almost synonymous to me . . . though respect *is* a more
    down-to-earth term, isn't it? But I'd really like to explore the
    word "trust" with you. It can mean different things to
    different people. What will you two mean when you promise
    to trust each other?
REBECCA: To me, trust means I can have confidence that Paul will
    do what he says he will . . . that I can rely on him.
ML: That he is a trustworthy person?
REBECCA: Yes. You can't trust someone who isn't trustworthy.
ML: That sounds as if in your view being trustworthy is a *general*
    personality trait.
PAUL: Don't you think it is? Some people are trustworthy, and
    others I wouldn't trust at all.
ML: That's true up to a point. But it's not very likely that *anyone* is
    100-per-cent trustworthy. We're human, after all. And it's
    rather foolhardy to be 100-per-cent *trusting,* too, wouldn't
    you say?
PAUL: I hope not, because I want to trust Rebecca completely.
ML: But she is a human being, and like all of us she has the poten-
    tial to make mistakes or simply forget.
REBECCA: I'm a little surprised. You make it sound as if trust is an
    unrealistic goal.
ML: Not at all, because almost no one is totally *un*reliable, either.
PAUL: I'm glad we brought this up. I can see the possibility for
    trouble ahead if Rebecca and I aren't clear on what we mean
    by trust. Can you help us?
ML: For one thing, there are many kinds and degrees of trust and

trustworthiness. They function in dozens of areas of marriage. But trust is not a global quality—and trustworthiness is not a generalized personality trait. Persons can be highly trustworthy in some areas, partly so in others, and utterly unreliable in still others. You soon learn just what you can and cannot count on in each other.

REBECCA: I'm thinking about something you told me the other day, Paul. You said you never counted on me to remember to bring the tickets when we're going to a play. It's a small flaw, but I'm not "trustworthy" about it.

ML: And I expect you have similar faults, Paul. But it would be wrong to label each other *untrustworthy* because you are unreliable in a few areas.

PAUL: No one would generalize from one or two areas to say, "I can't trust you at all."

ML: Oh, but they do! When trust is broken in one place or one way, it is quite common for the disappointed partner to say "I'll never be able to trust you again!"

ISOLATING AREAS OF TRUST

A husband or wife is particularly likely to make this leap from the specific to the general when a partner betrays trust in an emotionally significant sector of their relationship. This happened with a thirty-eight-year-old man who, after twelve years of marriage, found that his wife was having an affair. The couple had been in counseling for some months for a variety of difficulties, but sexual adjustment had not seemed to be among them. As a result, the husband was even more upset and disillusioned than if sex had been acknowledged as a problem. He was meeting with the counselor alone to talk out his shock and anger:

HUSBAND: I'll never be able to trust her again. How can I believe anything she tells me?

MARCIA LASSWELL: Are you really saying that since she deceived you about this, you can't ever again believe *anything* she says? For instance, will you doubt her when she says she put gas in the car? Or that your mother telephoned?

H: I might! Why not? How do I know what else she's lied about all this time? (He pauses) Anyway, what's putting gas in the car got to do with it? That's a hell of a long way from going to bed with another man!

ML: I know you're hurt, Anthony. But try to realize what you are saying. You are generalizing mistrust in one area of marriage to your entire life together. Of course, it's an important one to you. But it is also important to isolate Harriet's sexual behavior from all the other ways in which she still *is* trustworthy.

H: I don't see how that can work!

ML: Do you think she is still a good mother to your children? (Anthony hesitates, then nods reluctantly) Is she still careful about spending money? (Again he nods) She still goes to work every day? She is still loving toward your parents? She is still concerned about you? (To all of these Tony nods) Then there are many ways in which you can still count on her.

H: When you put it that way, I have to agree. It doesn't seem to make sense. But it *does,* I guess.

ML: What I am trying to show you is that trust itself has many dimensions. A relationship is not necessarily shattered beyond repair just because one part of it is broken. If enough is left intact, the broken part can be fixed.

The crucial first step this husband had to take in order to make whole again the fabric of his marriage was to isolate the area in which trust had been broken; to see his wife's affair, insofar as possible, as a separate unit of behavior which does not automatically contaminate their total relationship. Breaking a partner's trust in the sexual realm creates a big enough problem without compounding it further. If Anthony insisted on generalizing his mistrust and extending it to the rest of the marriage, there would soon be nothing left of it at all. What the couple needed to do (and what *was* done in subsequent counseling sessions) was to analyze the reasons behind the wife's liaison *separately*—to find out the signal it was sending about her needs, to discover what it said about her relationship with Anthony. *Something* had evidently changed in her life since she first promised fidelity, for no one breaks a promise without a reason. Indeed, part of trusting another person is to hear out his or her reasons for breaking a promise. The stakes are too high to throw trust away without exploring the motives behind its violation. Of course, the other person's motives do not always make sense—to you or to themselves, for that matter. As a result, one may find it hard to understand a partner's reasoning. But *trying* to understand may make it possible to accept, to forgive, and eventually to put back together the broken pieces of the marriage.

THE ABILITY TO TRUST

The ability to trust begins early in life. An infant *must* trust. A baby is forced to depend for its very survival on the willingness of others to provide round-the-clock care for months and years. Some children quickly learn *not* to trust. They are the ones raised in circumstances where care is inconsistent or grudging—or, at the outer limits, is virtually nonexistent or even replaced by cruelty. It may take many years to rebuild the quality of trust in a person—child or adult—who has been repeatedly hurt, disappointed, rejected. And even then, one incident, one slip-up, may bring the entire structure down again. Some experts also believe that there are a few rare individuals who never learn to trust. They do not simply *dis*trust as a result of repeated betrayals; their ability to trust is simply missing. They may even have a built-in *un*trust; an incapacity for comprehending the idea at all.

Yet there *must* be a measure of trust in any human relationship if it is to function. Essentially, an employer trusts his employees to work loyally and competently, and they trust him to pay the salary they have earned. A person who needs help with a specific problem—legal, medical, emotional, financial, marital—must trust the skill of the expert; the expert must trust the client to give all the pertinent facts and to follow advice or instructions. But between husband and wife there needs to be something more. They are not concerned only with each other's reliability, or honesty, or competence—they are concerned with the added dimension of *caring*. We trust a spouse to act in our best interests because she cares . . . because he wants us to be happy . . . because we know we need each other. It is the difference between what has been called the "commitment of obligation" and the "commitment of feeling."

To trust in the obligatory routines of daily living and working is far easier than to trust in areas where caring is involved. For to care, to be loving, makes one emotionally vulnerable. To be vulnerable to someone we love, and yet not be able to trust him or her is to be in an uncomfortable position. To be vulnerable *and* trusting—and then to have that trust betrayed—is a crushing blow. For some of us, then, the answer becomes: *If I'm not too trusting, I can't be badly deceived . . . If I don't allow myself to be emotionally open, then I can't be hurt.* But such emotional insulation carries a penalty. One cannot keep out hurt without also keeping out love. A nontrusting, nonvulnerable person seldom knows the satisfaction of touching a partner emotionally, or of being touched the same way. We often hear people who have built this protective wall say, "I just don't care any more . . . all the feeling is gone."

TRUST AND CHANGE

When we trust someone we say that we can "count on" him or her—to carry out responsibilities, to keep promises, to live up to our expectations. Given the fact that so much of our daily marital behavior is habitual, couples tend to "trust" each other almost automatically in those relatively predictable or routine aspects of marriage. Some therapists refer to this as "static" trust: counting on a partner to keep on doing pretty much what he or she has always done. But static trust exists on a delicate balance. It leaves little if any room for human error or, more important, for the possibility of change. Yet change in life and in marriage is inevitable. Thus trust that is based on the assumption that things will go on in the same way forever is a trust ripe for trouble.

The kind of trust that *can* cope with change may be called "flexible trust." It rests on both partners' willingness to be open and honest so that each can "count on" what the other says even in changing circumstances. The more open you are with each other, the greater such trust can be. One may not necessarily *like* what one's partner says or does . . . one may be distressed by the changes that are occurring . . . but at least one knows there will be no deception, no betrayal of trust.

Not everyone can handle, at the outset, the amount of honesty and tolerance that flexible trust requires. Past hurts and disappointments often stand in the way. So do hidden emotional insecurities. Just how much openness each of you can cope with is something you will have to find out for yourself. But it is wise to go slowly in the process. Trying to be too honest with each other too soon can damage a relationship. That's why we say: Don't ask your partner a question unless you are quite sure you want to hear the answer. If you don't want to know what you suspect, think twice about asking. Otherwise you force your partner "underground"—to be either deceptive or silent.

But though you may not reach *total* openness (probably no couple ever really does), you can each begin to be more open than perhaps you have been about things you thought you could never tell each other. And it is surprising how often your partner *already* knows what you believe is still a private bit of your life. The late Nathan Ackerman, a pioneer in family therapy, said that secrets a spouse thinks are too destructive to reveal are in fact usually not all that destructive *nor* secret. Indeed, couples in counseling often find a great sense of relief in getting such secrets out in the open—relief both for the person who tells them and also for the person who finally hears them said.

For example, a husband who was an inveterate gambler borrowed hundreds of dollars from friends to bet on a "sure thing" system at the race track. When his horses kept losing he borrowed more in an effort to recoup. Soon he was several thousand dollars in debt—an amount it would take him years to repay. The strain of carrying his burden of shame and worry, combined with the strain of keeping his secret from his wife, affected every aspect of his life. He made so many mistakes at work that he was in danger of losing his job. He alternately yelled at or ignored his wife and children. He lost interest in sex. Unable to sleep, he went out late each night for long, aimless walks. Eventually his distraught wife sought counseling on her own. At the therapist's urging she managed to get her husband to go with her to one session. After ten minutes of stony silence he suddenly spilled out the whole story. When he finished, he obviously expected his wife to condemn him. Instead, she reached out and tenderly took his hand:

WIFE: Why didn't you tell me before? I knew *something* was wrong, anyway. At least now I can help you. Before it was like having a ghost between us.

HUSBAND: I was afraid. I thought you would be furious. And I didn't want to worry you.

W: You didn't want to *worry* me? How could I not be worried when you act the way you do? First, I thought there was another woman . . . then I thought you had some terrible disease. Finally, I guessed it was probably a gambling debt . . .

H (surprised): You guessed that?

W: It wasn't so hard. You always like to gamble. I figured you had borrowed and lost . . . But I had no idea it was so much.

H: I should have told you. But I didn't want to hurt you.

W: It hurt more to know that you didn't think you could tell me. How can I help you if you won't tell me the truth?

H: Well, I don't feel good about what I've done, but it's a relief not to have to hide it any more.

W: And I'm relieved, too . . . to know it's nothing worse.

SETTING YOURSELF UP FOR DISAPPOINTMENT

We have said that trust involves "counting on" another person. That means, among other things, counting on him or her to meet our expectations. For instance, a couple talked about some rewarding behavior they had come to look forward to from each other:

WIFE: I know that every day when I get home from work Sam will have a chilled martini waiting for me. I really look forward to it.

HUSBAND: We started the custom right after we were married. I was in law school then, and I got home from class before Betty arrived from work. She was so pleased that I just kept on doing it . . . it's nine years now.

W: And every Sunday I make a special brunch. Sunday was the

one morning Sam didn't have to rush off to class or to work, so I would buy all sorts of delicacies and we'd sit and eat, and talk, for as long as we wanted.

H (laughing): Now, if Betty didn't fix a big brunch on Sunday I'd know she wanted a divorce!

Sam and Betty never actually planned their customs of the evening martini and the Sunday brunch. No demands had ever been made. It simply evolved out of habit into an "expectation" they both could count on. All too often, however, expectations can go awry. When they do, it is trust that suffers.

In the context of trust, what *is* an expectation? In effect, it is an assumption that certain specific behavior will take place. Some expectations are so routine, so automatic, that we *know* we can count on them to be fulfilled. Others have a high degree of probability, and we may anticipate with a reasonable amount of assurance that they will be met. But some expectations can be better described as *hopes:* "Peggy knows I need a new camera, and I expect she's going to give me one for Christmas." And still other expectations may be completely unrealistic; indeed, the person we expect to act in a particular way may not even *know* we expect him or her to act that way. Obviously, an unrealistic expectation is not likely to be fulfilled. And no one can meet an expectation he or she doesn't even know about. But the expectant partner may see such failures as a breach of trust. Never mind the reason: He or she *counted* on you, and you didn't come through.

This kind of confusion about expectations often has its roots in childhood. Young children have little ability to distinguish between realistic and unrealistic expectations; or to sense the differences among probabilities, possibilities, and just sheer hopes. As adults we are supposed to have learned how to make these distinctions. Yet many people continue to confuse what they want, or what they hope for, with what they can legitimately expect. *This is especially true for personal relationships.* John has no trouble realizing that while he *wants* to win a million dollars in a lottery, and obviously *hopes* he will, he certainly can't *expect* to win. If he does expect to, he must be prepared for disappointment. Yet John—and many men and women—have a great deal of difficulty separating wishes from hopes and hopes from expectations when they deal in feelings with a marital partner.

It is the failure to make those distinctions that sets a person up for disappointment—that lays the groundwork for him or her to conclude: "I can't trust you." Moreover, while most of us readily realize that wishes and hopes may often be unreasonable, we tend to think of expectations as well founded. Yet some of them are as fanciful as the most extravagant wish. For instance, we may have expectations of which we ourselves are not even aware, but which nevertheless color our thinking: Can a husband realistically expect his wife to act the way his mother did when he *does not consciously realize* this is what he seeks? More common is the expectation which we do not even bother to communicate. A good example was provided by the middle-aged woman who sighed with resignation as she told the counselor bleakly that she *knew* her husband would forget their wedding anniversary next week:

MARCIA LASSWELL: How can you be so sure?

WIFE: He always has, he always will.

ML: Why don't you remind him about it ahead of time?

W: I'd never lower myself to that! If he loves me, he ought to remember.

ML: It seems that remembering anniversaries is more important to you than it is to him—whatever the reason may be. So, if you won't remind him of it, and he always forgets it, you're just setting yourself up for another disappointment. You are going to get exactly what you anticipate . . . and precisely what you say you want to avoid. Does that make sense to you?

It is futile—and dangerously self-deluding—to believe that if a person loves you, he or she should intuitively know what you expect and spontaneously provide it. Disappointment is certain to follow. Indeed, being aware of feelings of disappointment is a good way to discover exactly when we have formed an unreasonable or unexpressed expectation. Ask yourself: *Why didn't my partner do what I was counting on him or her to do?* The honest answer is quite likely to be that he or she did not *know* what you wanted. This is a good starting point from which to identify your problem and begin to work it out.

It is a good feeling when something you want or hope for can be converted into an expectation that you know will be met. It makes you feel loved. And loving partners *try* to meet each other's expectations as often as possible. But everyone must be emotionally prepared to be denied an expectation from time to time. This seems perfectly reasonable when one watches what's happening from the outside, when one is an emotionally uninvolved observer. *How could Jim expect Martha to agree to have his mother move in with them permanently?* we say. *Her home wouldn't be her own any more!* But it is quite a different matter when it is *your* mother, and your partner says "No." Then we tend to see it as a denial of love, a personal rejection.

Taking an unmet expectation as an emotional rejection is a dangerous trap. Paradoxically, the couples who fall into it most often seem to be those who feel they are responsible for each other's happiness. The following case stands out as a prime example. Greg, a twenty-seven-year-old executive, wanted his wife to go back to college. She had quit after her freshman year to support them while Greg got his graduate degree in business administration. At first, Greg merely said it was "Kathy's turn to finish her education." He urged her to go into a business course similar to the one he had taken. He was "only thinking of her welfare." Later, he became more candid about his reasons. He wanted her to be able to hold her own intellectually with his friends and associates; and he wanted her to get a business degree so they would have interests in common. Kathy thought it all made good sense: "Having a degree will give me more confidence," she said.

Seemingly, the couple were on the way to fulfilling shared expectations. At least Greg and the counselor thought so. But it gradually became clear that Kathy had growing reservations about studying business. She didn't enjoy her classes. Her grades were passing but marginal. She was depressed. She began to think of herself as incompetent. And she blamed herself for "letting Greg down." At the counselor's suggestion Kathy took a series of interest and aptitude tests. The results showed she was much better suited, by skills and temperament, to a career in science. After some exploration Kathy found she liked botany best. She decided to make that her major. And she did extremely well in it.

Was Greg delighted? He was not. He was disappointed, and he

showed it by making sarcastic remarks about "the importance of botany to world progress." Finally, Greg accused Kathy of having "rejected" his ideas, his help—indeed, him*self*. Having invested so much of his ego in trying to arrange Kathy's life to his personal satisfaction—to meet *his* expectations rather than hers—Greg was taking Kathy's decision as a personal affront. He had a good deal of work to do before he would be able to realize that he had *set himself up* for this disappointment:

MARCIA LASSWELL: Greg, what kind of person do you want Kathy to be in the long run?

HUSBAND: Someone I can talk to. Someone who is interesting. Someone I can be proud of.

ML: When you were a boy, did your parents have any expectations about what they wanted you to be?

H: I'll say! My father bugged me for years trying to get me to study law. He was a partner in a law firm, and he wanted me to come into it . . . sort of take his place when he retired.

ML: And why did you resist?

H: I wasn't interested in law.

ML: Wasn't your father disappointed?

H: Huh? Oh, sure . . . for a while, I guess.

ML: Did he feel that you had rejected him . . . his way of life?

H: I don't think so. He never acted that way. Once he saw how well I was doing in business school . . . how much I liked it, and all . . . Well, I guess he was pleased for me.

ML: Then why can't you feel that way about Kathy's switch to botany? I know you're disappointed that she didn't choose *your* field. But if you look at it logically, won't you be better off if Kathy is a happy and satisfied botanist than if she were a depressed and reluctant businesswoman?

H: Well, I thought that if she cared about what's important to me, she would go along with my plan . . . But when you put it that way, I have to admit I wasn't being logical.

Because it was important for the future of their marriage that both Greg and Kathy understand where they made their mistakes, they pursued the matter in subsequent sessions. Kathy admitted that when she found she disliked the business course she had hesitated to say so frankly. "I didn't know what I really wanted," she said, "so it was easier just to go along with what Greg wanted." For his part, Greg took Kathy's acquiescence to mean he could *expect* her to follow his plan. The result? Kathy and Greg were setting themselves up for mutual disappointment. Ultimately, Greg was able to accept Kathy's decision without feeling that she had rejected *him*. He learned to trust her feelings in one area of their life together without assuming that they mirrored her feelings about all of it—or about him.

Nothing is so difficult and delicate as to rebuild marital trust once it has been broken. For that reason, if no other, it is important to identify and to deal with problems of trust and expectations before they get out of hand. Here are some suggestions for self-counseling approaches:

• Be clear in your own mind about the difference between wants and expectations. A child may want an ice cream cone and therefore—simply because he wants it—expect to get it. Adults are supposed to know better.

• Remember that some expectations are not "legitimate"—they may be only hopes or wishes in disguise.

• Make sure you communicate your expectations clearly. Don't assume your partner is a mind reader. When you feel hurt or disappointed by your spouse, immediately ask yourself: "What did I expect that I did not get?" When you have answered that, then ask yourself: "Did he or she *know* that I expected it?" To clear the air, and to avoid falling into a pattern of "setting yourself up for disappointment," you might say something like this: "What you did [or failed to do] upset me because I expected something else. I realize you didn't know I expected it. But now I will tell you what it is. Now you have a choice—knowing what I expect, you can do it or not."

• Never force your partner to meet your expectations by threats, or by using the "if-you-loved-me-you-would" technique. You can *ask* your partner to give you what you desire, but he or she must be free to do so willingly.

• You are entitled to be able to count on a partner's promise or agreement. That is one of the foundation stones of trust. When spouses promise each other to behave in a particular way, *not* to keep one's word is a serious matter. Of course, everyone is fallible; there can always be a slip-up or a lapse of memory. But if you find you have promised more than you feel able to deliver, it's vital to maintain trust by frankly saying: "I'm sorry, I promised too much. I can't do what I said." To go back on one's word with no explanation is untrustworthy behavior. If one has promised too much— or if circumstances have changed so that the promise can't be kept —it's wise to say so and then renegotiate your agreement.

• To trust another person, you must be able to trust yourself. If you know you can count on certain inner strengths—self-confidence, self-reliance—you will be less afraid of opening yourself to the vulnerability that comes with trusting. If you know you can cope with emotional hurt and pain, being vulnerable ceases to be so frightening.

Building marital trust is a slow, gradual, and often painful process. Attempts to rush it or to take short cuts may defeat your purpose; trust, like intimacy, cannot be forced. But when it is achieved, trust *itself* can become a way of dealing with other marital problems. For if self-disclosure encourages the growth of trust, trust in turn encourages the kind of self-disclosure that's needed for effective self-counseling.

8

"WHY ARE YOU TELLING ME THIS?"

A judge with something less than the wisdom of Solomon—and certainly less than an elementary knowledge of marriage—once "settled" a matrimonial dispute by ruling that a husband "need not listen" to his wife's conversation. (Just how the man was to go about that was not spelled out in the decision.) In these days of equal rights such a judge might grant a wife the reverse privilege. But even if blocking out a spouse's words were possible, most couples would agree it is a foolish tactic. The importance of good communication in marriage is clearly recognized. Indeed, enough has been said and written about it recently to fill several library shelves. Yet much of the communication about the need for communication is poorly communicated.

There are, for example, complicated techniques designed to teach couples how to talk to and understand each other. There are a variety of "rules" (often conflicting ones) for "verbal interaction," and a slew of sociological theories about "meta-communication" (which just means talking about talking). All this may be meaningful and even helpful to marital therapists; but to the ordinary husband and wife trying to figure out why they have difficulty getting ideas and feelings across to each other, the rules and theories are usually confusing. In practice, we've found they have a "chilling effect"—they make people think that good marital communication is an abstruse intellectual exercise, or requires complex technical skills.

The essential element in marriage talk is the *feeling* behind the words.

Effective communication between spouses depends not so much on *what* is said as *why* and *how* it is said.

To hear beyond the words, to "hear" the emotion behind them, is basic to understanding what they actually mean. There are so many possible ways to react to another's remarks that we often respond inappropriately. The key to appropriate response is a single question that should always be asked—silently, if not openly: "Why are you telling me this?"

For instance, one evening not long ago two marital therapists who are married to each other were enjoying a quiet dinner together when the husband started to tell at great length about a new client he had seen that day. Ordinarily his wife would have been interested in hearing everything he had to say. But there were a number of reasons why, at that particular moment, she grew impatient. For one thing, she had put in a long workday teaching students and listening to her own clients. She had had a surfeit of words. Then, too, she had seen little of her husband the past few days: one or the other had been away on business or working late. It seemed to the wife that there were more interesting personal matters they could discuss. Yet she realized she was tired and tense—and she didn't want to shut off a conversation that might be important to her husband just because she was irritable.

"Tom," she interrupted. "I'm wondering why you are telling me all this."

"Why?" he asked, surprised.

"I need to know how to listen to you. If you're asking for advice about what you ought to do, I'll listen more carefully and try to tell you what I think. But if you're making conversation to entertain me, or to pass the time—I'd rather talk about something else."

"To tell you the truth," Tom said, after a thoughtful silence, "I'm not quite sure why I *am* going on so much about it." Then he considered the matter further. "Well, I *would* like your opinion—maybe I'm too involved with the case to see all issues at stake."

"That's what I needed to know. Now I know how to listen to what you are saying."

The fact is that conveying information is perhaps the least significant function of marital conversation. True, it makes up the bulk of the wordage two people exchange over the years. But it is scarcely as important to their relationship as the sharing of feelings. Studies of marital conversation patterns show that it is almost entirely concerned with routine affairs—"What did you do today, dear?" "Oh, nothing much . . . what did *you* do?" . . . "Was there anything in the mail?" . . . "The plumber came to fix the sink." One exception is the first year or so of marriage, when couples still share ideas, plan for goals, probe each other's emotions. And there seems to be a partial return to that pattern in the later years, when children have grown and gone. But during the long stretch in between—when daily pressures are greatest, problems most likely to occur, and good communication most necessary—it is precisely then that couples usually fail to communicate feelings, fail to sense what each other's words really mean. Indeed, they often cling to the bare exchange of information as a way to *avoid* getting into an exploration of feelings.

Even couples who instinctively realize how important it is to understand the emotional needs behind each other's remarks find it hard to ask, "Why are you telling me this?" "That's all very well for a husband and wife who are marriage counselors," you may say. "They are trained to talk that way. But can the average couple be expected to react similarly?" Yes, the skills of good marital communication can be learned, and applied through self-counseling in much the same way that a therapist would apply them. For instance, a couple in therapy for some months said they were having trouble communicating.

MARCIA LASSWELL: How do you see the problem?

WIFE: Paul just goes silent on me most of the time. He must think I can read his mind. And when I try to tell him what I've been doing, or how I feel, he acts bored. I wonder if he cares at all what goes on with me.

HUSBAND: I care! It's just—well, I never know what you want from me.

ML: Paul, do you think you're expected to respond in some particular way when Joanne tells you something?

H: Well, yes . . . I guess I do. But I can never figure out which way!

ML: Did you ever think of asking her *why* she's telling you whatever she is?

W: What do you mean?

ML: There are many different reasons for communicating. To inform. To amuse. To get rid of angry feelings. To get an opinion. And lots more. If Paul knows *why* you tell him something, Joanne, then he will know *how* to listen to you . . . how to respond.

w: Sometimes I just want to get something off my chest. You know, just *talk* about it. It isn't that I want Paul to offer a solution or give me an opinion. But if he just seemed interested, that would help . . . If he looked at me and asked a question or two.

ML: And other times you might hope for a different reaction?

w: Of course.

ML: So, it would probably help both of you if Paul knew the purpose of your communication.

H: But how do I find that out?

ML: You ask.

H: Ask? How?

ML: There's nothing mysterious or complicated about it. When Joanne is talking to you, and you aren't sure what kind of response she is seeking, you simply say—"Why are you telling me this?"

H: I'd feel foolish.

ML: Not after the first few times. Not if it became a habit. Certainly not if it helped you both to get along better.

The "Whys" Behind the Telling

For some people, communication is a way of trying *to achieve empathy with a partner*—to know that the other person "feels with" him or her. It's not usually necessary to "fish" for empathy when *positive* feelings are involved; most everyone is more than willing to share in or respond to expressions of joy, love, success. It's harder to get someone to share in our negative feelings, our blue moods. But that often is exactly when communicative sharing is most wanted. This sort of experience from a case in our files is not unusual:

HUSBAND: My wife pays no attention to half the things I say. I get the feeling I'm talking to myself.

WIFE: Half of them aren't worth answering.

MARCIA LASSWELL: Can you give me an example?

W: Well, the other Sunday we planned to visit friends and play tennis, but it started to rain and we had to call the whole thing off. Alex was so depressed he wouldn't even try to think of what else we could do. All he did was look out of the window and gripe about what a shame it was how the day was ruined.

H: And all *she* did was keep telling me I was behaving like a child. I said, "Doesn't it bother *you* that the rain loused up our plans?" She said, "No, you ought to be able to adjust to disappointments if you're grown up."

ML: That's reasonable, isn't it?

H: Yes, sure . . . But that wasn't the point.

ML: What *was* the point?

H (hesitantly): Mostly, I think, to have her say something so I'd know she was as disappointed as I was . . . not to be so damned cheerful when I felt let down.

ML: Suppose your wife had said, "What a shame it's raining! And it would have been so much fun to play tennis!" Would that have made you feel better?

H: Yes! That's all I wanted . . . just one sentence that showed she felt the same as I did.

W: Well, of course I did! Did I have to say so out loud?

ML: Yes, since you obviously didn't convey your feelings to Alex the way you did respond.

For most couples that kind of verbalized empathy might not be necessary. But for this husband, his wife's calm acceptance of the spoiled day could have been interpreted to mean that she actually didn't mind that it was spoiled . . . perhaps she was even secretly pleased. He needed the reassurance of knowing that she did indeed empathize with his feelings. That is what he was telling her. She either did not pick up the clue, or chose to disregard it.

Another answer to "Why are you telling me this?" is the desire *to share experiences as well as feelings.*

More is involved here than an exchange of information. A husband may need to talk about what happened on the job, or a wife to recount her routine at home or at work, not so much to fill each other in on the mundane facts—after all, they don't vary a great deal from day to day—as to bring each more fully into the other's life. We are apart from each other so much these days—in time, in space, in tasks, in thoughts—it often seems as if married couples are more co-workers than life-sharers. Telling "what happened" is one way to close this gap. A couple we know—he's a third-grade teacher—fondly refer to their daily pre-dinner conversation as "show and tell" time. The details of who said what to whom are not always interesting to a spouse who doesn't know the other people involved. What *is* interesting is the report of your own feelings and reactions. If you concentrate on your responses to whatever happened, your spouse is more likely to remain interested.

Sharing experiences with those who care is a great dispeller of loneliness. There is the existential fact that each of us, bounded inside our own skin, is ultimately alone. Neither being "joined" in wedlock nor anything else can make two people one person. Communicating with someone we love is a way to bridge that separateness. A divorced man—a writer friend who has recently ended a fifteen-year marriage—made the point this way:

> I had the most wonderful news the other day. My literary agent called to tell me that my new book had been chosen by one of the major book clubs. The instant I hung up the phone I rushed into the other room to tell my wife—and it was many seconds before I realized I didn't have one any more. I can't tell you how depressed . . . how lonely . . . I felt. There I was, going to be famous and rich, and I had no one who would really care, really know what this meant to me.

This need for contact stays with us from infancy, when an adult's tender care makes the world seem to be a good place. To be accepted by school friends becomes the next strong motivator of children's behavior. Not to be "one of the gang" is a painful experience in rejection. As adults we are still threatened by it, and we seek someone who cares enough about us to listen when we need to share good or bad news.

The ventilation of anger and pain is a third motive that underlies the need to unburden oneself verbally. Here is a young bride talking:

> During the first year of our marriage, Don was interning at a city hospital. Interns work endless hours, and when Don had a chance to come home he was too exhausted to do much talking. He usually just flopped in a chair and watched TV. This one time, however, he paced grimly around our little apartment. When I asked what was wrong he kept saying, "Nothing," but in such a violently *controlled* voice that I knew whatever it was must be terrible. After a while he started talking in a monotone, almost as if I weren't there. He had been doing his tour of duty in obstetrics, helping in a routine delivery. "It was an accident," he said. "Nobody knows how it happened, but the anesthetic exploded. They'd just taken the baby, and then there was a flash and a noise and the mother and the baby died—bingo! Just like that!" I was horrified. *Why does Don have to tell me about such things?* I thought. *Someday I'll be having our baby.* As if Don were reading my mind he looked up at me and I saw he was crying. "I didn't want to tell you," he said, "but I couldn't help it." I was still stunned, but I knew what Don needed . . . what he wanted but couldn't ask for. I went to him and held him and stroked him until he was calm. A few months later Don said that was the moment he really knew I loved him.

Men have as much need to express their emotions as women, yet the weight of custom and tradition still prevents many men from releasing their dependent feelings. Anger is more acceptable. It is somehow considered more "manly" for a man to vent his rages or resentments, especially those connected with his job. But a man needs to feel free to talk about his other feelings, too; a wise wife will encourage him to do that with her.

Learning how to listen when your partner is "ventilating" takes a skill all its own. It requires more than sympathy—it demands the ability to maintain your own emotional balance while you listen so that you do not get depressed when your partner is down, or angry when he or she is angry. You become a sounding board for a ventilating partner. Generally, you are not expected to take any action. You don't have to fix things. Just listen. A woman who has learned this lesson well says: "One of the important things I learned in marital therapy is that when Jim comes home from the office in a rage he isn't mad at *me*. I used to be defensive and either get angry or clam up. Now I know he needs to sound off, so I can listen and stay even-tempered."

Obviously not everything we choose to tell one another flows from noble motives. Human nature being what it is, words are also used as weapons: to criticize, to undercut, to belittle, to hurt. Frequently, we deny what we're doing while we're doing it by wrapping the words in guilt-disclaiming phrases: *"I'm telling you this for your own good . . ." "I don't like to criticize you, but . . ." "You're forcing me to say this."* But neither speaker nor listener is deceived.

For effective self-counseling it is important to distinguish between the various "whys" that underlie destructive communication patterns. The willful and deliberate use of words to hurt another is inexcusable. It is one thing for a man to point out, while he and his wife are getting dressed for a dinner party, that her dress has a spot on the shoulder she hasn't noticed. Or that it doesn't do justice to her figure. But it is quite another matter to wait until one's wife is about to walk into the host's home before saying, "That dress really doesn't look good on you." Belittling or critical comments often reflect a person's deep self-unhappiness. When one's ego is beaten down, one tends to compensate by trying to beat down somebody else's ego. A man who is out of work may try to bolster his self-esteem by being supercritical of his wife, or overly demanding of his children. His harsh words are actually a cry for help. Understandably, if you are the one being beaten down it is hard to respond with sympathy. But to ask: "Why are you saying this to me?" may help you both to realize the real message behind the hurtful words.

By now it must be evident that most answers to "Why are you telling me this?"—to achieve empathy, to share the good things that happen in life and to ventilate the distressing ones, to find a link across the gap of loneliness—are all manifestations of a single basic human requirement: *ego support from those we love.* Against the assaults and trials of the outside world, ego support is at once our bulwark, our refuge, and our reserve of strength. Indeed, getting and giving ego (or emotional) support to each other may be a fundamental function of marriage.

THE FOUR LEVELS OF EGO SUPPORT

What is "ego support"? It is a kind of reinforcement for a person's feelings or beliefs about himself or herself. It is positive feedback that says "you are adequate" . . . "you are a good person" . . . "you are lovable." It is *not* criticism and it is *not* indifference (which is a form of rejection). Some people tend to think of ego support as an all-or-nothing matter: *If you aren't for me, you're against me.* As a result they take the least criticism, the smallest objection, the slightest hesitancy as a sign of *total* nonsupport.

It is extremely important—if you are going to be effective at self-counseling—to realize this is an unfounded and misleading conclusion. Out of our counseling experience we have developed a theory that identifies four levels of ego support. Each level is significant in its own way, and there are enough gradations between them to allow for great flexibility. The theory had its genesis in the case of a woman client, an interior decorator who worked in a department store. She sought help because she felt she got very little support from her husband in any area of her life. She wanted to know how to handle what she referred to as her "constant disappointments." Her husband joined her in one counseling session:

MARCIA LASSWELL: Can you give me an example of something that took place recently that made you feel you weren't getting the support you want?

WIFE: Oh, I will suggest doing something and he comes up with a lot of reasons for *not* doing it. Like the other day I said I might take a few days off from work to go visit my sister. Vince said: "You were just up there two months ago."

HUSBAND: Well, you were. But I didn't say don't go, did I?

W: You didn't even ask why I wanted to go again so soon, or give me credit for having a reason.

H: I can't get very excited about your visiting your sister. What did you expect me to do? Cheer? Every time you go, I manage okay with the kids and the house. No one stops you.

ML: Let's stick to the main point. What *did* you want from Vince?

W: It would be nice if he'd say he thought it was a good idea, and act like he wanted me to go.

ML: Even if he doesn't particularly want you to go?

W: I don't understand what you mean.

ML: It sounds to me that what you wanted was for Vince not only to *act* as if he was glad you were going, but actually *feel glad,* too. It might be nice for you if he did feel happy about it, but evidently he doesn't. However, that does not mean that you aren't getting *any* support from him. There are several levels of support. Not standing in your way when you are going to do something he doesn't like is actually one form of support.

W: I can't see that at all.

ML: Let's use an analogy to your work. Let's say a customer comes in and picks out furniture and fabrics that you like, too. It's a joy to help her co-ordinate things because you agree with everything she chooses. You support her 100 per cent. That's nice when it happens—but it's also a very easy kind of support to give.

W: Yes, it is. I can see that.

ML: Now, another customer comes in and knows exactly what she wants, only this time you think her selections are ugly. But by helping her co-ordinate them, the result turns out to be "well-done ugly." It's surely not what *you* would have chosen but if that's what she wants, you'll help her get it.

W: I get plenty of those customers. It's really a matter of personal taste and style. Even decorators disagree.

ML: Right. Now, a third customer comes in who has such poor taste that you can't go along with it. She picks out fabrics that will be wrong for the style of furniture. What she insists on is going to be a mess. As a decorator, you give up and let her do what she wants. You don't actively oppose her, but you don't refuse to show her what is available.

W: It's hard for me to deal with people like that. They have horrible taste; but they think it's great.

ML: And finally, a man comes in who so offends you by what he

wants in his apartment that you refuse to help him. You tell
him the store doesn't carry what he wants.

w: Well, I couldn't do that in my job. I'd have to help him.

ML: That last example would be no support at all—maybe even
thwarting his plans. That wouldn't go in business, I'll agree.
But it happens all the time in marriage.

H: But that isn't what *I* did.

ML: No, you didn't. You actually gave support. And you didn't
give the easy kind. You gave the kind your wife said was
hard to give. You didn't like what she wanted to do, but you
didn't stand in her way. You even helped by indicating you'd
take over with the kids and the house while she was gone.

w: I never thought of that as support before. I wanted the 100-
per-cent-agreement kind, didn't I?

ML: Most people do—until they realize that giving support when
you *don't* agree is much harder . . . is a much greater emotional gift.

To clarify how the four levels of support can be distinguished,
let's summarize each one:

Level 1: You are in total agreement with your partner's
goals or ideas, and are willing to support him or her 100 per cent.
This is the kind of ego support all of us want. It is the sort most of
us consider the *only* one that's worth while. Yet it is, paradoxically, the easiest to give. Supporting what one agrees with in the
first place does not make a huge demand on one's ethics or concerns or love.

Level 2: You do not agree with what your partner wants to
do, but you will nevertheless support him or her to whatever extent you can. We might label this the "Voltaire" attitude, consistent with the French philosopher's position that "I disapprove of
what you say, but I will defend to the death your right to say it."
Level 2 support is based on essential respect for one's partner's
good sense and individuality.

Level 3: You disagree quite seriously with your partner, and
you cannot in good conscience lend any kind of support. However,

you will not create problems or raise obstacles. Level 3 is a "hands-off" position.

Level 4: You not only disagree but you will also do whatever you can to dissuade your partner, or even thwart his or her plans. This is no support at all.

It's not very often that two people actually want the same thing, at exactly the same time, with exactly the same amount of enthusiasm—and yet, if the Level 1 response isn't forthcoming it's like a dash of cold water. It's great to receive 100-per-cent support; it's easy to give when you truly feel that way, but phony if you don't, of course. The best kind of support is usually that which reflects the way you honestly feel. To pretend Level 1 enthusiasm when none is felt becomes unnecessary if you both recognize that Levels 2 and 3 are also valuable gifts. (However, there may be times when sensitivity to your partner's needs should come ahead of total frankness. In those moments you should try to give the kind of support you know is *needed*—regardless of your own feelings.)

The ability to identify the *reasons* behind your spouse's remarks is a first step toward being able to provide the quality of ego support he or she is seeking. An equally vital second step is to improve your skill at interpreting the *true* content of the messages.

A key concept in Sigmund Freud's theories of psychoanalysis is that a dream consists of two parts: the "manifest content"—what the action of the dream seems to be about; and the "latent content"—its inner meaning, which is simultaneously masked yet revealed by the symbols of the dream. In much the same way there can be manifest and latent content in the things we say to one another. For example, a woman leafing through the newspaper advertisements remarks to her husband, "We need a new sofa." She may mean exactly what she says; the manifest and latent content of her words may be identical. On the other hand her statement may have a number of hidden meanings. She may be saying they need *another* sofa. She may be saying she's bored with or ashamed of the old one. She may be attacking her husband because he doesn't share her interest in the home, or because he doesn't earn enough for them to afford decent furniture. If he answers, "I don't think we need one," then it's her turn to guess what *he* really means. Is he saying they can't afford it? Or that they can afford it but shouldn't spend the money? Does he want to open a discussion or close it off? Is he waiting to be convinced or trying to bury the whole subject?

In short, to know why a person is telling you something you need to be able to analyze how the words reveal—or conceal—attitudes and feelings. And not only words. Messages are contained in nonverbal signals as well: gestures, facial expressions, voice tones, body postures. Is there, for instance, a husband or wife who does not wonder if there is an unspoken message in the turn of a body toward or away from one in bed?

Experts in body language—"kinesics" is its technical name—have proven that what we do with our bodies can communicate as much or more than words. Moreover, kinesic research shows that sensitivity to body-language clues is a learned skill. Women generally are better at this than men. Women have been socialized to watch for signs in others that they can react to—some even say to be "person pleasers." But men who work at jobs where sensitivity to others is necessary have also developed that ability. Many psychiatrists, actors, teachers, and salesmen are trained to read body language with a high degree of accuracy. So are counselors. One woman client, for example, used to sit with her legs crossed and used a swinging motion of the crossed leg to punctuate her speech. Her leg would move up and down with an affirmative statement and from side to side for a negative one. One day she answered a question with "No" but her leg moved up and down. She later admitted that she had not been telling the truth. But her leg was. In self-counseling, watch for valuable body-language clues.

CLARIFYING THE MESSAGE BEHIND THE WORDS

A counselor trying to help a couple improve their communication faces a paradox. Because the counselor must work with words, he or she creates still one more verbal layer, another set of messages and meanings to be interpreted. By adding one more person (the therapist) to the problem-solving session, the communication network gets more complex. So in that respect, self-counseling couples have an advantage: they can eliminate the third voice that may complicate matters. Therapists attempt to get a couple talking directly to each other as soon as possible in counseling sessions. But most couples with problems do not communicate well at the outset. When communication does take place it is often vague, full of ambiguous or judgmental statements. Each partner will talk *about* the other to the therapist rather than to the partner directly. Changing this pattern is one of the early tasks of therapy. Most of the techniques that counselors use to improve communication can easily be used in self-counseling. Here are some of the ways in which you can take a new look at your marital conversation:

• To what extent do my spouse and I mean the same thing by the words we use?

If that strikes you as a ridiculous question, remember that while a couple may both *speak* English, they often do not *talk* the same language at all. An example from a case history shows how the confusion arises: A woman asks her husband to stop on his way home from work to "pick up one or two things" for her. He readily agrees, expecting—as most men would—that she is referring to a last-minute grocery item, perhaps a bottle of wine, or something from the drugstore. But the wife's "one or two things" turn out to be a large bundle of groceries, two dresses from the cleaners, a bunch of leaves from the florist, and the iron she left to be repaired at the appliance store. By the time the man gets home with his awkward burdens, he is fuming. His wife cannot understand why he should be irritated. After all, he agreed to do it. Didn't he realize what she meant?

The misinterpretation syndrome works the other way around as well. "The other day my husband was fixing something underneath the hood of our car," a wife says. "He was having trouble getting the flashlight to stay in exactly the spot where he needed it, so he said, 'Honey, will you just hold this a second?' Naturally, I stopped what I was doing and went over to help him. Well, for the next *ten* minutes I was given a dozen instructions on how to hold the flashlight, where to aim the beam, which tool to hand my husband next, where to find the offset screwdriver he needed. That was *his* idea of 'hold this a second'!"

Without being sexist about it, there are differences between the way men and women use words. And as long as they are unaware that these differences exist, men and women will continue to interpret the same words differently.

- Do I tend to make snap judgments about the emotional significance of my spouse's remarks?

A wife's question—"What time will you be home tonight?"—may set up automatic resentment in some men. *She's checking on me again.* Or, *I can't have a moment's freedom.* And she may indeed be trying to exercise control. But it's useful to examine other possible emotional meanings that may lie behind that question. Maybe she is concerned because her husband has been working too hard. Perhaps she's planning a special dinner and needs to know when to start cooking it. She may even be trying to say, without knowing how, *"Hurry home, I miss you when you're gone."* Instead of leaping to false conclusions, cultivate the patience to ask *silently:* "Why are you asking me this?" And you may decide to ask out loud: "When would you like me to be here?"

- Do I project my own feelings into my partner's words?

Each of us knows what *we* mean when we use certain words, phrases, tones. Or we know what our parents meant by them; or our best friend. That being so, many of us "project" this information—and assume that a spouse who uses them means the same thing. Recently a young wife told us that she was afraid to ask her husband to fix anything around the house because whenever he worked on a project he yelled and cursed and flew into a temper. A chat with the man revealed that he didn't mind fixing things at all—he rather enjoyed it. He just got annoyed when he dropped the hammer while he was up on a ladder, or when the wall wouldn't hold a screw. "It helps to cuss," he explained. His wife had assumed that kind of language meant he was angry with her. Once she knew the real purpose the words served, she was less disturbed by them.

We have a strong tendency to believe that the meaning we give to someone's words or actions is the *right* meaning—the *only* meaning. This is what happens when we attempt "mind reading." A particularly uncommunicative husband shrugged his shoulders as his only reply to one of his wife's questions. The therapist asked him what the shrug meant. Before he could answer his wife said, "I know what it means. It means, 'Go to hell.'" When the husband finally managed to speak, he said it meant, "I really don't know how to answer since I've never thought about it before." Quite a difference in how they saw what he did.

To illustrate in another way how projection interferes with understanding, let's eavesdrop on the Ellsworths as they try to decide whether to go to the movies. Neither husband nor wife has a strong preference one way or the other. Finally Mary says, "I don't care . . . I'll do whatever you like." Does this please or even placate Jon? No, it convinces him that Mary is angry—because it is exactly the kind of remark *he* is likely to make when he feels, *We're going to do what you want anyway so why discuss it?* Irritated, Jon gets sarcastic: "You think I always get my way, don't you?" This upsets Mary. She really wanted Jon to choose; she thought she was being more than agreeable. What could have been a pleasant evening is now spoiled.

All of these kinds of misunderstandings and misinterpretations can be avoided if a couple cultivates the habit of "proving out" a conversation sentence by sentence. This takes time and patience, and though it often seems awkward—or even simple-minded—it is a tested counseling technique. It goes under many names. One therapist calls it "the art of asking." He teaches each spouse to ask the other after every sentence (or every word, if necessary) exactly what he or she meant, intended to mean, or felt. When the explanation is given, each spouse repeats it back to the other to make sure there has been no gap in their understanding. Psychologist Carl Rogers trains couples in a similar "echo game." In his version, A may not state his views until he has summarized B's remarks to B's complete satisfaction, and vice versa. Other counselors refer to the technique in technological terms; they call it a "communication feedback loop." By any name it is a strong force for clarity. It may be a necessary, if cumbersome, step to re-establish constructive communication between two people who say, "We can't talk to each other any more."

NINE WAYS TO ENHANCE SUPPORTIVENESS

Earlier in this chapter we made the point that the basic answer to "Why are you telling me this?" is the need for ego support. In dealing with communication, therefore, you are actually trying to improve the skills that go into mutual emotional supportiveness. Much of what we have already said about marital communication has involved these skills, explicitly or implicitly. As a guide to your own self-counseling activity, however, here are additional suggestions for couples who want to explore and improve their mutual ego-support responses.

1.   Set aside a special time and place when you can talk and listen without interruption or distraction—like the family who had "show and tell" every evening before dinner—not merely to fill each other in on the news of the day but also to provide a sounding board for each other. A major complaint many couples have is that one or both spouses lack the patience or serenity to listen.

2.   "Why are you telling me this?" is only one part of the double-barreled question you should always bear in mind. The other part is: "Why am *I* telling *you* this?" Examine your motives for the statements you make. It will help you to see whether you are trying to be constructive or critical, asking for help or making a demand, offering support or doing a subtle put-down.

3.   Learn how to detect the clues that indicate when your partner wants your support but is unable to ask for it. Ask questions to show that you are interested and concerned; or to find out what crankiness, edginess, or moody silence means. A perceptive husband reports that he always knows—often even before his wife does—when she is worried. "Her way of spending money changes. She's usually thrifty but when something weighs on her mind, she goes on a buying spree." Maybe your partner starts to gain weight or to drink more than usual. The young intern who was so troubled by the delivery-room accident was fortunate to have a wife able to sense that he needed emotional support even though he could not ask for it.

4.   Being supportive does not mean you must totally subordinate your own ideas, values, or good sense. Criticism itself can be supportive if it is offered in the right way, at the right time. Sometimes we really do tell a friend something for his or her own good. But the motive behind the criticism should be to help the situation become better—not to destroy or to cause pain. Always ask yourself, "What do I want to accomplish?" before leveling a criticism. If you are *asked* for your candid opinion you may feel freer about

speaking out frankly. Not always, though. Sometimes people ask for your opinion when they really want your approval. A good rule of thumb for dealing with this is: If the act is not yet committed and your opinion is asked, the truth will probably be welcome. (*I'm thinking of quitting my job. What do you think?*) If the act is already committed, approval is most likely sought. (*I quit my job today. Do you think I did the right thing?*)

5. If you and your spouse use words as weapons to wound each other with, make an effort to find out why. When you know the underlying reason—self-justification? revenge? ego-buttressing? unspoken grievances?—you can begin to deal with *that*. Attacking each other is going to close rather than keep open the lines of communication. When partners have fallen into the habit of name-calling and verbally assaulting each other, marital therapists call a truce. They explain that open communication requires a safe atmosphere, not a hostile one. Until the couple cease wounding with words they will probably not make progress in improving their marriage.

6. Try to avoid using "tune-out" words when you talk together. Certain words or phrases have negative emotional meanings for every couple. These are words like—"mother-in-law" or "money," "fishing trip" or "sex life"—designed (consciously or not) to raise the other person's hackles. But raised hackles interfere with empathy and understanding. They get in the way of attentive listening. On occasion, this turns into a game-playing ploy in which the partners hit below the belt until one of them gets angry. The other then says, "I was only teasing." The hostility is plain enough, and the game is not much fun. Sarcasm is another hostile way of attempting to communicate. The sarcastic partner withdraws from the anger he or she has provoked to the safety of "Where's your sense of humor? I'm only joking."

7. Develop the art of attentive listening. As social critic William Whyte pointed out several years ago, "the mere act of listening may be far more important than anything we have to say." Yet, as we have seen, few people are truly competent at listening with the "third ear"—picking up the emotional content beneath the surface flow of words. To do it, one must concentrate on what is being said.

Even on a purely technical basis listening is a difficult art. Studies show that the average person mentally grasps only about a third of what he or she hears, and remembers accurately only half of that third. Moreover, we tend to screen out what we don't *want* to hear—or think we do not need to hear. Physiologically, we can listen *five times as fast* as we can speak. Thus in the time it takes A to say 125 words to B, B has "brain room" for 600 words. The excess capacity is usually wasted or misused in wool-gathering, tuning out, or getting your rebuttal ready. If you experiment with a tape recorder, you can actually hear this happening—hear yourself answering almost before the other person is through talking. You were, in effect, so busy planning what you were going to say you did not listen carefully. Better to use that extra "brain room" to pay attention to the speaker.

Psychologically, marital listening is hampered by bad habits. *Boredom* is one. When a husband launches into complaints about his job, a wife who has heard it all before puts her ears on automatic pilot. Yet perhaps *this* time the husband is saying something new, something serious. *Narrowness* is another bad listening habit. It involves choosing to hear only those words that convey familiar or emotionally agreeable content. The narrow listener automatically rejects what he or she dislikes hearing—an obviously self-defeating skill: We ought to know as much as possible about whatever we have to deal with. Since information from your partner—whether you like hearing it or not—is necessary to the problem-solving process, it's essential to listen to *all* that he or she has to say. There is also the *"defensive"* listener who manages to twist whatever is said into a personal attack:

HUSBAND: Damn it, I'm late and my car is out of gas!
WIFE: Don't blame me. I didn't drive it last.

OR

WIFE: Groceries are getting so high, I don't see how we're going to make ends meet.
HUSBAND: I'm working as many hours a day as I can but it never seems to be enough to suit you.

A defensive listener can even turn a comment on the weather into something personal. One wife reported that when, on the day of the big "homecoming" football game, she said, "Oh no, it's raining, what a shame!" her husband snarled, "I got fifty-yard-line seats and you want me to make the sun shine, too?"

8. Don't overdo the "sympathy bit" in an effort to be supersupportive. When a person has had a depressing or anger-making experience, he or she usually wants to ventilate that emotion and know that you are listening sympathetically. But offering unsolicited advice can be counterproductive. "Nothing is so irritating," a wife said recently, "as to gripe about a household problem and then have my husband tell me how I should solve it! It took years before I could convince him that when I want his advice I'll ask for it—but when I'm upset I want him to listen and nod and let me get it off my chest!"

To get as hurt or angry as your partner is also a poor way to offer support. "When my husband seems to take over my feelings—even in a well-meaning way—it makes me feel like an incompetent child," a woman counseling client remarked. "I want him to sympathize. I want him to tell me I'm right. But I don't want him to fight my fight for me. I can handle that myself."

9. Train yourself in the art of reading "verbal cues." More agony is caused by missed implications and *mis*-interpretations than almost any other communication flaw. Garbled talk leads to garbled actions, and garbled actions to a relationship trapped in cross-purposes. A few years ago a couple who were on the verge of divorce came for counseling. During one session they were talking about the tensions that had built up over their conflicting ideas about how often they should have sex. Gloria thought they did it too often; David, too seldom. Gloria had tentatively agreed to try to be more willing. In the following excerpt from the case transcript, the couple are discussing what happened the previous night.

HUSBAND: I was watching TV and I heard Gloria say "I'm tired, I'm going to bed." And that meant to me, "I'm going to sleep, don't bother me."

MARCIA LASSWELL: Okay, Gloria, what *did* you mean?

WIFE: He should have known I wanted him to come upstairs pretty soon.

ML: Now, David, could Gloria have meant that?

H: If she did, why didn't she say so?

ML: All right, suppose she said, "I'm going upstairs; are you com-
　　ing up?" What would you have answered?

H: I might have said, "As soon as the news is over."

ML: And what would that have meant to you, Gloria?

W: I'd have thought he wasn't interested and I would have gone to
　　sleep.

H: But that's wrong. I would have meant—"I'll be up when the
　　news is over—so *don't* go to sleep!"

ML: But that's not what you *said*. Or, anyway, it's not how Gloria
　　heard it. I'm trying to show you how ambiguous you are most
　　of the time . . . how you try to read minds, and read them
　　wrong, and then act on the basis of these misinterpretations.

WHY ARE YOU NOT TELLING ME ANYTHING?

A brief word needs to be said about silence. Husbands and
wives who over long periods of time do not share their thoughts
and feelings are in even more trouble than those who must struggle
to understand each other's words. The syndrome is a familiar one:
The man who brings work home every night and buries himself in
it until his wife has gone to sleep; the woman who surrounds herself constantly with household chores, civic duties, and responsibilities to the children so she doesn't have to talk to her husband.
Some of these people are silent because they have identified with
their own silent parents. They simply never learned how to relate
through conversation.

But if there are problems in a marriage, discussion is necessary.
The silent partner will just have to start talking—using "I" statements to tell how he or she feels. The more verbal partner should
learn to listen, and to respect the effort the silent partner is making. Sometimes writing down what is to be said and having the
other person read it helps a couple to break the silent pattern. Or,
taping the message and playing it back is a way to begin. Some silent people make a virtue of the vice. "I don't dump my troubles
on him," a wife might say. "I try not to get into arguments around
the house," a husband might protest. But all too often these tacit
compacts to keep silent camouflage fears that to talk to each other
—to confront reality—will be too threatening or destructive.

There is one more pattern of silence that is common enough to be a major cause of communication problems. Many people keep their thoughts to themselves until they make a "pronouncement" that comes as a shock to the other person. "It was like a bolt out of the blue," a mystified husband told a therapist. "She told me she was quitting her job and taking a new position with another firm. It means a whole new way of life for her, and I don't see how she can do that so impulsively." What he didn't know was that his wife had been thinking about this change for months, talking it over with trusted business associates but not with him. Her decision was not impulsive. It was carefully planned. But the wife was a silent thinker who never made a serious statement until she had thought it over to herself. She had to learn that if she expected her husband to adjust to her decisions she couldn't spring them on him. He needed the same amount of time to absorb the changes as she allowed herself. In this instance the problem was compounded by the fact that the husband tended to *think out loud*. If something occurred to him he was apt to say it, even though he had not given it much thought. A day or so later he might announce that he had changed his mind; and later still say he'd changed it once again. To his silent-thinking wife, his words did not count for much. After all, when *she* said something it was well-thought out or it didn't get said. The husband needed to learn to warn his wife that his statement was tentative and she shouldn't take it as a final decision.

A silent marriage usually needs professional counseling because if you aren't talking, you can't do self-counseling. The dictionary definition of "communication" is revealing in this connection. The word, it says, originates in the concept of sharing, linking together, opening up to one another. Silence is a closing—and, more than that, a foreclosing of self-knowledge. Significant are the words of the biblical sage: "Speak, that I may know thee."

9

SEX AND OTHER INTIMACIES

A man and woman may be close to each other in every physical way, yet remain emotional strangers. To lock away one's thoughts and feelings inside the strongbox of the mind is to deprive a partner of the most significant gift one can offer—the intimacy that goes beyond all others. Even the pragmatic dictionary recognizes this. "Sexual intercourse" is the secondary definition of the word "intimacy." Its primary meaning is the "close personal relationship" that springs from the "inmost self." Thus, intimacy between husband and wife cuts across the totality of a marriage, not just its sexual aspect. It is, perhaps, what we really mean (but do not realize we mean) by "love."

A chord of truth about intimacy is struck midway through *Fiddler on the Roof*. That classic of the musical theater tells the story of a traditional Jewish family in a Czarist Russian village. The hero and his wife have been wed for twenty-five years after a marriage arranged, as was the custom, by a matchmaker. For all that time they have lived together, worked together, raised children, shared total physical intimacy. Now the husband startles his wife by asking, in song, "Do You Love Me?" After all these years, she answers in effect, *Don't you know that?* That's not the point, he implies: *I want to hear you say it.* By voicing the words *I love you* his wife will give him what he has till then unknowingly yearned for—the greater intimacy of sharing her feelings.

This intimacy that goes beyond sex presents difficulties for many couples. We all need it, we all want it. But not all of us know how to find it, nor are able to give it. In self-counseling, intimacy can be one of the knottiest areas to deal with since differences in our ability to give and receive intimacy often stem from deep psychological causes. A marriage empty of intimacy, for whatever reason, is likely to intensify doubt about our own worth and adequacy—a doubt that gets translated into a further retreat from intimacy and sets up a cycle of isolation.

But couples can make a beginning, at least, at improving their ability truly to share an intimate relationship by better understanding the levels of intimacy; by learning to recognize some of the barriers to it; and by developing the skill to overcome these barriers.

WHAT INTIMACY IS, AND ISN'T

There's been a good deal of foolishness put forth about intimacy. Some would have you believe that while it is a bonus in marriage its absence is not fatal, that a couple can find sufficient satisfaction in a "colleague" relationship where both persons function independently but get on well together. Others hold intimacy to be the only essential element of a good marriage. In the reality of wedlock, the truth would seem to fall somewhere between these extremes. Even the most functional/congenial couple do not have an intimate relationship, in our sense of the word, if they seldom are emotionally joined.

Conversely, we don't expect any couple would score 100 per cent on an "intimacy rating," if there were such a scale. Nor should they. Each individual rightly reserves close-held emotional space for private thoughts and feelings. Couples who assume that there is always *complete* intimacy in a good marriage thus naturally feel, from time to time, that something is wrong in their relationship. They have set a standard for themselves (or had it set by outsiders) that is impossible to achieve. Moreover, intimacy manifests itself in many forms: a smile across a room, a shared joke, a family ritual, a kiss, a touch, sex, even in a certain inflection of the voice. How intimate a couple are, and what forms their intimacy takes, depends on how they "negotiate" the difference between their individual desires for it. Intimacy cannot be a one-way proposition. Obviously, a marriage between an emotionally giving (or needy) woman married to a very private man will have a hard time achieving a degree of intimacy acceptable to both. But it is equally difficult in the case of, say, a very giving woman married to a very intimacy-dependent man; for then all the emotional flow will be going in one direction.

As a practical matter, the level of intimacy between husband and wife is constantly changing. Moments of intense closeness intersperse with periods of varying emotional distance. Try this experiment. Draw two circles on a sheet of paper. One represents you, the other your spouse. Where they intersect and overlap represents your area of intimacy. For example, during a particularly good sexual experience the circles may overlap almost completely, like this:

But there also may be times when intercourse, though still satisfying, is not quite such an intense merging experience. One of you may be worried, or tired, or just not as interested as the other. The circles in that case might look this way:

Yet the next evening, at a large noisy party—or just across a quiet living room—you may each look up from what you are doing and meet each other's eyes in a spontaneous exchange of silent affection. At that instant the circles will again be virtually superimposed—

—and you are just as intimately linked as you were in that earlier act of sex.

During much of the twenty-four hours, as a couple go about the routines of living, their circles may barely touch.

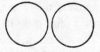

After a bitter argument, they may be widely separated:

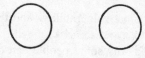

And the silent sharing of a mood can bring them close again. Some years ago a writer friend described what he called "one of the most intimate moments of my married life." He and his wife were reading the papers on a lazy Sunday morning over second cups of coffee while the FM radio played in the background. "Suddenly," he said, "the music of Mozart flooded the room. Without exchanging a word or even a glance, my wife and I simultaneously got up from our chairs, moved to the middle of the room, bowed to each other, and began to improvise the steps of a minuet. It all happened as if we had been one person. I shall never forget how close we felt."

In short, the circles constantly shift as each person gives and receives, withholds and blocks out.

BARRIERS TO INTIMACY

It may seem strange that anyone should want to avoid intimacy in marriage. Yet many people not only seek to avoid it but secretly fear it. Therapists believe the main reason is that intimacy, like trust, inevitably implies *vulnerability*. They are two sides of the same coin. Emotional sharing requires self-disclosure, and for many of us the idea of opening up our inmost centers is a scary prospect. Suppose we get hurt? Suppose we are rejected? Suppose we open up to find and to reveal to our partner that there is little or nothing inside?

Schopenhauer's parable about the porcupines which drew together for warmth but separated when their quills pricked each other illustrates the pull-and-push interplay of intimacy and vulnerability. Pained, the animals move apart; then, feeling the chill of the air they move close again, only to be hurt once more in the act of sharing warmth. We are often told that hate is the opposite of love, remoteness the reverse of intimacy. But it appears the real antagonist of both is the fear of being vulnerable to hurt, rejection, or disillusionment.

One protection against vulnerability—and thus a secondary barrier to intimacy—is to avoid the risk of self-disclosure by masking your true self. That's why some people can be comfortable emotionally so long as they can play the "role" of husband and wife. Doing the conventional and saying the expected things, we are saved from having to deal with the real feelings of real people. Sadly, it's all too easy to get on life's treadmill and keep running so steadily or so fast that we can find no time for intimacy. For men and women who have a poor opinion of themselves to begin with, the marital "role" is a convenient cloak to hide insecurities and weak self-images. One wife put it this way: "I don't feel free to be myself, because I'm afraid my husband wouldn't like me." But where is intimacy if all that a man is being intimate with is a facade of his wife? Is their "intimacy" based on what she lets him see? What she thinks is "acceptable"? And how does she know whether he will like her or not unless she shows him who she really is?

The retreat into role-playing is often an outgrowth of the artifices some couples adopt in their dating days. Ideally, courtship should be the time when men and women reveal themselves to each other with increasing intimacy. But even today—when so many courting conventions have gone by the boards and young couples dissemble less and level more—even now they still tend to conceal realities that might threaten their relationship. And when the *part* one plays succeeds in attracting and holding the person one wants, it gets progressively harder to step out of that character. But by dodging true intimacy in courtship we make it harder to achieve in marriage. "The more I am myself, the more you are free to be yourself," observes psychologist Jess Lair. "But I have got to be real to somebody, or they are not going to be real to me in return."

Even sexual intercourse defies intimacy when two people become actors in bed. Sociologist Robert Bell, a researcher into the sexual behavior of women, reports the reaction of a wife who for years faked orgasm so her husband would not feel a failure as a lover: "Now I am trapped," she said. "I would like to be honest with him because that would be a start at solving our difficulty. But it would mean admitting I deceived him all this time." Like all other kinds of intimacy, sexual intimacy depends on maximum *mutual* openness.

INTIMACY AND SEX

A pathetic paradox of these sexually "free" times is that Americans are making love more but enjoying it less. The average young man and woman experience their first sexual intercourse at an increasingly early age. Ever-fewer brides, and of course, grooms, are virgins at their first wedding. Marital sex takes place more often. One study of 10,000 women found that between 1965 and 1970, coital frequency increased from an average of 6.8 times in a four-week period to 8.2 times—a 21-per-cent jump. Extra-marital sex is also on the rise.

Yet at the same time there is marked dissatisfaction with the rewards of all this sexual activity. William Masters and Virginia Johnson, the pioneer sex therapists, estimate that half the married couples in the United States have sexual problems. Marriage counselors say that four of every five couples they see report some sexual difficulties. True, one reason for these statistics is the freer sexual climate itself. People expect more from sex, and are more willing to seek help when they are disappointed. And some of the problems result from physical difficulties, or ignorance, or negative conditioning about sex during childhood. But much sexual unhappiness grows directly out of the fear of intimacy. In fact, some couples develop sexual problems as a result of the stress one or both partners feel about being emotionally committed to an intimate relationship. For these people, sex may be good before and early in marriage. But when the realization hits that a good marriage demands ever-higher degrees of intimacy, there may be a retreat from sex. A case in point involved a young husband who felt emotionally and physically cheated. His wife had turned out to be quite different from the woman he had courted. He believed she had deceived him into marriage. He was particularly unhappy about the change in their sex life.

MARCIA LASSWELL: You mean you had a good sexual relationship before you were married, and now it's not going well at all?

HUSBAND: Right! Ann was great in bed and I thought she really enjoyed sex. When she got sick on our honeymoon that seemed to start the problem. Suddenly she was always tired, or not in the mood, and *now* she says she never liked sex and never had an orgasm.

ML: Ann, can you tell me what *was* going on with your sexual feelings before you married?

WIFE: What Rob says is true. I didn't enjoy it, but I pretended to because I wanted to please him. I thought maybe I could learn to like sex if I *acted* like I did. I know it sounds silly, but I acted the way I had seen in some movies—but it never worked for me.

ML: And you never felt you could share your true feelings with Rob?

W: To tell you the truth, I don't think I knew what they were. I was in love, and I kept thinking that would be enough to get me over the problem. After I got sick, I found it was a relief not to have to put on an act any more. That was when I first realized I must not even *like* sex.

Ann's problem came from self-alienation, but Rob read it as deliberate deception. His sense of being cheated was easy to understand—even for Ann—since she clearly had let him believe something that was not true. But it is also easy to understand how she could have allowed this to happen: she was not sufficiently in touch with herself to be able to share her intimate feelings. Ann's admission of her true reactions to intimacy—sexual and otherwise—was necessary for the couple to begin dealing with their problem.

Sexual "distancing" often goes with a general absence of marital intimacy. Its crisis symptom may be infidelity. Nearly one third of all counseling cases mention an act of unfaithfulness—or a continuing affair—as a "presenting symptom." Almost always the offending spouse is "shocked," and sees the infidelity as a gratuitous sexual betrayal of an otherwise adequate marriage. In some instances that may be true. Yet most of the time infidelity is not so much a search for sex as it is for emotional intimacy. A couple who can face that fact—and do something about it—have a good chance not only to survive the infidelity but to grow closer.

While sexual distancing is almost always a sign of intimacy problems, sexual contact is not always a sign of emotional closeness. That is another paradox self-counseling couples need to bear in mind. For example, there are marriages in which sex is the only good thing the couple share, and is sufficiently rewarding to hold together a relationship that lacks most other assets. Even men and women who are separated or divorced may still be drawn together sexually. For other couples, intercourse may represent the search for an antidote to loneliness, the "skin hunger" that desperately needs assuaging by human touch. It may confirm a person's sense of masculinity or femininity. It may offer reassurance that one is still vigorous and desirable. Or it may be a frantic effort to prove one still actually *exists*. Widows and widowers are often shocked to find that quite soon after a spouse's death they want—or form—a new sexual liaison. Similarly, there's an upsurge of sexual activity after major disasters. In both instances people are denying death, expressing the life force, saying with their bodies: "*I* am still here."

Too, sex can be a weapon in a marital power struggle. Here is how one husband frankly described a marriage where sex was perverted into a travesty of intimacy:

I suppose I wanted to be the boss too much. I ordered the meals, I doled out the household money, I made the decisions. Finally, she did the only thing she could, I guess—she wouldn't go to bed with me. After a few months without sex I stopped giving her any money at all. Pretty soon she said she couldn't buy food, she couldn't go anywhere. She started crying. "What do you expect me to do?" she said. I told her, flat: "Come to bed." She didn't say a word, just began to unzip her

dress and walk toward the bedroom. The sex was good,
and I started giving her money again.

Withholding sex—being "too tired" or having a "headache"—is
a standard method for turning an intimate act into a power struggle. Spoiling sex—being passive or brusque, repressing a climax or
ejaculating too quickly—are somewhat crueler refinements of the
technique. One woman drove her husband to fury by making casual remarks about the day's events during intercourse.

Sometimes couples quarrel in order to feel sexy. Making up in
bed after a fight is a common marital pattern. It is reassuring when
the bond of intimacy survives an argument. But if it is often done
deliberately one needs to ask *why* quarreling is a turn-on. Marital
therapist Laura Singer has observed that "it may be a way for a
couple to distance themselves from each other to avoid true merging . . . Or the act may be an extension of the fight. People may
perceive a fight as firing their libido, but what it really fires is their
hostility."

All these "uses" or "mis-uses" of sex distort its function as the
most intimate link in marriage. Even more startling, however, is
the use of sex as an outright *substitute* for intimacy. A person who
is so alienated as to fear any close relationship may turn to sex as
the only nonthreatening way to be with another person. When
there routinely is physical contact with no emotional attachments,
the act of love becomes the *denial* of intimacy.

INTIMACY AND LOVE

A remark marriage counselors frequently hear is, "I love her
[him] as a person, but I'm not *in* love." This usually turns
out to mean that a particular quality the speaker expects from a
love relationship is missing or has changed. For example, a group
of married couples in counseling, encouraged to talk about their
ideas of love, made these comments:

WIFE: My husband is a good provider, a good father, a consid-
    erate man. But he never says "I love you" and he hasn't
    given me a kiss in years—not even during sex.

HUSBAND: I'm not the romantic type. I show my love by working to support my family. My wife never has to worry about money, or where I am at night. I'm a real family man.

2ND WIFE: Well, I'd trade any time. Actions speak louder than words. I hear "I love you" several times a day but it means nothing because my husband is irresponsible.

2ND HUSBAND: How much I love my wife is separate from other things. I tell her I love her because I *do*. But she seems to think when I take a fling at the race track and lose it means I love her less.

In short, people define love in different ways. We can classify the basic concepts of love under six major headings:

romantic love seeks a total emotional relationship with the partner and expects it to provide a constant series of emotional peaks. There is a powerful physical attraction to the loved one, usually from the very first meeting. "Love at first sight" is characteristic. Obviously, the intensity of that first attraction cannot be maintained at the same high level for a lifetime; but those who define love in romantic terms say that the original excitement is frequently rekindled: "I've been married to her twenty years and I still catch my breath at how beautiful she is"; or, "When my husband walks in the door there is no question that he excites me just as he did when we first met."

self-centered love views it as an enjoyable game and employs a wide range of tactics and strategies to keep the game interesting. Persons who define love this way usually show a good deal of self-control and self-sufficiency. They make few demands on the loved one, and do not like demands made of them, either. Such persons do not look for an "ideal"; they can love a variety of types. Their approach to an intimate relationship is almost casual, and they tend to avoid intense expressions of love. They are more likely to say: "Of course I love her, but I don't have to make a big fuss about it," or, "I love my husband very much but I always hold back a little so he won't take me for granted."

intense-dependency love justifies making enormous emotional demands on the partner. A man or woman in this category reacts to the smallest emotional slight with fierce jealousy or anxiety, for he or she seems to have an insatiable need not only for affection but also for reassurance. "Tell me you love me" is a frequent plaint. Absences enforced by business trips are miserable times for such a person. Separate vacations are unthinkable: "How can you love anyone and want to be away from them?"

thou-centered love is unconditionally giving. The partner need not return affection in the same way as it is given, nor to the same extent. This kind of lover often is considerably self-sacrificing; yet the result is not martyrdom but a pleasurable "better-to-give-than-to-receive" attitude. Thou-centered love is sometimes called "unconditional love": "There is *nothing* you could do to make me stop loving you."

best-friends love is emotionally predictable, companionable, and mutually supportive. It is usually slow to develop: "One day I realized I must love her—we had so much in common," is how one man described his decision to marry a woman he had known for four years. Sex is not important in the early stages of a "best friends" relationship. Even if a "best friend" spouse gets divorced, he or she may well continue to want to remain close to the former mate.

logical-sensible love emphasizes the practical values of a stable relationship: "I could never love anyone I wouldn't consider a suitable spouse." Such lovers often know exactly what kind of a partner they are looking for, and will wait patiently for the one who meets most (not necessarily all) of their requirements.

Very few of us are what might be called "pure" examples of any single category of love styles. Most of us are a mix of two or even more of them. The most frequently encountered combinations are romantic/self-centered; romantic/intense-dependency; best friends/logical-sensible, or self-centered/logical-sensible. And there are some men and women who have a bit of every love style in their emotional make-up. Which style is emphasized or becomes dominant seems to depend on the characteristics of the partner.

The important consequence of these different ways of thinking and feeling about love is that each person loves according to his or her own definition. That means most of us love our partner the way *we* want or expect to be loved, and not the way he or she wants or expects to be loved. When partners' definitions conflict, each is likely to feel unfulfilled.

This may be the one situation where the Golden Rule—"Do unto others as you would have others do unto you"—is not the right approach. For when husband and wife interpret love from different emotional perspectives, the quality of marital intimacy suffers. For example, a woman who sees love as a romantic and intensely interdependent state of affairs may be upset when it levels off from heights of passion to a steadier but blander pattern of caring. Such a wife may read that change to mean that her "best-friends" love-style husband is "falling out of love," since by *her* definition he is certainly no longer *"in"* love.

When love styles conflict, furthermore, actions that one partner takes to *show* love are often not *perceived* by the other partner as loving. A simple example is provided by the couple who were always upset by the presents they gave to and received from each other. "I don't think Ray loves me any more . . . he certainly never shows it," was how Marian began a meeting with the counselor. She and her husband had been married for eight years. At first, the woman said, Ray used to call her from the office to say he was thinking of her; he would often bring home flowers or plan surprise evenings out. "But there's none of that any more," Marian concluded grimly.

Ray was not essentially a romantic person. He admitted that he had played the "role" of lover during courtship and the early days of marriage because he thought that was how things should be done. But after a year or so he found it more natural to be himself. To Ray, this meant showing love in a sensible "best-friends" way. Instead of flowers, he would bring home a new kitchen gadget. Instead of phoning from the office he concentrated on his work in order to get a promotion and a raise. "By now," Ray said, "Marian ought to *know* I love her—why do I have to keep saying it?"

But a can opener or a knife sharpener did not strike Ray's wife as a love token. She enjoyed giving him sentimental, impractical gifts and could not understand why this annoyed him. "It's a waste," Ray said. "How often will I wear a smoking jacket? How many sets of cuff links do I need?"

To help this couple learn that husbands and wives need to love each other as the other wants to be loved, the counselor explained the various categories of loving and showed Ray and Marian how they were each behaving according to their own definitions:

MARCIA LASSWELL: If you want to be loved, you must *say* what makes you feel loved. That is the only way you will ever learn what each of you thinks of as a loving act. Marian, you have to tell Ray that flowers, or champagne, or something you would not get for yourself makes you feel loved. And you, Ray, need to learn to listen and accept that need of hers. Marian, you have to realize that a velvet smoking jacket does not mean love to Ray. What *would* mean love to you, Ray?

HUSBAND (after a moment): You know those dead trees in the back yard, Marian? (She nods, puzzled) How about a chain saw!

Of course, this conflict in definitions of love is often far more complex. In some cases incompatible love styles can lead to incredible emotional tangles. Not long ago, for instance, an unhappy couple were referred for marital counseling by the wife's concerned parents. Herb was twenty-eight, Carol was thirty-two; they had been married for eighteen months.

MARCIA LASSWELL: Why did your parents ask you to have counseling?

WIFE (blurting it out): It's simple! *He* wants a divorce and I don't.

ML: Is that correct, Herb?

HUSBAND (calmly): Yes, it is.

Carol, it developed, had been married before for three years. When her first husband "began acting strangely" Herb—who was their closest friend—visited frequently and tried to be helpful. But all he saw was Carol getting more upset and bewildered. One weekend, when her husband was away on a fishing trip, Carol called Herb and said she was lonely, asked him to take her out to dinner. She chose a place that was dimly lit and had music for dancing:

WIFE: I suppose you could say I set out to seduce him that night. I acted sexy. When we got home I invited him in for a drink. It didn't take me long to get him in bed.

MARCIA LASSWELL: Do you know why you did that?

W: I think so. Realizing I could still attract a man like Herb gave me a lot of courage. In fact, enough courage to leave my husband.

ML: So, you two continued to see each other, and then got married. How did it happen?

HUSBAND: I felt she had left her husband *because* of me. And I felt guilty about betraying my friendship with him—although I must say *he* didn't seem too upset by what happened. One thing just sort of led to another . . . I figured Carol expected me to marry her, and I suppose I thought I *ought* to. I didn't want to just run out on her.

ML: And why do you want a divorce now?

H: I don't feel toward Carol the way I should. What it amounts to is, I don't love her any more.

W (to Herb): How can you say that? You don't love anyone else, do you? You still like sex with me. You say you like the way I look, you like to take me out to show me off.

H: I *know* all those things . . . you're right. But it still seems wrong to me to *pretend* I love you when I *feel* that I don't. Anyway, not *my* way. It's not honest. The only fair thing I can do is divorce you.

W (hopelessly): Fair! That's your idea of fair?

Paradoxically, it *was* Herb's idea of "fair." This husband and wife had quite different definitions of love. Carol, a romantic, needed the kind of affection and reassurance that Herb could not provide. His way of loving was to be a good friend, to sacrifice himself if necessary. At one time that way met Carol's need. Now, it did not. Herb had married Carol rather than disappoint her. Now he felt he should divorce her since he could no longer love her as he realized she wanted to be loved.

Just as marital therapists pay particular attention to each spouse's definition of love in order to find a basis for integrating a couple's ideas of intimacy, a self-counseling couple also need to clarify their definitions, to identify their styles of loving. At the end of this chapter is a Love Scale Questionnaire you can use for that purpose.* Answer each question carefully and rate yourself according to the scoring instructions. The result can be a valuable self-counseling aid to help you and your spouse determine your personal concepts of love and intimacy.

EXPRESSING INTIMACY

Some husbands and wives are genuinely puzzled by the suggestion that they try to raise the intimacy level of their marriage. They agree with the theory but they do not know how to put it into practice. They seem to assume that a talent for sharing feelings is an inborn skill which can't be learned. Or that it takes "too much time" to cultivate. Or that their responsibilities keep them too much on the go, or too far apart, to be able to create a basis for true intimacy. We like to tell such people about a couple we know who have been married nine years. From the start Geri and Martin have been separated by half the world more than six months every year. Martin's business requires him to make long swings through Asia and the Middle East.

"I think we are closer to each other than many couples we know who are always together," Martin says. "When I come home we have so much information to exchange . . . so many new ideas to share . . . that we are completely involved on every level. We are fresh and important to each other physically, intellectually, and emotionally."

"When we were first married I went with Martin three or four times," Geri says, "so I know his trips are not fun. They are exhausting and often boring. Most of the time I spent alone in a hotel room while Martin tended to business. Now when he's away he is more thoughtful of me. He phones several times a week. He

---

* This questionnaire is an adaptation of a counseling test designed by Thomas and Marcia Lasswell. It was first presented at the 1975 Annual Meeting of the American Association of Marriage and Family Counselors.

writes long letters that let me see more deeply into his mind than if we were talking in the same room. Of course, I get lonely while Martin's away. But I plan ahead for theater and concert tickets. I let our friends know I'm available for dinner invitations. And I find I'm self-reliant—which makes me feel better about myself when Martin gets back. I spend a lot of time *thinking* about our life together, planning its possible futures. Martin does the same. When he comes home we have all that to explore together."

That's an unusual situation, of course. But there are any number of ways every couple can find to enhance and to express their mutual intimacy:

• Confiding in your spouse is an aspect of intimacy. Think back and ask yourself whether you often tell a friend or neighbor something you feel you cannot or do not want to tell your wife or husband. If you do, perhaps you should ask whether you are being emotionally fair to your partner—and why you are shutting him or her out, or shutting yourself away.

• Sharing "trivialities" is a way of increasing intimacy. Some people feel it's "boring" to tell a spouse all the little things that occur during the day. But marriage is essentially made up of these small details; they are the "nuts and bolts" of living together. True, they are usually routine. But if you wait for some major event to happen you may wait quite a while.

• Intimate behavior does not have to involve only grand passion or high drama. Intimacy is built as well (if not more soundly) on lighter, slighter actions: reading aloud; putting a loving note in a lunch box; giving a small but unexpected present; doing a chore the other person hates (without being asked); telling the other person when you have had a warm thought about him or her.

• Verbal communication is an important part of intimacy because unless we can put feelings into words our partners may never know we have them. Even an argument can contribute to marital intimacy. If a couple can have an honest fight without letting it deteriorate into aggression or anger, it often leaves them feeling closer when it's over. As one couple said after a furious battle: "You can get mad and know it's *because you care* about each other." Conversely, poor communication can handicap a couple's efforts to be close. One husband and wife each year go on a wilderness camping trip. It uses up a lot of their energy and money. And they have a terrible time on the trip because both of them hate camping. Why do they do it? Early in the marriage their communication channels were blocked. Each thinks the other loves camping.

• While sex is the peak physical expression of intimacy, it's essential to remember that there can be many kinds of marital sex. There can be an intense spiritual or emotional merging. There can be sex that makes you feel like the most desirable man or woman in the world. There is casual love-making, playful "seduction," intercourse for the release of tension, reluctant sex, or sex on the purely physical "let's do it" level. One brings a different expectation of intimacy to each kind of sexual experience, and it is important for both partners to know what kind of expectation the other has for each particular experience.

The emphasis on sexual technique in recent years has cut many couples off from true intimacy. They get so caught up in mechanics and methods that they lose sight of the need for feelings and concerns. Good physical sex is obviously important—but no two persons' cycle of desire coincides exactly all the time. Not even the perfect orgasm is any guarantee of interpersonal intimacy. For instance, two of every three wives who said (in a recent survey by Dr. Bell) that their marriage was "good" or "very good" also said they almost always reached a satisfying sexual climax. "But," asks Dr. Bell, "which is cause and which effect?" Orgasmic sex can make a good marriage better; but a good marriage, with a high level of emotional intimacy, can also make for more or better orgasms.

• Many men and women find pleasure in varying degrees of physical intimacy short of sexual intercourse. That's why touching is such a key factor in conveying intimate feelings. Americans avoid touching. They tend to think of body contact not in terms of comfort and affection, but in terms of sex or combat—both of which are prickly with cultural and psychological taboos. Thus a wife may come to resent a husband's touch because she thinks all it means is that he wants sex—"he only touches me when he wants to sleep with me." She hesitates to touch him for fear *he* will think *she* wants sex.

Yet touching is the most natural act in the world. It is an infant's first experience at birth and the main avenue of communication for many months afterward—hands changing, feeding, bathing, rocking, holding. In one famous experiment a psychologist showed the importance of what he called "contact comfort" when he proved that baby monkeys preferred to cling to a "mother figure" built of rubber and soft cloth that did not give milk rather than one built of wire that did. Human skin has hundreds of thousands of submicroscopic nerve endings that sense dozens of different kinds of touches. No wonder a touch can calm anxiety, ease pain, soothe fear, provide emotional security. Indeed, touch is the main sensory avenue by which our need for intimacy is satisfied.

If you have hesitated to express or receive intimacy through touching but would like to experiment with it, try these steps:

1. Discuss the idea first with your partner. Nothing is more disconcerting than when one person suddenly and without explanation becomes a "toucher."

2. Begin with simple physical contacts that are customary in many families: a good-morning and good-night kiss, a hug in greeting or farewell.

3. Become more aware of your spouse's physical presence. Many couples become so familiar with each other's bodies that, paradoxically, they forget how those bodies *really* look and feel.

4. Touch yourself more often to develop a sense of body awareness. We do it automatically while drying after a bath, shaving, putting on make-up. But we should learn to do it consciously on occasion.

5. Touching should never be an implied demand to be touched in return, or a camouflage for clinging to another person.

6. Learn to be sensitive to when the other person wants—or does not want—to be touched. The important thing is to respect each other's feelings about it.

Is it better to experience intimacy at the risk of some hurt, or to avoid it in order to feel safe?

That is what economists call a "cost-reward equation." As with all such questions, the answer lies in the balance between how much it costs to get the reward we desire. In a sense, every chapter in this book is about how to minimize costs and maximize rewards. But nowhere is such help more needed than in the area of emotional intimacy. To a vulnerable person it always *seems* safer to keep feelings at arm's length. But retreating from intimacy is no guarantee that you will not be hurt by someone, somehow, anyway. In the long run, reaching out and opening up is not only more rewarding but also less risky.

THE LOVE-SCALE QUESTIONNAIRE

Answer each of the following questions true or false in terms of your feelings about the love relationship in your marriage. If you are not now married, respond in terms of your most significant past love relationship.

1. T/F I believe that "love at first sight" is possible.
2. T/F I did not realize that I was in love until I actually had been for some time.
3. T/F When things aren't going right with us, my stomach gets upset.
4. T/F From a practical point of view, I must consider what a person is going to become in life before I commit myself to loving him/her.
5. T/F You cannot have love unless you have first had *caring* for a while.
6. T/F It's always a good idea to keep your partner a little uncertain about how committed you are to him/her.
7. T/F The first time we kissed or rubbed cheeks, I felt a definite genital response (lubrication, erection).
8. T/F I still have good friendships with almost everyone with whom I have ever been involved in a love relationship.
9. T/F I try to use my strength to help my partner through difficult times, even when he/she is being unreasonable.
10. T/F If one of us has to suffer illness or misfortune, I would rather it be me than my partner.
11. T/F Part of the fun of being in love is testing my skill at keeping it going smoothly and getting what I want from it at the same time.

12. T/F   It is best to love someone with a similar background.
13. T/F   We kissed each other soon after we met because we both wanted to.
14. T/F   When my partner doesn't pay attention to me I feel sick all over.
15. T/F   I cannot be happy unless I put my partner's happiness before my own.
16. T/F   Usually the first thing that attracts my attention to a person is his/her pleasing physical appearance.
17. T/F   The best kind of love grows out of a long friendship.
18. T/F   At the first touch of my partner's hand I knew that love was a real possibility.
19. T/F   If I separated from my partner I would go out of my way to see that he/she was okay.
20. T/F   I cannot relax if I suspect that he/she is with someone else.
21. T/F   At least once I have had to plan carefully to keep two of my lovers from finding out about each other.
22. T/F   I have always been able to get over love affairs pretty easily and quickly.
23. T/F   The best part of love is living together, building a home together, and rearing children together.
24. T/F   I am usually willing to sacrifice my wishes to let my partner achieve his/hers.
25. T/F   A main consideration in choosing a partner is whether he/she will be a good parent.
26. T/F   Sex shouldn't be rushed into; it will happen naturally when intimacy has grown enough.
27. T/F   I enjoy flirting with attractive people.
28. T/F   My partner would get upset if she/he knew some of the things I've done with other people.
29. T/F   Before I ever fell in love, I had a pretty clear physical picture of what my true love would be like.
30. T/F   If my partner had a baby by someone else I would want to raise it, love it, and care for it as if it were my own.
31. T/F   It is hard to say exactly when we fell in love.
32. T/F   I couldn't truly love anyone I would not be willing to marry.

33. T/F   Even though I don't want to be jealous, I can't help it when he/she pays attention to someone else.

34. T/F   I would rather break up with my partner than stand in the way of his/her happiness.

35. T/F   I wouldn't date anyone I couldn't fall in love with.

36. T/F   At least once when a love affair was over, I knew realistically I couldn't see the person again without still feeling love.

37. T/F   Whatever I own is my partner's to use as he/she chooses.

38. T/F   If my partner ignores me for a while, I sometimes do really stupid things to try to get his/her attention back.

39. T/F   A main consideration in choosing a mate is how he/she will affect my career or future security.

40. T/F   The best love relationships are the ones that last longest.

SCORING: The only answers that need to be considered are the "True" responses. The questions are designed to give equal representation to the six categories of love styles.

"True" answers to questions numbered 2, 5, 8, 17, 23, 25, 31, and 40 indicate the "best-friends" kind of love.

"True" answers to questions 3, 14, 20, 33, 36, and 38 indicate an "intense-dependency" love style.

"True" answers to questions 9, 10, 15, 19, 24, 30, 34, and 37 characterize "thou-centered" love.

"True" answers to questions 1, 7, 13, 16, 18, and 29 are indicative of "romantic" or sensual love.

"True" answers to questions 4, 12, 26, 32, 35, and 39 are characteristic of the "logical-sensible" love style.

"True" answers to questions 6, 11, 21, 22, 27, and 28 indicate a "self-centered" or game-playing style of love.

INTERPRETATION: Remember that rarely is anyone a "pure" example of a single type of love style. Most likely your scores will show a mixture of the various categories—but with one or two categories having a predominant number of "true" responses. Your test profile will probably show some "true" answers in all the classifications, but with peak scores in two or three of them. For example, say you have answered "True" to five questions in the "best-friends" category and to four questions in the "logical-sensible" one. We could then reasonably assume that you are a person who is extremely practical in terms of whom you can love, and how you love them; but that you also will want to make the person you love your closest friend.

Here is another illustration: Say you have answered "True" to four questions in the "thou-centered" category and to four in the "romantic" group, and also to two questions in each of the other classifications. It is reasonable to interpret this to mean that you felt a strong physical attraction to your partner at the outset of your relationship; and that you believe that if your love is a true one it will overcome every obstacle—even to the point of giving each other up if that will make you both happier.

While the test is highly indicative of your personal concept of love—what it means to you, and how you show it—it is not an infallible guide. And only a counselor trained in interpreting the test can be certain of the significance of the results. But even as a self-counseling device the test is useful in revealing how a couple's attitudes toward love may mesh or clash.

10

WHO'S IN CHARGE?

How Couples Deal with Decisions

If you were to attend a convention of marriage counselors or specialists in family relations, we're sure you would agree that they are among the kindest and gentlest of people. This does not stop them, however, from devising Machiavellian social experiments—games that no one can win, quizzes to which there are neither right nor wrong answers, dilemmas to which there are no correct solutions.

The purpose of these stratagems is to learn more about how married couples behave when they are faced with a stressful situation. One such test is a "game" called SIMFAM—"Simulated Family Activity Measurement." It was developed to find out how a husband and wife make and carry out decisions in a crisis. Let's watch one couple as they play it.

At one end of a small "playing area" resembling a shuffleboard court are two targets—one for John and one for Mary. Each target has a pair of red and green lights. John and Mary have been told that they are taking part in an experiment in "learning skills." Every time they both make a correct "move" in the game, the experimenter says, the green light will flash; every time they make an incorrect move the red light will go on. But the couple deliberately have not been given the rules of the game. They are supposed to learn these, it is explained to them, by discovering which of their actions turns on the green light. After each "inning" of play, their score is posted prominently alongside the score of an "average couple" to show them how well or poorly they are doing.

John and Mary enjoy the challenge of the game. They confer

frequently as the lights flash to determine which of their moves were right and to figure out what the basic rules are. They are pleased when the green bulb lights up often enough so that their score is considerably higher than that of the "average" couple. About midway through the game, however, the pattern changes. Now, almost no move that John and Mary make produces a green light. They play more frantically because time is running out and their score is falling well below the standard that they have been told is average.

What John and Mary *don't* know is that there are *no* rules for SIMFAM. Their actions and choices have no effect at all on the green and red lights. Those are secretly being manipulated by the experimenters. Moreover, there is no "typical" score and the "average couple" is a myth. But without this information, John and Mary naturally assume that *they* are suddenly doing something wrong, and that *they* are now making incorrect decisions.

How do they react to this simulated "crisis"? Do they shift to another pattern of decision-making? Do they cling stubbornly to the one they have been using even though it obviously no longer works? Do they turn to each other for guidance and direction? Does each try his and her own ideas? Does one of them try to take over the decision-making process, countermanding the other's suggestions? Does one spouse denounce the other for a poor choice of moves? Do one or both of them just give up in the face of confusion and failure?

Whatever John and Mary do now gives important clues to how their decision-making process might be affected in a real crisis in their life. Also, it provides another significant bit of data that will help the experimenters to build a theory of marital decision-making. SIMFAM results indicate that if one spouse is highly dominant, the couple will continue to accept that person's decisions even though they consistently prove "wrong." If the couple have what is called an "egalitarian" marriage—that is, if they normally share the tasks and decisions of daily life—they tend to go on consulting with each other, to test each other's choices, to shift smoothly between them the responsibility for effective decision-making in this minor "crisis."

A couple's ability to work out mutually agreeable and effective ways of handling decisions is clearly one of the most important day-to-day skills a marriage needs. No family can function successfully if every question that comes up, every choice that must be made, every action to be taken has to be thrashed out from scratch. Yet despite—or because of—its importance, decision-making is one of the most troublesome and irritating areas a couple must deal with.

Every couple sooner or later works out a pattern for reaching marital decisions. The catch is that many of these patterns are self-defeating, or inefficient, or both a cause and a result of other conflicts. Most husbands and wives are reluctant to face this truth. Most of us like to think of ourselves as reasonable persons—open to discussion, willing to be convinced by facts, ready to make compromises. Ask any couple how they make decisions and assign responsibilities for routine family tasks. The answer is almost sure to be some variation of: "Oh, we try to work things out rationally . . ."

Yet in practice most couples do *not* follow—do not even *have*—a rational basis for decision-making. Moreover, they are not aware of this lack. As a test, ask yourself and your spouse these questions right now and see how many you can answer and how well you agree:

- Who makes most decisions in your family?
- Do you have any guidelines to distinguish between a "minor" decision and a "major" one?
- Do you have any standard procedure for settling arguments when you disagree on a decision?
- How do you decide which household chores each of you will handle?
- In which areas of family life do you have the right to make decisions unilaterally, without consulting your spouse? How did you decide *that?*
- Do you make the decisions you want to make, or just the ones your spouse does *not* want to make?
- Are you truly "in charge" of those matters about which you have the right to decide? Or has your spouse merely abdicated from them, or tacitly given you permission to manage them?

- Do you have any "veto power" over each other's decisions and, if so, on what sort of basis?

If you can answer any of these questions with a degree of certainty, you are unusual. When we talk with married couples, in or out of counseling, it's apparent that most of them cannot respond to the questions accurately and have seldom even thought about such matters. Couples don't know why they're successful at decision-making—if they are. They don't know why they fail at it—if they do. They are for the most part unaware that their attitudes toward decision-making may conflict. And—perhaps most significant—what they *think* takes place between them when decisions are being made is usually quite different from what actually happens.

For example, Ralph and Doris believed they made decisions in a logical and orderly way. So when Ralph was offered a better job with his firm's branch in another state, he wanted his wife to have an equal voice in a decision that would mean major changes in the whole family's life. Ralph suggested they each write down pros and cons about the move, and then compare their lists. The couple was astonished when their lists did not have one item in common. Ralph had noted only those points concerning his career and the family's financial situation. Doris's list concentrated on questions of housing, schools, social adjustments. Instead of the "reasoned discussion" they had expected, they found themselves in a shouting match about who was being selfish, who was being ungrateful, and "whoever said a wife *had* to go where her husband wanted, anyway?" By the time they called a counselor the couple were like two mules—each unwilling to budge. Each thought the other was being manipulative and self-serving.

WIFE: I think Ralph had his mind made up before he asked for my opinion. Then when he realized I disagreed with him, he got angry and said we were going whether I liked it or not. Ralph is thinking only of himself.

HUSBAND: And you're not? You are using the children as a weapon to make me feel guilty. Why should I feel guilty? It's not just "my career" that will benefit. The promotion and the extra money will be good for all of us.

MARCIA LASSWELL: The fact that neither of you listed any of the pros or cons the other one wrote down indicates a real lack of understanding. I think you need to try harder to sense how the other person sees this possible move. Did you have your mind made up before you asked Doris for her opinion?

H: No, I really didn't. I wanted her opinion. But I thought we'd be talking about what this would mean in terms of my future, of our finances, how we might come out if we had to sell our home and buy another—things like that.

ML: Why didn't you have any of those on your list, Doris?

W: I just told you. I figured Ralph had his mind made up, and I wanted to show him there were other things to consider.

H: She was trying to make me feel guilty . . . to make me feel I was asking everyone to sacrifice for my sake. Then I was supposed to back down and she would have gotten her way.

W: Ralph doesn't care if the children have to adjust to a new school, or find new friends. I would have been willing to discuss the whole thing reasonably if he hadn't started saying we *had* to go. I wanted him to know there were other things to think about besides his job.

The closer one looks at such maneuverings in marital decision-making, the more they take on the choreography of a minuet. The partners bow and sway and step about each other in turn, careful not to seem too aggressive nor too yielding, and above all not to step on each other's toes. But when the music stops and the minuet is over, they are back in the same position from which they started. Ralph and Doris had backed away from each other to the point where they were about to stop dancing altogether—to cease to be partners. Marriage, of course, must *move*—backward if not forward—and that motion is the sum of all the daily decisions a couple makes.

A husband and wife who continue to dance around the need to work out ways for dealing realistically with decisions are in trouble. Most couples know this, even if only subconsciously. Why, then, do they continue to avoid coming to grips with the problems of decision-making?

We believe it is because they also realize—and also on a subconscious level—that the question of "who decides what" is actually a question of *who holds power* in the marriage. And that issue so disturbs most couples that they prefer not to confront it.

But it cannot be avoided. It can be camouflaged, overlooked, misinterpreted, ignored. But not avoided. In every marriage there is, willy-nilly, some kind of balance of power between the spouses. It manifests itself most clearly in the way couples reach decisions and assign tasks. A British expert on family relationships, Ronald V. Sampson, has observed that each of us seeks "to order his life and his relations with others on the basis of love or on the basis of power." Love and power operate like opposite ends of a seesaw. If power is the main drive for our behavior, love is diminished; if love predominates, there should be a minimum of power struggles. The attempt to escape having to make the choice is futile, Sampson says. As most counselors will confirm, this clash between power and love is at the heart of conflict over decisions. Or, to put it another way, decision-making is a key aspect of what sociologists call the "family power structure." It's important, therefore, to take a closer look at this structure.

In old-fashioned marriage, when the roles of men and women were sharply defined, the areas under each spouse's control fell into place almost automatically. Some were dictated by custom and tradition, some by law, some by the special skills and shared expectations of husband and wife. Today these guidelines are in disarray. Customs have changed. Laws have given women a broad measure of equal rights and freedom from traditional controls. Household and job skills are no longer linked so closely to sex roles. And even expectations are no longer necessarily shared. A man, for instance, may *expect* that his wife will be sexually faithful, but she may believe in "open" relationships and expect the right to sexual freedom. He may expect her to stay home and take care of the family, but she may expect to build a career; conversely a wife may expect her husband to provide total financial support while he may expect her to work and share the economic burden.

With tradition replaced by flexibility, and dependence giving way to personal independence, what are the new sources of marital power? Family experts believe that power rests today with the spouse who has the most "resources." One of the first studies of family power, made by sociologists Robert O. Blood and Donald M. Wolfe, asked 900 middle-class couples which spouse decided how much to spend on food, what car to buy, where to go on vacation, what doctor to select for the children, and similar questions. Blood and Wolfe found that the spouse who earned more, or who had a better education, or who was more competent in dealing with society—in short, the spouse with the most resources—was the one who made most of the decisions.

But as researchers dug deeper into the question, this "resource" theory of marital power was refined. We know now that it is not just a person's earning capacity or financial know-how or college diploma that determines his or her power-standing in a marriage. Today, one's "resources" can include physical attractiveness, sexual skills, social status, and a host of similar intangible assets. There are even circumstances in which a weakness, a dependency, a failing, can serve as a reservoir of power. A wife with a chronic illness can exert enormous control over a solicitous husband. A man's guilt over a single infidelity—whether his wife knows about it or not—can be a major hidden power "resource" for her.

A University of Southern California sociologist, David M. Heer, has carried this refinement even further. He takes the position that marital power depends in large part on which partner has the better "market value." Thus, if a woman believes her husband is in a stronger position than she is to leave and make a new life for himself, she is at a power disadvantage. Conversely, if a man feels that his wife is more desirable, a "better catch" than he is, then the balance of power lies with her. In other words, whoever *needs* the marriage most tends to strike a power bargain—to yield some control to keep from losing everything.

Moreover—and this is a critical point—it does not matter whether these beliefs are borne out by the facts. It is only necessary that one partner *think* (or imagine) that the other has a better "market value." Often the partner who thinks of himself or herself as the least desirable or capable suffers from a poor self-concept. The partner who is assigned a high "market value" is not, in fact, that much better. Marital counseling in such cases amounts to giving each partner a more realistic view of the other. It may help the insecure spouse to see how a negative self-image has kept him or her from functioning as an equal in the marriage. For instance, not long ago a most intelligent and attractive young woman, married to an attorney in a major law firm, sought therapy because she rarely had an orgasm during intercourse. She was depressed about herself, and said she wouldn't blame her husband if he "gave up" on her—especially when he was so generous. Just recently, the woman said, he had paid for a painting class she wanted to take. He had "approved" her entering the course so long as it didn't interfere with her homemaking duties. The woman, totally in awe of her husband, saw nothing wrong in this. Indeed, she felt fortunate that he was "allowing" her to study painting at all. In that same counseling session the woman guiltily said that though her husband would do anything to please her sexually, she always took "too long" to become aroused:

MARCIA LASSWELL: What do you think about when you're having sex?

WIFE: That my husband must be getting worn out . . . that he's bored . . . that I'm a poor sex partner. I'm afraid if I don't respond he'll lose all interest in me.

ML: And find someone else?

W: I guess I am afraid of that. He's around attractive women all day.

ML: But you're attractive, too, you know.

W: I am? I don't feel that I am.

ML: I suspect those negative feelings cause you to put a lot of pressure on yourself to respond sexually to feel "adequate." But you really defeat yourself when you try too hard. You can't concentrate on your sexual feelings, and that blocks out your orgasms. Try to concentrate on how you *feel*—not on whether having an orgasm makes you a good wife.

Therapy helped this woman to realize that her sexual performance was not a measure of how adequate a person she was. This in turn led her to understand that she had yielded to her husband in nearly every decision-making aspect of their lives. Once she stopped thinking of herself as inferior to him, not only was sex better but the couple gradually reached a more truly intimate and equal relationship.

A counselor working with a couple who are having difficulties with decisions looks for the pattern of power balance in their marriage. This is also a sensible and feasible starting point for self-counseling. What is important is: 1) to learn to recognize the pattern you use; and 2) to apply that insight to the way in which you both deal with decisions, negotiate conflicts about them, or initiate changes in your decision-making techniques. The best way to begin is to ask yourself questions.

Do we divide responsibilities and control on the basis of traditional role expectations? In this arrangement each partner knows what he or she is responsible for doing. Usually the husband earns the living (or the major part of it), manages family finances, takes care of the car, does household repairs, mows the lawn, takes out the garbage—and makes the decisions involved in carrying out those tasks. The wife cooks, does housework, cares for the children, and, nowadays, may also work at a job. This pattern can work efficiently unless a spouse begins to question the extent or the value of the specific "power" areas he or she controls. It can also function well for a couple with young children; but it holds the seeds of difficulty when the children get older and a mother prepares to return (or actually returns) to work. Problems may arise then in connection with decisions a woman no longer wants to *have* to make. If, for instance, she works all day, grocery-shopping on the way home may be enough of a chore without her having to decide each night's menu as well. Conversely, problems may come up concerning decisions she now feels she ought to share. As a working wife she may well be unlikely to accept her husband's unilateral judgments about family finances. If she drives to her job, she may have considerably more to say about whether the family car needs new brake linings or not.

In other words, changes in a couple's lifestyle inevitably create the need for changes in their decision-making pattern. But many couples fail to realize this in time—or ever. They are puzzled when conflicts about decisions increase. This kind of "slippage" often causes serious trouble in marriages where the feminist movement is a major influence on a woman's ideals or actions. (We'll discuss ways couples can deal with such dislocations in Chapter 12.)

Do we share authority for making decisions on the basis of which of us is best equipped to do so at any given time? This kind of power pattern has many names: "parallel," "equalitarian," "alternative." If your marriage is of this type, you and your partner are able to shift control from one to the other, depending on which of you has the knowledge, skill, or interest required for the particular job at hand or decision at issue. It is a highly efficient pattern. It allows for personal growth without creating anxiety in the spouse. It imposes no artificial restrictions.

Sharing the power to make decisions also has its drawbacks, however. One is that a husband and wife may each be so involved in his or her own interests and areas of control that they become *too* detached from each other. Moving on parallel tracks without making a real effort to keep "in touch" can lead to alienation. This often happens, for example, when a father abdicates nearly all the parenting responsibilities to the mother. If a child asks permission to sleep at a friend's house, or to go on a weekend hike, the father says, "Ask your mother." She in turn feels burdened at having all these decisions thrust on her. But because her husband is out of touch with the child's routine and activities—partly from choice but partly from the way the couple's system operates—he does not feel he is in a position to make sensible decisions. Here is how we approached such a dilemma in a recent counseling situation:

WIFE: I'm tired of being the one who makes *all* the decisions about the children. They ask you something when you're not even busy and you send them to me—no matter how busy *I* am.

HUSBAND: I don't know what you want them to do.

MARCIA LASSWELL: So you put everything concerning the children on Karen's shoulders?

H: When I try to offer advice, or get upset about their behavior, Karen gets mad. So I just stay out of it.

ML: Is that true, Karen?

W: I *have* blown up a couple of times when you were especially critical, Hank. But you only get involved if it's to *criticize*. I figure since you don't take an interest in the kids any other time, you should keep out then, too.

ML: Power to decide things concerning the children is so clearly

held by you, Karen, that Hank has simply given up in that
area.

w: I guess you're right. But you know, now that the boys are getting older I really need your help, Hank.

ML: Are you willing to get more involved, Hank? (He nods
agreement) Then let's see next time how both of you can
change the pattern of your decision-making about the children's affairs.

*Do we avoid or abdicate entirely the responsibility for making
any decisions?* Amazingly enough, many couples do not so much
make decisions as merely *allow* them to happen. This fear of making choices—it's been called "decidophobia"—can be so emotionally overwhelming that even the most critical matters are postponed until events themselves force a decision. For example, not
long ago a researcher was quizzing couples who expected their first
child within the next few weeks. To his astonishment many couples had not yet decided what to name the baby, whether to
breast-feed or bottle-feed, whether to hire a practical nurse when
mother and child came home from the hospital, whether or not to
use a commercial diaper service. Indeed, some couples had not
even discussed these matters. "They simply refused to admit," the
researcher said, "that *someone* would have to make all these
choices—and very soon, too."

We frequently encounter marriages where one partner is angry
because the other constantly evades decisions:

WIFE: My husband refuses to take responsibility for anything. He
says he does not want to be "bothered."

HUSBAND: I'm an investment counselor. All day long I make important decisions for clients involving huge sums of money.
When I get home, frankly, I don't care what we do, or where
we go. I am tired of making decisions.

w: But then, if something *I* decide turns out poorly, you criticize
me. I don't think that's fair.

MARCIA LASSWELL: Mark, at your firm you have a number of people to whom you delegate work, don't you?

H: Yes. But what's that got to do with anything?

ML: One of the cardinal rules of delegation is that you don't turn over work—or decisions—to anyone who can't be trusted to do a good job.

H: And you're saying I shouldn't turn over decisions to Ruth if I feel I can't trust her to make the right ones?

ML: Well, I think that's part of the picture. Any time you "turn over" decisions to Ruth, or just default on them so she *has* to decide, then I think grousing about the outcome is unfair.

H: So I'm supposed to keep my mouth shut even if I don't agree with her decisions?

ML: *Or* you could help with the decision-making. I suspect that if we studied the matter we'd find there are some decisions you really don't care if she makes . . . and a few that involve you a little bit . . . and others where the outcome matters a good deal to you. Unless you want Ruth to make all the decisions on her own, you'd better work up the energy to sort these out, and make your preferences known in things that do matter to you.

Decision by default is a routine pattern for many couples. One spouse defers to the other (or they juggle a choice between them like a hot potato) out of fatigue, apathy, a feeling of incompetence, an aversion to argument or even to discussion. One wife remarked: "In our case, the one to whom a decision matters *least* will usually yield to the other." This sometimes saves time or stress when minor choices are at stake, or when a spouse *truly* has no preference. The danger is that a couple may become locked into this pattern and decide *important* issues the same way.

In an ideal world, the answer to "who's in charge?" of marital decisions and responsibilities would be based neither on one spouse's power nor the other's apathy, but on the expertise and rationality of both. Since we do not live in an ideal world, we must do the best we can to establish personal patterns for decision-making that will meet our own special needs. The following suggestions may provide useful guidelines for doing that:

A husband and wife should explore together the ways in which they handle decisions. Pick a time to do this when there are no important decisions waiting to be made.

You can discuss your decision-making methods more objectively and more reasonably if you are not at the same time under the pressure of having to make a decision. There is less of a tendency, then, to get into questions of power and control. You will be better able to stick to the point of finding out how you actually go about making a decision.

As a start, ask yourselves these questions: How did you decide how many children to have? Who decides how the household tasks are to be divided? Who decides (be honest now) when you will have sex? Who decides how the money is spent? How did you decide the last three times which movie to see or where to eat when you were going out to dinner? Would you say one or the other of you made virtually all of these decisions? Did you share in the decisions according to some formula? What was it? See if there is a consistent pattern that you both agree is operating.

Avoid getting locked into set patterns of decision-making.

If you know the kind of pattern you tend to use most often—and if it does not work as well as you would like—experiment with other approaches. One couple in marital therapy was given the "homework" assignment of finding out if they had a decision-making pattern. Much to their surprise they found one that bothered them considerably:

HUSBAND: We sort of keep score. I found that if Sue picked out the movie Friday night, I'd say it was my turn on Sunday.

WIFE: I did that, too. Jim watched Monday night football on TV so I insisted on choosing a program for Tuesday night. I'm not sure I like this system—it seems childish.

MARCIA LASSWELL: A lot of couples have this need to keep the power balance equal. It works well enough on decisions such as the ones you've described. But couples can get into trouble if this is the *only* system they have. Do you use this for major decisions, too?

H: I'm afraid we do. Our bedroom furniture is a crazy example. Sue picked out the bed so I said I should pick out the chairs. She bought a bureau and I took my turn at the tables. No co-ordination at all—and the furniture really shows it! But until now we thought we were co-operating!

W: I think we need some advice on how to make decisions another way. I don't like playing this game.

Be versatile—develop a repertoire of techniques that can be used for different kinds of decisions.

Research shows that couples tend to use a single pattern for *all* issues or choices. A husband and wife who always argue will do so as intensely over whether to have the Joneses for dinner as they will over whether to buy a new house. Another couple, who seldom make a decision without discussion and compromise, will spend as much time debating which movie to see as which investment to make.

Do you really know how your spouse deals with decisions, or are you merely making assumptions?

Witness this revealing interchange between a husband and wife in one of their early counseling sessions:

MARCIA LASSWELL: Do you have any problems or conflicts about making decisions?

HUSBAND: No, that's the one area where we don't argue. We've agreed that whichever one of us feels more strongly about something can make the decision about it.

ML (to wife): Would you agree with that?

WIFE: I guess I'll have to confess. If he thinks I care a great deal about a particular thing, he opposes the idea. So I've learned *not* to express strong feelings in favor of it. If I want a decision to go my way . . . or if I want him to agree with me, I try to seem indifferent.

ML: Then you're saying that the pattern is just the opposite of what your husband says it is.

W: Yes, if I act like I don't care, he loses interest in making the decision and says, "It doesn't matter to me, you decide." So, I do.

Just as one nation tacitly recognizes another's "sphere of influence," and avoids trying to exert power or control over it, spouses can agree on areas of living which are most important to each and agree not to intrude when a decision must be made.

Spheres of influence or authority develop out of a person's special interests, background, or know-how. A man may have final say about which car to buy and a woman about which rug to buy. It's important to recognize, though, that as the once-sharp demarcation between traditional male and female "roles" gets fuzzier, areas of authority are no longer inevitably sex-linked. Moreover, many matters that might *seem* sex-linked often overlap both male and female concerns. If a couple about to have a baby are deciding whether to buy a washer-dryer or have commercial diaper service, both partners have a legitimate stake in the verdict—because one would have to do the washing and one would have to pay the bills.

Where frequent or recurrent decisions need to be made, agreement on some arbitrary system can save a good deal of discussion.

Example A: When one couple bought a larger house, they agreed the husband would be responsible for all financial matters and the wife for all home purchases. To avoid constant squabbling over whether they could afford to buy specific items, they set a dollar limit—the wife could spend up to $100 per item without consulting her husband.

Example B: This couple had conflicting ideas about what to do on vacation. The husband was an avid sight-seer; the wife preferred to spend her time at the pool or beach. To eliminate daily friction they agreed in advance to a "my day—your day" compromise. On her day they both swam and sunbathed; on his day they took tours and visited museums. A cautionary note: such "turn-taking" can function well over the long haul only if both spouses are mature enough to avoid the feeling they are making "sacrifices." Otherwise, one runs the risk of keeping track of who owes whom the next decision. When used as the *only* decision-making method, it can lead to intense competition. One partner may try to outdo the other to see who can get or give the most. To believe you are *giving* the most can make you feel martyred or resentful. To feel that you are *getting* the most can trigger feelings of guilt or inadequacy.

You may not be deliberately attempting to "manipulate" deci-

sions in your favor but you may be doing so without realizing it.

It is possible, for example, to control decisions by creating circumstances that force the other person to make the choices you want him or her to make. For example, a young husband wants to quit his dead-end job and go to law school. His wife fears their savings won't last long enough to see them through the three years of study. Because she cannot openly argue with him (after all, that would be obviously selfish), she says: "Bill can do whatever he wants. It's his life, after all. He just has to be sure there's enough money coming in to support us." A seemingly reasonable concern —yet a weapon with which she can manipulate his final choice.

Even though you may have settled on a decision-making pattern (or patterns) that works well now, be aware that as life-cycle changes occur you may need also to change the ways you make decisions.

A husband who makes most of the decisions may find that as his career demands more and more of his time, he expects his wife to be more active in decision-making. Or, as mentioned earlier, when children grow older their father needs to become more involved in decisions affecting their lives. Women who have made most of the home decisions may go to work and find their time too limited to do all of the deciding. A working wife who contributes to the family finances may want more say in money decisions.

If you find that you are in frequent conflict over the division of family responsibilities, here are two techniques that can help to sort out the problem.

First, both you and your partner should list the tasks to be done. Now list who you believe is *supposed* to do what. Then make a list of who *actually* does what. Comparing them will show the areas where expectations are not being met. It will also reveal any "gaps" in the assignments, thereby eliminating the "Didn't-you-take-care-of-that"/"No-I-thought-you-were-going-to-do-it" arguments.

Second, draw up a "task division" chart that will enable you to decide "who does what" on a rational basis. List all household chores and family responsibilities you can think of. Then, for each one, ask yourselves these questions:

1. Who has more time to do this?
2. Who is better at doing this? (the more expert, the more practiced)
3. For whom is this task more convenient (inconvenient)? Who has the more flexible schedule?
4. Who likes (or doesn't mind) doing this?
5. Who hates doing this?
6. Who is more concerned with getting this done?

If you answer these questions honestly, you can assign yourselves tasks in a realistic fashion. Moreover, this can be a family project, with children choosing certain jobs and trading off ones they "hate" for ones they don't mind as much. One youngster actually volunteered to clean the bathroom if she never had to vacuum again.

Ask yourselves what are the major decisions each of you feels you make. What are the minor ones?

This may seem simple, but spouses frequently disagree on what is major and what is minor. A couple in counseling typifies what happens:

HUSBAND (to wife): You decide everything. You spend almost all our money . . . you run the house . . . decide everything about the children . . . whom we have as guests . . . whether we'll eat out or you'll cook . . . I don't decide anything important.

WIFE: Those are things you've never wanted to be bothered with. As I see it, you never thought they were important. I think *you* make the *big* decisions.

H: Like what?

W: You decide when we go on vacation every year. Whether you know it or not, you decide what we eat since I cook what I know you like. And you really decide what time we eat, what time we go to bed and get up, and when we have sex. Now, tell me you don't make the major decisions.

There is no one formula that couples can use to determine what falls into a major or minor category. In counseling groups it is not unusual for couples to disagree with one another about what the big decisions really are. Some couples feel there are so few momentous marital decisions that the partner who makes the bulk of the small decisions that set the style of day-to-day living is the powerful partner. Areas that many couples agree *are* major include *sex; residence* (neighborhood, type of housing, schools for children, amount of income spent on housing); *children* (whether or not to have any and how many, names, guidance, and discipline); *finances* (how money is earned, spent, and saved); *friends and relatives* (how often they are seen, spending holidays with them, gifts given and received).

Finally, it's essential to realize that the spouse who *makes* decisions is not necessarily the spouse who *controls* them. The key question ultimately is, "Who *decides* who decides?"

Husbands or wives often "delegate" decision areas to their partners so that while the actual decision is made by one, there is no doubt that the other holds the power. As we have pointed out, sometimes the "weaker" partner may actually have his or her mate jumping through hoops. A "helpless" husband may ask his wife to lay out his clothing every morning so that his socks, shoes, tie, shirt, and suit will co-ordinate. *She decides* what he will wear, but *he has decided* she is to be his "valet." A "depressed" wife may have everyone in the household catering to her "bad" days. Many books and articles have been written telling wives how to fool husbands into believing they are "lords and masters" by appearing to defer to them on the surface. This game-playing backfires in the long run. Finding the patterns you use to make decisions, altering them to suit your needs, and having a variety of decision-making methods to use for different circumstances are the realistic and effective techniques that make a marriage function well.

II

TIME TO BE US, YOU AND ME

A husband defends himself: "My wife says I'm always going into another room to read. Believe me, I would if I could. When I decide to go bowling, Ella decides to come with me. If I want to go for a walk, *she* wants to go for a walk. If I go to bed early, she goes to bed early. I think if I had to have an operation she would check into the hospital with me!"

A wife complains: "He's on the road all week, and on weekends he says he needs to be by himself to relax. We are never together. We never do anything together."

Another wife: "I'm desperate for time by myself. It's reached the point where I have to shut myself in the bathroom if I want to be alone."

A busy executive and his lawyer-wife: "We operate on a hectic schedule. If we didn't actually make appointments with each other . . . set aside a time to lunch or dine together . . . we could go for days without any contact."

Napoleon Bonaparte, to a man seeking a favor: "You can ask me for anything you like—except time."

Time to talk or be quiet, time to play together or to work side by side, time for sex, time for solitude, time to be spouse, parent, lover, but also time to be one's self—all these "times" are vital ingredients of marriage. Sorting them out to everyone's satisfaction can present problems. Some years ago the word "togetherness" was coined. It stood for an ideal of family closeness that was supposed to provide benefits for all. A sense of family unity and sharing is of course a positive value. But when it is overdone—as togetherness often was—it tends to stifle personal interests, overwhelm individual needs, substitute sameness for compatibility. Similarly, while a measure of "separateness" between partners is healthy for a marriage too much of it can be damaging.

The fact is that marital congeniality depends not so much on the amount of time a couple actually are together or apart, as it does on whether they *agree* on how to make that allocation, on how much time they feel they want or ought to share or keep separate. It depends, too, on the *quality* of that time—again without relation to whether they spend most of it jointly or not. For instance, there are men and women who share every evening and weekend, yet who feel lonely and alienated because that time is empty, unfulfilling. Others may have only half an hour or so a day to be together but find that brief period emotionally rewarding.

Thus, such questions as, "What is enough togetherness?" or, "How much time alone does a person need?" miss the point. Some couples get along well because they see a lot of each other. Some are equally content because they are apart a good deal. One study reports the average married couple "talk meaningfully" with each other only twenty-seven minutes a week. For some this may be enough, for others so pitifully little as to be a major concern. For example, the wife of a busy surgeon says that when she and her husband go to a party (which isn't often to begin with) she eavesdrops on his conversation: "I find out most of what I know about him by listening to what he tells other people."

Moreover, different marriages—and different life-stages of the same marriage—encounter different problems. For one couple the question may be how to allow one partner the privacy he or she needs without having the other feel rejected. For another couple it may be the difficulty of trying to preserve more time together in the face of demands from children, friends, jobs, family. Still a third couple, who always "did everything with the children," may need in their older years to learn how to be alone together. Counselors find that most people usually fail to identify these problems accurately. A wife or husband complains that sex is too infrequent, or communication nonexistent, or a job too time-consuming, when the real issue is their inability to manage marital time or to agree on how it should be used.

Know Where Your Time Goes

A first step toward cutting through this confusion is to find out exactly how you *do* use your time. Most people have only a vague and largely inaccurate idea. We usually suggest to couples in marital therapy that they keep a detailed log of their time for at least two weeks. That is also a sensible approach for self-counseling couples.

Keeping track of how you spend each day need not be complicated nor burdensome. The simplest way is to rule a page into twenty-four segments and make a note of what you do in each hour. It isn't necessary to keep a stop-watch-type record, noting that you took five minutes out from an hour of work or shopping for a coffee break. But it is necessary to list "major" deviations, such as interrupting an "hour" of conversation with your spouse to make a twenty-minute telephone call. If you persevere for a day or two the timekeeping will become routine. When the 14 days are over, an analysis of how you used those 336 hours should be extremely revealing. For the first time, probably, you will have a definite answer to that plaintive query, "Where does the time go?" And that answer can help you to understand your spouse's complaints, and to make constructive changes in time use that can help to ease them.

For example, one husband's gripe was that after dinner his wife always had so many chores to do that she never sat and talked with him. Moreover, he said, by the time they went to bed she was almost always too tired to make love. The woman denied his charge—and honestly meant her denial. After keeping a time chart for two weeks, however, she had to admit that he was right, that she did spend several hours each night doing laundry, sewing, writing letters, even polishing silver. With the facts in black and white, this woman was able to rearrange her schedule to get some of these things done during the day, freeing more evening time to be with her husband. In another instance, a salesman learned from his record-keeping that after work, sleep, and commuting time were added up, he had only twenty-one hours a week to eat, bathe, dress, and be with his family. By cutting his work schedule an hour a day, and sleeping half an hour less each night, he gained 50 per cent more time to spend with his wife and children.

It is important to realize that the patterns of frenetic overactivity that keep spouses apart are not always the result of poor scheduling. It can be a device, deliberate or subconscious, to *avoid* spending time with one's partner. If that is the case, neither record-keeping nor rescheduling will help. The difficulty is not a matter of managing time, nor of finding mutually agreeable ways to allocate it, but a deeper conflict in your relationship. When counseling or self-counseling succeeds in coping with it, the time imbalance will very likely equalize itself.

"I Need Time to Be Me"

American marriages are unique in their emphasis on the state of being "coupled." This is not just another version of togetherness; it is the premise that in a good marriage a husband and wife must be invariably packaged as a twosome. In much of the world couples are expected to have separate identities; each partner is free to see personal friends or indulge individual interests without either of them feeling that this reflects poorly on their relationship. But in this country marriage traditionally forces two individuals— Ted and Sue—into a linked unit—Ted-and-Sue—as if in preparation for the next sailing of the Ark. Couples are invited to social gatherings as a pair. Separate vacations? *There must be something wrong between them,* go the whispers. There is a definite implication that couplehood equals happiness, and that to want a significant amount of time alone is a sign of marital trouble. Only recently have the feminist and humanist movements made some progress toward changing these ideas.

No wonder, then, that one of the myths of marriage is that it necessarily does away with individuality and privacy. Men and women begin to speak of "giving up my freedom"; or they start to use such words as "allow" or "let" when talking about what their partners can do within the framework of marital restrictions. "I'd like to work but my husband won't let me" . . . "I can't get out in the evening because my wife doesn't allow that."

There is another side to that coin, as well. Many of us feel apologetic if we *want* to be alone, go off by ourselves, do something as an individual rather than half of a pair. The irrational feeling persists that "in a good marriage I *shouldn't* want to be alone, I *shouldn't* need something beyond what he or she can give me." It is often difficult to say, "I want some privacy . . . I want some freedom," without making one's spouse feel rejected. One young wife says she had to "fight and connive" for three years before her husband understood that her wish to be alone at times was not a slap at him. When he did accept this he showed it by converting a walk-in closet into a room just for her. Yet the desire for privacy or for a reasonable measure of independence does *not* reflect upon the other person. It is your need. It concerns only you.

Most of us are with other people all day—in buses and car pools, at work, in school, in stores—and we come home to families who need and want attention. Everyone knows the need to escape the pressure cooker of everyday life, to refresh body and spirit in solitude, to be alone to think. "I go in the back yard and pull weeds because nobody bothers me there" . . . "I drive around in the car because it is the only place I can be by myself." We understand that feeling. What we don't understand so well is the need for privacy *as a personality trait*.

There are people who have a "normal" wish to be alone from time to time. Psychologists don't know why some of us crave solitude and others crave companionship. Some think the need for time to be alone is the hallmark of a well-adjusted person. Others call it the sign of a neurotic "loner." Stress intensifies both reactions: when "affiliative" persons are upset they seek company; "loners" go off by themselves. Even birth order (which we mentioned earlier as having a lasting effect on adult personality) is involved. An only or oldest child tends to want companionship when under stress; a middle child, who has had more than enough of other people around, tends to seek privacy. In a marriage, that combination can lead to trouble.

Like so many personality differences, however, there is no right or wrong about them. Much of the tension that grows out of this kind of conflict is due to the way husbands and wives approach it. Demanding privacy often arouses irritation (and suspicion). Demanding companionship is often counterproductive. A couple can learn, however, how to explore each other's motives and reactions in order to reach an understanding. The following cases show how two couples, with quite different privacy needs, finally were able to express and resolve them:

HUSBAND: I really have to get out of the house some nights . . . just for a walk to the drugstore on the pretext of buying cigars.

MARCIA LASSWELL: On the pretext? Can't you say you need to be alone for a while?

H: I'd feel guilty. Susan's home all day with the kids. I know she hates for me to leave her alone when I don't have to.

WIFE: That's true. But I can understand your need to be alone, now that you bring it out in the open. I could use some time to myself, too. (She hesitates an instant, then plunges ahead) I'm going to tell you something, Clark, that I never had the courage to say before. When you go on out-of-town business trips . . . I'm *glad*. I miss you, but I'm glad. I love being alone after the children are in bed, not having to set my time around your schedule.

ML: How do you feel about this revelation, Clark?

H: I have two reactions. One is relief, because I can stop feeling guilty about going away. The other is annoyance that you didn't tell me this sooner. Think of all the guilt I could have avoided.

Clark and Susan could mesh their individual needs for privacy with relative ease because they were basically in agreement with each other about wanting time alone. All they needed was to be honest with each other. If one partner wants more time alone and the other seeks more togetherness, the task of working out a mutually acceptable arrangement is obviously harder. But not impossible. Here's how Gwen and Eric, a childless couple in their thirties, went about it. Eric's original complaint was that Gwen had "too many activities." Not only was she a busy, involved person, but she also wanted a good deal of time to herself. Clearly, she had little time left for Eric. Gwen, for her part, diagnosed their problem as centering in Eric's insistence that she conform to *his* schedule and, therefore, restrict her own choices.

WIFE: The problem, as I see it, is that you want me to be available at your beck and call, Eric. But I can't just drop what I'm doing when you're ready for companionship.

MARCIA LASSWELL: I hear *two* problems. One, you are both very busy and meshing schedules is not easy. Two, you feel that Eric wants you to do the adjusting to *his* schedule. Is this correct?

HUSBAND: Right on *one;* wrong on *two.* Maybe you feel I want you to do all the adjusting, Gwen, but I don't. I think we both need to set aside time to be together—even if we have to mark it on the calendar. I'm willing to do this.

W: I don't think anyone ought to have to schedule time together! I have enough scheduling in my life without programming our personal lives, too. That should be spontaneous.

ML: There's just one thing wrong with that notion, Gwen. As busy as you and Eric are, if you leave your time together to "spontaneity," it's not likely to happen. I'll agree that programming *what* you do in your time together is best left to a certain amount of spontaneity; but I don't think you can leave deciding *when* to be together entirely to chance.

H: Things seem to come up to whittle away at our days off, even our vacations. Somehow, we always wind up with almost no time together.

W (reluctantly): You're right, now that I think about it.

ML: Eric, you said before that you feel Gwen needs more time alone than you do. I'd like to get some idea of what you are both talking about in the way of actual hours. How much time a week would you like to spend alone with Gwen?

H: I really would like at least two hours every evening and most of the weekend. But I know that's more than Gwen wants.

ML: Let Gwen speak for herself. What do you consider to be a good amount of time to spend alone with Eric?

W: Oh, I'd like to talk while we're fixing dinner and eating. You know, to catch up on the day's events. We usually clean up the kitchen together, but then I like to get busy with my projects. That is how I relax. Saturdays and Sundays are pure heaven to me because I don't have anyone to answer to. I resent the idea of scheduling those two days around Eric. It's the difference between sharing my time and sharing my *self*.

ML: The amount of privacy we need is often a result of personality as much as the kind of life we lead. Usually, the pattern goes back to childhood. How was privacy handled at home when you were a child, Gwen?

W: I never had *enough*. Since I can remember, I've always wanted a room of my own. But I never had one. I used to sit in a tree when I was a kid to read. My mother used to call me and I wouldn't answer. I've always been this way. That's why I like the way my life is now.

ML: But Eric isn't happy, and since we've already established that you love and want to stay married to each other, there has to be some compromise. The result won't be *exactly* the way either one of you wants it to be, but we'll hope to find a pattern that gives you both *some* of what you want—more togetherness for Eric without seriously encroaching on Gwen's need for privacy. Can we work out a plan where you, Gwen, spend more time with Eric during the week in return for Eric's promise to let you have an equal amount of time to yourself on weekends.

H (after Gwen nods): If I could *count* on some time every week, and you would give it freely, I could freely give you privacy the other times.

In the compromise Eric didn't get as much togetherness as he would have liked, nor Gwen as much privacy as she would have liked. But they were able to recognize that in marriage there is no such thing as total freedom . . . that "winning" doesn't work. Eric got more of Gwen's companionship in return for being more understanding about her need for privacy. A fair exchange.

Controlling the "Outsiders" in Your Marriage

A different dilemma confronts the couple who agree they want and need to be together more, but find most of their time spoken for by the demands of children, family, friends, colleagues, bosses, and even co-workers in civic and community affairs. Even though all of these people are "outsiders"—tangential to the core relationship—their claims on marital time are at best important and at worst unavoidable. On top of this, moreover, is piled what sociologist Arlene Skolnick calls "the horde of seemingly irrelevant trivia —missing buttons, lost keys, dental appointments, PTA meetings, broken washing machines—that determine the time, energy, and moods" a couple have to give to each other. In addition, all this pulling and pushing from the outside is more erratic and uncontrollable than the influence of spouses on each other. Because we can't predict when or how these time pressures will crop up, they tend to be especially irritating when they do. An important point to bear in mind about these "outside" factors is that while it may seem each one causes a different kind of stress, the stresses all have a common base: intrusion on the marriage—physical, financial, or emotional. As a result, they can usually be dealt with in the same fundamental ways.

How can a couple satisfy the essential claims of these "outsiders" and still satisfy their desire for time together? We've combined a number of useful techniques for doing that, culled from the experiences of several hundred couples. One or more of these may be adaptable to meet your special situation:

Comparing calendars. "We all lead hectic lives, so we keep a 'family calendar.' Every Sunday night we sit down together to look for blocks of open time which we can match to one another's plans. If my son needs a ride to his Little League game on Saturday, for instance, we look to see who has free time to drive him— my husband, my daughter, or me. If no one does, he has to find his own ride. When my husband and I locate a mutual block of open time, we put an 'X' through it. That means it is reserved for us to share alone. The children understand, since through our discussions they've seen how hard it is for us to find time together. We may go to a movie, to lunch, or just listen to records. Sometimes we discuss personal matters. Sometimes we have sex. The important thing is that we *know* we will have those undisturbed hours."

Programming the week or month. "We don't like the idea of scheduling our obligations first and taking whatever time is left over for ourselves. So we plan well in advance. Mealtimes and Sunday morning are set aside for family. One night a week I go to a Scout meeting with my son, and he and I do something together for a few hours each Saturday. Since my wife doesn't work she can be with him every day when he comes home from school. Twice a month, on a Friday or Saturday, my wife and I go out. One weekend every other month we go away on a mini-vacation to get away from everything and feel close to each other. We go away for three weeks in the summer—two weeks as a family and one week without our son. Our plan probably sounds rigid and artificial—but my wife and I find it's the only way to make sure we don't grow apart."

Staying unencumbered. "We have had to learn to protect ourselves so we can have time together. Neither of us likes to plan ahead much; we'd rather decide at the last minute to do something. But we know that to make that work we have to avoid getting tied up with invitations and responsibilities. So we're not joiners, and we have told our friends to ask us only to informal gatherings; if we cancel at the last minute it won't matter. I guess you could call us selfish. But we're lucky to have friends who understand."

No one can deny that having good friends adds to the satisfactions of marriage. There are many things a woman gets from another woman, a man from another man, that they cannot get from their spouses. But it is also important to realize that friendships can sometimes be time-devourers encroaching on your privacy, your togetherness, and your personal identity. For instance, we talked earlier about the American habit of viewing a husband and wife as an indivisible unit. This attitude gets carried over into friendship formation. A husband may have a night out with the "boys," a wife may go shopping with the "girls"—but when it comes to making friends they almost always do so as a couple. Only when all *four* spouses are fond of *one another* are they likely to become good friends. Moreover, every study of friendship and marriage has shown that if a husband or wife has an individual friend—especially of the opposite sex—it causes considerable marital strain. What this means, of course, is that opportunity for personal growth and exploration—"time to be me"—is greatly lessened.

Having a large circle of friends can lead to constant intrusions on your time together as well as your personal times alone. Unless, of course, they are the kind of people who respect your rules for "staying unencumbered." One wife described what can happen when they don't: "I know we're lucky to have five couples we consider close friends. But when I tell my husband I'd like to spend *some* time alone with *him,* he says I'm antisocial. How can I convince him it's important to our marriage to have a little emotional privacy, some experiences only the two of us share?"

Consider, too, the possibility that a couple who spend most of their time with friends—either many casual ones or a few intimate ones—may be subconsciously trying to cover up or to escape from conflicts in their marriage. The presence of "outsiders," no matter how close, short-circuits the intimate talk a marriage needs to get problems out in the open where they can be dealt with rather than avoided.

A final point: When two couples become "inseparable" the intensity of that relationship may overwhelm a marriage. Some years ago we knew two such couples. They were together most evenings, every weekend and vacation. They even hooked up their homes by wireless intercom so they could talk to each other at any time. After three years one husband was transferred to a distant city by his company. The couple left behind were desolated. They had cut themselves off from other people, forgotten the art of making new friendships. Worse, they found nothing to say to or do with each other. With no inner resources of its own, that marriage quickly shattered.

Learning to say "No." "We have gained a tremendous amount of extra time to be together by cultivating the ability to say 'no.' Both of us had a bad habit of taking on too many responsibilities. One day I woke up to the fact that I often hurt my family by taking time away from them to do something for someone I really didn't give a damn about. My wife did that, too. We talked it over and hit upon a plan we call 'buying' time. When someone asks us to be on a committee or join a club, we tell them that we will let them know in an hour, or a day, or however long we need to decide if we want to do it. Then we think about it; talk it over with each other; figure out what we'd have to give up if we accepted; then we decide. It's amazing how much more often we say no—and feel *good* about it!"

Admittedly, it is difficult to turn down requests for help, requests that flatter us. It's particularly difficult for a woman. Even in these days of personhood and self-assertion some people expect a woman to be more self-sacrificing than a man. When a woman raises this point in counseling we suggest that the next time she feels tempted or obligated to say "yes," she run through a mental checklist to determine *why* she feels that way: Is it to polish her image or the family's status in the community? Is it to win approval? To bolster self-doubts? To avoid criticism? To keep from hurting other people's feelings? To be "one up," to have a favor owed to her?

When you are using self-counseling to sort out problems about marital time, add this critical question to the list: "Where do I rank my marriage in my list of priorities?" If you believe it ranks high, then ask yourself how much time you spend nourishing it.

Marital Time—Not Only How Much, but How Good?

Continuing physical and emotional contact is essential to a vital marriage. But the quality of that contact is as important as its quantity. Filling your days with too much activity, shared or otherwise, can cause tension and fatigue to undermine the time you spend together. So often we save our best efforts and energies for "outsiders" and give each other the dregs that remain. True, home should be a refuge from life's pressures, a place where you can "let go" and "let down." But if *all* that a husband or wife gets from each other is an exhausted zombie or a complaining bundle of nerves, it's not fair.

The quality of a couple's time together is directly proportionate to the number of "hook-up points"—shared interests—that link their lives. That's why growing apart is such a major marital problem—especially for older couples who no longer have what might be called the *built-in* hook-up points of children, home-building, job advancement. A couple can try to remedy this by scheduling more shared time. But without mutual interests that time often proves boring, tense, even anxiety-producing. A fifty-one-year-old legal secretary and her engineer husband, fifty-five, encountered this problem after the last of their three children got married. Even though they sought counseling, they seemed at first resigned to loneliness:

WIFE: We tried to set aside special periods of time to spend together, but we didn't *do* anything with them.

HUSBAND: Laura was never interested in my work, and I admit I'm not interested in hers. I enjoy solitary hobbies and she likes being with people. The children, the house—they kept us going. But now . . . I don't think we know how to be close any more.

W: He's right. We really don't enjoy being together that much.

MARCIA LASSWELL: But I gather you did agree on a certain amount of time you felt you ought to share?

H: Well, we figured it was necessary to keep from drifting totally apart. We settled on three nights a week and all Sunday. But we both feel it's wasted time.

ML: How did you spend that time last week?

W: One night we watched TV—a complete waste of time! Another night we made love, but who needs a whole evening for that! The third night we tried to tell each other what went on during the day, at work, but that bored both of us. Sunday we went to the museum. That was okay. But you can go to just so many museums.

ML: Sometimes, when couples grow apart as you have, it helps to think back to your courtship and newlywed days, to recall what you enjoyed then. I'd like you to do something for me right now. Here's paper and pencils. Each of you write down whatever you can remember you liked to do together in the past. Then make a second list of things you always wanted to do but never got around to. Then make a third list of activities you do now, either alone or with each other, that you'd like to do more often.

By matching both versions of the three lists, this couple found two activities from the past that each would still enjoy—listening to concerts and picnicking in the woods. They also came up with two things each wanted to do but never had—learn to sail and go to auctions. The third list showed both wanted to visit art galleries and antique stores more often than they already did. Thus, in ten minutes, this couple discovered six shared interests to fill, interestingly, the time they wanted to spend together.

Another middle-aged couple, also concerned about being alone together, were terrified when they were due to leave for a week at an Arizona dude ranch on the first vacation they had ever taken without their children. "I don't know what we'll talk about," the wife said. "We haven't had a conversation in years except at the bridge table." The first night at the ranch they met another couple, also devoted bridge players. "We had a fantastic time," the husband reported when they got home. "We played bridge with these other folks all week . . . We never had time to be alone." Obviously this is not an ideal or permanent solution for this couple's problem. But since there are plenty of bridge players around, and the couple is rarely alone, their marriage can coast along amicably on this one interest that they share.

Clearly, the quality of the time a couple share depends on the efforts they make to build bridges to each other. Moreover, those bridges must be started in the early years of marriage—and with a deliberate eye on how they will stand up in the later years. Like everything else in marriage, the ability to be together contentedly must be practiced. Previous experience counts!

GUIDEPOSTS FOR SELF-COUNSELING PROGRESS

1. It is easy to pay lip service to the idea that keeping "spaces between your togetherness" is good for your marriage. It is often hard to accept and carry that out in daily life. It will help if you can bear in mind that the more you respect your own need for privacy and time alone, the less hurt or threatened you will be by your spouse's need to be separate.

2. Try not to let time together deteriorate into problem-solving sessions. Shared time is to explore intimacy, develop empathy. Concentrate on getting to know each other better rather than on how to pay for Johnny's braces or whether the car will last another year.

3. Does he or she want more "togetherness" than you do? Or vice versa? Consider ways in which you can be "alone"—do your own thing—but still be together. For example: reading in the same room; exploring the same museum, but visiting different exhibits

and then meeting to exchange reactions; listening to records with earphones on; on a vacation trip, alternate the days in which each of you can decide what you both will do. Conversely, there are ways to be "together" even if you are alone: think about the other person; plan a surprise for him; write a letter to her; call him on the telephone; learn about something she's interested in.

4.   Don't feel guilty about being selfish of your time together. When you exclude the children from your activities, tell them why. Make a point of granting them privacy and personal time too, so they understand how important you think it is. If your parents or other relatives feel you are shutting them out of your life, point out that a husband and wife's loyalties belong to each other first. There are emergencies, of course—an adolescent's emotional crisis, an aging parent's illness—when your own time may have to go by the board. Still, as one woman put it, "I do my best to meet their needs . . . but I must have an instinct for my own survival."

5.   In somewhat the same way, learning to say "no" will come more easily if you can stop thinking of yourself primarily in "roles" other than husband or wife. A woman who considers her chief identity is "mother" will be hard-pressed to stop doing things for her child. A man who sees himself mainly as "wage-earner" or a potential corporate executive does not find it easy to turn down requests from his boss or his company, or to give up business-oriented social life that takes too much away from marital time.

6.   You'd be surprised by what can happen when you make a sincere effort to share a spouse's interest that you think you hate. One woman complained endlessly in counseling sessions because her husband left her alone every Sunday to indulge his passion for golfing. To every suggestion that she try golf herself she said, "I hate the game, it's stupid!" Eventually she agreed to go with him one Sunday—not to play but to try to understand why he enjoyed it so much. "It was the most marvelous day!" she said. "I never realized how interesting it is to *walk* a golf course—the woods, the ponds, the fairways." She still hated golf, but she loved hiking the course.

7.   No couple ever solve all the delicate conflicts that arise in the constantly shifting dynamics of marital togetherness and marital privacy. There is almost never enough time to provide all the time we'd like to be me, you, and us. That being the case, the important decision to make is to value the time you *do* have.

12

CAN EVERY MARRIAGE
BE "LIBERATED"?

More and more couples need help nowadays to cope with problems arising out of the changes that have taken place in our ideas about a woman's role in life and in marriage. The difficulties are basically familiar to counselors. But they often manifest themselves in new guises and with increased intensity as one or both partners put into practice some of the principles of a "liberated" marriage.

The problems are by no means limited to husbands and wives who *disagree* as to whether these changes should be made at all. Couples who accept or even embrace the concept of marital equality have just as much trouble when they try to carry it out in daily life. For example, one young couple who enthusiastically entered into a dual-career marriage found themselves at odds when the consequences of their choice left both of them feeling "cheated." Ellen and David were married just after Ellen was graduated high in her class at a California medical school. She was offered an internship by two top-rated hospitals, one in Los Angeles and one in San Francisco. Since David had a good job with a major Los Angeles law firm, he fully expected Ellen would choose to intern in the same city. Instead, over his violent objections, she took the San Francisco opening. Seven months later their marriage, which had started out so bravely, was a shambles:

DAVID: Of course I want Ellen to have her career, to make her own choices. But I thought she would make them with some concern for our marriage. After all, she chose *me,* too—not just medicine . . . We see each other about once every two weeks, and that's only because I fly up to San Francisco to do it. When we are together she's so tired she doesn't want to talk or go out. We have virtually no social life and damn near no sex life.

ELLEN: Am I asking so much? Two years out of a lifetime? Dave knows what it means to a young doctor to have the chance to intern in this hospital. But he just nags about everything. Why doesn't he quit his job and get one up here if he misses me so much!

That couple's problem is compounded by the disillusionment both of them feel at the way their high hopes for a "liberated" relationship have run afoul of conventional realities. Counselors are concerned about such dilemmas. They agree that it is good for men and women to have a variety of marital options, to seek growth and satisfaction in marriage rather than merely to carry out stereotyped sex roles. But they also know that there are few guidelines to help couples deal with the new tensions that result. Our feeling is that the changes can be made to work with a minimum of problems if couples aim for *mutual* "liberation." Conflict between the sexes is not built into our psyches. Nor is it necessarily the result of clashing ideologies—"militant feminism" versus "male chauvinism." Rather, the conflict is a symptom of a lack of balance and function between the partners. In that sense, a liberated marriage is not so different from a conventional one. But a liberated couple have higher expectations; when a conflict does arise their disillusionment makes it harder for them to handle it.

It might be a good idea at this point to define what we mean by "liberation." Couples often use the word as a synonym for "equality." Yet the words have different meanings. Equality connotes an evenness of strengths and values. It is feasible in marriage if husband and wife see each other as partners "holding the same rank." "Yes, I earn money at my job, but my wife contributes equally with what she does at home," is how one man views it. "I know it would take nearly my entire paycheck to hire someone to do what she does." We have a personal view of what "liberation" means in marriage. It may not suit feminists nor male chauvinists; it has little to do with so-called sexual "freedoms" or with theories of "alternative family forms." To us, liberation in marriage means simply that both partners are free from constraint—released from the "oppression" of prescribed marital behavior.

This concept troubles many men and women, especially those who cannot handle change well to begin with. They read it, incorrectly, as a release from any kind of responsibility for or commitment to each other. Naturally, this is frightening. If you fear that your partner is going to go off in unpredictable directions, or have vastly different attitudes and goals, you are quite likely to react defensively. But liberation does *not* mean abandoning all structure. No form of marriage in social history has existed for long without some rules, some agreements about the exchange of duties and supports. There are always mutual obligations. But they don't always have to be the same programmed ones for each man and woman. In a liberated marriage, partners accept each other as individuals with the right to choose and make their own arrangement for duties, supports, and responsibilities. Men are freed from the constraints of rigid "masculine" roles just as women are freed from the "feminine" ones. A liberated marriage replaces narrow definitions of acceptable behavior with more human values. A liberated spouse is not necessarily one who has a career, or leaves home, or has a sexually "open" marriage. A liberated spouse is one who is free to choose a lifestyle that best meets his or her goals.

To make such a liberated marriage work, husbands and wives need to have a real awareness of that concept. They also need to realize that liberation is *basically* a matter of choices—and that the opportunity for choices varies at different stages in a marriage. One couple discussed this with the counselor:

WIFE: Doesn't "liberated marriage" mean that a wife is working and earning money? Isn't it easier that way?

MARCIA LASSWELL: It generally seems to be, but it's not *necessary* for a woman to have a job to be liberated. There are many women who choose the job of homemaker. They like it. They consider it important . . . more important to them than being an attorney or a secretary, say. The only thing that is necessary for a housewife to feel liberated is that her choice be her own.

HUSBAND: But men don't have any choice. They have to work to support their family whether they want to or not.

ML: I agree that for those men who don't like their work, or would rather be doing something else, it's just as much of a trap. That's why I tell couples that in a truly liberated marriage both of them would have more freedom to choose. Unfortunately, not all of us can do just as we want. But we all *can* make changes toward that end. Even small changes in a positive direction can help if they are consistent.

W: If I understand you correctly, Mrs. Lasswell, you are saying that not everyone can hope for liberation—that circumstances sometimes make it so we *can't* choose.

ML: For the time being, at least, that is often the case. But remember that circumstances change. *You* can change them. Just because your choices in life are limited today doesn't mean they will always be . . . that you will never be able to choose.

One circumstance that limits a couple's choices is having to care for young children. Many parents tend to feel that for mother to stay at home and for father to earn the living is the most functional —if not the preferred—marital model. As youngsters get older a mother finds more time is available for her personal interests. She may begin to ask what she wants from life after her children have left home, and to plan for that new goal. Some women go to work, others go to school to prepare for a career. But these changes often lead to conflict in the marriage. For example, at thirty-five Liza Baker feels she wants to go back and finish the nurse-training program she had quit years ago when she married Alvin Baker. The couple's two children are now fourteen and twelve; in a few years they will be off to college or to jobs. But Liza is not sure how Al will react to the idea of her spending twenty hours a week, many of them in evening classes, away from home. She is pleased when he says, "I think it's a good idea and I'm all for it." But then Alvin adds the crusher: "You do anything you want—just so long as everything keeps running smoothly around here."

WIFE (to the counselor): In other words I am free to do whatever I can fit in the time that's left after I've been a full-time homemaker, wife, and mother! Do you think that's fair?

MARCIA LASSWELL: What do *you* think, Alvin? *Is* that fair?

HUSBAND: Fairness works both ways. Is it fair that I have to live in a house that's never straightened out, never organized? Is it fair that Liza never has time to go out with me, or have our friends over? Is it fair that she's always too tired to make love to me?

W: I can't do everything. There aren't enough hours in the day.

H: You don't *have* to go to nursing school, you know. Your first responsibility is in the home.

ML: Wait a minute, Alvin. You're acting as judge and jury. Let's see the choices both of you have . . . break the problem down to see if you can find a compromise. First of all, let's look at the roles you both have to fit: husband and wife, father and mother, businessman and homemaker.

H: And community work. I was active in the United Fund campaign last year. And don't forget what I do at home—keeping up the yard and making repairs.

ML: And Liza is a student nurse. You are busy people. But let's take a look at what you both do that is absolutely essential.

W: Well, we're both parents. We can't quit that.

ML: And you're both husband and wife, which is quite separate from your parenting roles. Also, you each have a job. But it sounds to me, Liza, as if you'd like to change jobs . . . to resign as homemaker and become a nurse.

H: She can't quit just like that!

ML: Agreed, the housework does have to be done. So if Liza resigns you'll have to come up with a way to handle that. But right now, let's answer the question of whether Liza has a *right* to choose her life's work. Must she be stuck with one job all her life—like it or not? Must she hold down *two* jobs so that she can do one of them that she enjoys?

H: But who does the housework? I don't have time. And if I do it, then *I'll* be holding down two jobs.

ML: That wouldn't be any more fair for you than it is for Liza. Perhaps homemaking is something neither one of you really wants to do, or has time for. Let's see if we can figure out another way to get the housework done.

Alvin was understandably reluctant to give up an arrangement that was comfortable and functional for him. Yet he was not blind to Liza's aspirations, and to how important it was for her to have a chance to fulfill them. Alvin sensed that if his wife had to give up school, or could continue going only if she handled the equivalent of two full-time jobs, it would not be in the long-run best interests of either of them.

Like most couples who move toward a measure of liberation in their marriage, the Bakers were forced to face the problems that come up when men and women break out of roles they have learned and known so well. It's an uneasy transition even for couples who have a good relationship. Those whose marriages are shaky to begin with will almost surely have trouble. The first concern couples express almost always has to do with "Who'll do the housework?" This surprises a counselor, because it is perhaps the least difficult of all the problems a couple will have to solve. An obvious answer is to hire a replacement—but it's costly and not easy to find the right person.

How, then, can you handle the homemaking dilemma? *The first rule is to separate housekeeping duties from child care.* Mothers who have to work know the difficulties of finding an adequate day-care center or a "substitute mother." Right now there is *no* good answer to this problem for working parents. But both father and mother should share the responsibility for whatever compromise solution they develop. For example, some couples try to arrange their work schedules so that one of them is always home, or at least when the youngsters are most likely to need them. Fathers who voluntarily become much more involved with parenting when mothers work find that the rewards of a closer relationship with their children more than make up for the added responsibility. "I can wipe a runny nose and help with arithmetic as well as my wife can," one man said. Another reported that the high point of his fatherhood came when his seven-year-old daughter needed a costume for a school play and—though her mother was in the room—automatically asked him to make it: "I was no longer just somebody who went out every morning to a mysterious job and earned something called money. I was a parent who could fill a specific need of hers."

Another couple ran the following advertisement in their local newspaper:

> Wanted: a grandmother who can give loving attention
> to three small boys after school. Cookies and milk sup-

plied. No housework—only homework. If you are what
we need, we'll pay what you need. Call after 6 P.M. or
weekends.

They had so many replies that they could have supplied several
families with "grandmas." Still other couples get free live-in help
by offering room and/or board to a college student in exchange
for baby-sitting or help with older children. Talk to other dual-job
couples to see what they are doing about child care. And don't let
anyone tell you that children of working mothers have more behavior problems, or turn out less well than those whose mothers
are always at home. Whether a mother works is *not* a crucial factor in a child's adjustment. What counts is the *quality* of the care
the youngster gets, and whether it has been the mother's *choice* to
work.

Even if you don't have children, of course, there is still the daily
housework to manage. A dual-career couple should list all the
tasks that are strictly homemaking. Then do some streamlining:

• How many can you cross off the list entirely? Using no-iron
fabrics, buying ready-to-use foods, having items delivered, shopping by mail—all these short cuts may cost a bit extra but they will
save even more valuable time and energy.

• Can you alter your standards? Your home does not always
have to look as if a photographer for *Perfect Homes* magazine is
about to take a picture of it. Clutter is not dirt; dust is not filth.
One couple decided to make beds only on weekends, or when they
were having company. Another couple simplified entertaining:
"Guests will eat almost anything if the conversation is good," they
said.

• Should you hire help or try to have the family share the
work? There are many kinds of hired help besides cleaning persons. Equipment such as electrical appliances or power tools—as
well as floor waxers, car washers, and lawn-care services—can be
rented. The rest of the housework can be parceled out among the
family, and even small children can be depended upon to do simple chores.

It should be emphasized that working wives do not have a mo-
nopoly on liberated marriages. Wives who do not work outside the

home also are reaching for new growth experiences that involve choice and change—and, as a result, some marital conflict. For these women, moving out of conventional female role-behavior usually means starting (or returning to) school or college; becoming involved at leadership levels in civic or community activities; or—perhaps as a result of consciousness-raising experiences—striving to develop a heightened sense of self, of putting into daily practice the new awareness that being wife and mother does not preclude also being a self-fulfilling individual.

The changes that a liberated couple must cope with in readjusting the routine functions of family life are simple compared to the changes that grow out of a woman's knowledge of her new resources. In many marriages—especially those based on power rather than on love—a woman's access to these resources can cause fundamental changes in emotional balance. The most obvious and probably the most immediately significant such resource is money of one's own.

Because our society has fallen into the trap of considering only income-producing work as "important," the partner who earns the major share of a family's money traditionally assumes the right to make the family's major decisions. For the most part this means the man is in charge. But as more and more wives begin to contribute important sums to family income, the shift in power is creating new problems or causing long-simmering ones to boil over: "I don't have to take guff from my husband now that I don't have to depend on him for my security," one woman said. Another put it more delicately and constructively: "I know now that I'm married to Jim because I *want* to be. It's hard to know that when you are totally dependent on a man." Still a third wife told how she was able for the first time in her marriage to stand up to her husband:

> One night we had a terrible fight and he said he had had
> enough, he was leaving. Earlier in our marriage I would
> have been scared to death. I would have just caved in
> and begged him to stay. But now I know I can take care
> of myself. So I said, "I don't want you to leave, but if
> you feel that you must, all right." Then I asked if he

> wanted me to spend the night with a friend while he packed his things. For about a minute he just looked at me as if he had never seen me before. Then he said, "I want to stay with you."

It is extremely difficult for both husbands and wives to adjust to such shifts in the power balance of a marriage. The first "heady" feelings of being in control—or the first depressing feelings of having lost some control—usually give way, in a good relationship, to a mutual search for some method by which balance can be re-established. One couple who came to the counselor with this problem worked it out admirably. Sally and Bill had been married when she was nineteen and he was twenty-nine. Sally had never worked, and Bill had always earned a good salary. By virtue of his financial power, plus the age difference between the couple, Bill took over as "head of the house" without challenge. Then, two years ago, with her children in school all day, Sally got a job managing an artists' co-operative gallery:

WIFE: I enjoyed the work so much that I scarcely thought about the money. All during the first year I just handed Bill my paycheck every week. It never occurred to me that I could keep it, or use it for things I wanted.

MARCIA LASSWELL: What happened to change this?

HUSBAND: What happened was that Sally started to get ideas.

ML: What kinds of ideas?

H: About spending money. I'd been using her pay to make some investments, build up a cushion for the future.

W: I didn't object to that. But I *did* think that since we had my extra income we could use some of it for special purposes. For instance, I wanted our daughter to have dance lessons, but Bill said that was a waste. I wanted to buy a few appliances that would make it easier for me to cook dinner when I got home from work, but Bill said that was being extravagant.

H: I still say so! I was willing to help you cook.

W: You were willing to sit in the kitchen with a drink and talk to me while I cooked!

ML: I don't think this is helping much. Let's stick to solving the problem. Tell me where you are in your thinking right now.

W: I kept wondering, "Why do I argue with Bill about this? It's money I earn, and I ought to be free to do whatever I want with it." So last payday I didn't give him my check, and he had a fit!

ML: Is that a valid description of your reaction, Bill?

H: Well, I got awfully mad. I mean, after all that time your wife suddenly starts holding out on you.

W: Then he *stole* it!

H: I saw the check lying on her bureau. I thought she'd forgotten to give it to me, so I took it and deposited it in the bank, like always.

W: We fought some more about *that*. Finally we decided we had better get some help before things go from bad to worse.

ML: It sounds as though they *have* gotten fairly serious . . . Well, I gather that you two lived comfortably enough on one income before you started working, Sally. So your money doesn't have to go toward necessities. Then what does your money mean to you, Sally?

W: Well . . . it gives me some rights, doesn't it? I don't like to turn this into a "my money/your money" kind of thing. I'm willing for our salaries to be "our" money. But I want some of the decisions about using it to be "ours," too.

With some help from the counselor, Sally and Bill worked out a compromise that satisfied both of them. Sally agreed to cash her paycheck and give Bill half of the mney to use for savings and investments. The other half was Sally's to do with as she chose. One of the first things she did was to enroll their daughter in a dance class. For the first time, she was asserting the power that her salary gave her. But by agreeing to the fifty-fifty division of her income, she was signaling her husband that she was not trying to take away all of the power that was so important to him.

Couples who deal with this kind of conflict through self-counseling need to approach it with much the same techniques that we suggested for dealing with conflicts over decision-making:

  • Learn to make and accept changes in the patterns of family decision-making.

• Be as versatile and flexible as possible in negotiating compromises.

• Avoid getting locked in a struggle for power.

A liberated marriage holds the potential for another kind of conflict. It centers about a concern that men and women have always had, but which is now heightened by women's new freedom: whether one's partner will find another person more interesting or more sexually attractive.

According to some of the more enthusiastic spokesmen for liberated relationships, jealousy is becoming an outdated emotion. In an era when women are increasingly claiming the right to as much sexual choice and freedom as men have traditionally had . . . when an "open marriage" may well include the privilege of having extra-marital relationships . . . some authorities are saying that jealousy is no longer relevant. Yet therapists find that more couples than ever are troubled by jealous feelings, and are searching for ways to deal with them. Just as a woman who stayed at home tended to wonder about her husband's secretary, or how he spent the evenings on out-of-town business trips, so now some husbands are wondering about their working wives' relationships with the men they meet on the job. This is not a fanciful concern. Recent surveys indicate that while the percentage of *all* wives who have had an extra-marital affair is rising, the figures for working wives are almost double that of nonworking wives.

In a world where we are so at the mercy of rapid change, it is little wonder that we seek stability and certainty in our most intimate relationship. Anything that seems likely to interfere becomes a threat. And jealousy—perhaps best defined as suspicion or resentment of someone you feel may be a rival—is an understandable response to such a threat. What could be more normal than to be jealous if a relationship you value seems to be in jeopardy?

Yet many men and women believe it is wrong—even "bad"—to feel jealous of a spouse. It is a painful emotion to confront. And besides, they say, what can we do about the situation anyway? Opening up that can of worms begins to seem like a thoroughly destructive act. But counselors know that if jealous feelings are dealt with properly there can be constructive results. The fact is that *no* feeling can be categorized as "right" or "wrong," "good"

or "bad." Rather, feelings are signals or symptoms of complex reactions. Just as pain alerts us to a physical problem and spurs us
to do something about it, so jealousy may be one way of calling
our attention to an emotional problem we might not otherwise recognize or want to face. What matters is not that we *are* jealous,
but whether we can find out *why*—and then how we deal with the
jealousy and what we can learn about ourselves.

One couple had been married only eight months when they
sought counseling to help them work through a problem of jealousy. Linda, a recent law school graduate, was clerking in a large
law firm while waiting to take her bar examination. When she
made increasingly frequent references to Tom, an unmarried junior partner in the firm, Paul grew jealous:

> Linda never mentioned what he looked like . . . that's
> what first made me suspicious. All she ever talked about
> was Tom's grasp of the law, his skill at preparing briefs.
> But I wanted to think Linda's emphasis on his ability
> was a way of covering up what really interested her in
> Tom. I used to wallow in mental images of the two of
> them nuzzling in the law library. I finally met Tom at
> the firm's Christmas party.
>
> The moment I saw him I knew he wasn't the kind of
> man Linda found physically attractive. But she seemed
> mesmerized by him. They talked and laughed together
> all evening. Every once in a while Linda would ask me if
> I was having a good time, but otherwise she ignored me.
> When we got home I exploded. Linda apologized for
> neglecting me but she said she couldn't understand why I
> was so upset. "Because you're so damned involved with
> Tom!" I said. "He's interesting and I learn a lot from
> him," Linda answered. "But surely you don't think I'm in
> love with him?" "No," I said. "Then what in heaven's
> name are you jealous *about?*" she asked. And I couldn't
> answer.

But the question stuck in Paul's mind. Instead of brooding
about his suspicions, he and the counselor began to probe for the
hidden well-spring of his jealousy. As they explored, Paul dis-

covered—and eventually was able to face up to—insecurities in himself:

> I had always worried that I wasn't clever or educated enough to be interesting to Linda, and I guess I never tried to be. I realized the reason I *had* to think Tom attracted her physically was that then I could compete. If it was his mind she liked, I was licked.

With this much insight into the real reasons for his jealous feelings, Paul was able to do something positive. On the counselor's suggestion he took an adult-education course on "Law for the Layman." Just being able to talk to Linda in her own language—to share something connected with her work even in a small way—gave him a good bit of the confidence he needed. Linda was surprised; but she was also touched and pleased. As a result Paul was able to confide in Linda about his feelings of insecurity and jealousy, and to enlist her help in overcoming them.

Partners in dual-career marriages often raise the question of being jealous of a spouse's time. Some husbands and wives seem to feel that any time spent on individual pursuits . . . time spent away from one's spouse . . . is an emotional affront. "You think marriage means you will be together, and then look at what happens," said a man who was married less than a year. "Janie and I have half an hour together at breakfast—when neither of us is coherent anyway. We don't see each other again until six-thirty at night. After dinner, we each have a bunch of household chores. Then we go to bed. I'm shocked at how little time we *do* have to be together without rushing, without always having something to do. And that's why I'm jealous of the time she spends with other people all day! I am afraid that if this keeps up we'll grow apart."

In another instance, a thirty-two-year-old woman tells the counselor that her husband accuses her of working long hours—evenings and occasionally weekends—because she prefers to be with her colleagues rather than with him. "He knows there's no *man* to be jealous of," she said. "Do you know who he's really jealous of? Me! I work those long hours because I have a responsible job . . . and because I want to get my next promotion. He didn't object when I first went to work, but now I think he is upset because I am doing so well. Better than he is, by the way. If it goes on like this I'm going to leave him. I can't respect a man who is jealous of me for being successful."

In all its manifestations, jealousy often springs from self-doubt, a lack of self-esteem, feelings of inadequacy—all the things marital therapists lump under the heading of "low self-image." For example, when men and women talk to counselors about what makes them jealous, only a few mention philandering or sexual infidelity. Instead they describe situations that threaten their self-esteem: "He talks with old friends about things I don't know, and I feel left out" . . . "She tells me about all the good times she had before she met me with her old boy friends" . . . "He talks about his work and I don't understand it" . . . "Everybody clusters around her at a party and ignores me."

What can you do with these feelings of jealousy? To begin with, don't become a victim of the conventional attitude that jealousy is an inevitably negative, destructive reaction to an emotional conflict. If you allow this to happen—if you use jealousy to punish a partner, to get attention, to excuse self-pity, to provoke, to start arguments—then it will probably live up to its reputation and corrode matters even more. But if jealousy is channeled into a positive approach, it can lead to constructive ends. It can, for instance, motivate us to take a closer and more intelligent look at our emotional needs. It can spur us to do something positive about our real or imagined shortcomings. It can make us work harder at a relationship. It can even move us to voice an honest cry for help—to say, "I love you . . . I want you . . . I'm afraid of what I think is happening and I need you to help me stop it."

It makes sense to take a new look at jealousy from this perspective. Specifically, examine your jealous feelings and ask yourself questions about them—questions that may help you discover what the feelings are all about. Ask yourself: What am I jealous of? Or, of whom am I jealous? Does my spouse know how I feel? Am I being realistic? What am I getting out of my behavior? What do I *want* to get out of it? One husband used these questions in a self-counseling process to analyze his surge of jealousy at a party where his wife (who enjoys harmless flirting) spent much of the evening in animated conversation with a good-looking man: "Why is Dorothy so involved with that man? I asked myself. Obviously she is having a good time. Do *I* discuss with her anything that interests her that much? Maybe I should try a bit harder, be less conversationally predictable . . . Do I love her? Yes. If I didn't, why would it matter *how* animatedly she talked to someone else? . . . Since I do love her, why shouldn't I be pleased that she is enjoying herself? Don't I want her to have a good time? Of course. Do I think because she is enjoying the conversation that she is arranging a tryst with Good-looking Fellow? Obviously not. Once I realized that my wife's conversation with another man took nothing away from me—in fact, it pointed to a way I could improve our relationship—I also realized that there was no reason for me to be jealous."

In traditional marriage, men and women functioned on an "exchange" basis. Each carried out his and her responsibilities in exchange for the other doing the same. On the surface, liberated marriage is doing away with this sex-role "contract." Essentially, however, the contract still exists. Only rather than exchanging goods and services, liberated couples are exchanging love and understanding. Instead of living together to carry out practical obligations, liberated husbands and wives see their main purpose as supporting each other's emotional growth and well-being.

It is this opportunity to help each other grow—and to enjoy each other's growth—that is the essence of a truly liberated marriage. Too often the emphasis is incorrectly placed on liberating woman at man's expense. But the measure of a successful liberated relationship is how well it provides for the emotional satisfaction of *both* partners, how well it enables each to reach his or her goals in life. True, liberation of this kind creates problems. It means a couple must plan and negotiate, argue and compromise, deal with a host of unexpected feelings and reactions. But those couples who are already finding it a good way to live report that the gains are worth the troubles. When you have real and free choices, you can no longer blame each other for unhappiness or frustration. It is truly a no-fault marriage.

13

PROFESSIONAL HELP

When You Need It,
How to Get It

We have distilled the techniques of the marital therapist so that you can apply them to your marriage through self-counseling. How effectively we—and you—have achieved this goal may not be immediately apparent or measurable. The relaxation of tensions, the easing of conflicts, the resolution of problems—these are not matters that can be accomplished quickly. The gauge of success may not even be whether a specific fact has been dealt with or a particular difficulty cleared away. Rather, it may be simply a sense of gradual change for the better in one or both partners' attitudes or behavior, or in their relationship. Does a husband say or do things that are constructively different from what he said or did before self-counseling? Does a wife show more insight or empathy? Do couples act out of new knowledge of themselves and of each other?

If you can answer "yes" to any of these questions, even in the smallest degree, it is likely that continued work with self-counseling techniques will lead to further marital growth. As one woman said after testing these approaches in her own family for several months: "We still have our troubles but we're learning how to handle them better. It's not *great,* of course, but most of the time, now, I enjoy my marriage!"

For some relationships, however, self-counseling may prove to be ultimately ineffective. In such marriages—and we'll detail their characteristics in a moment—there comes a time when the only sensible action is to seek professional help.

How can anyone tell when that time is? How can you identify

the boundary lines that differentiate a conflict that can be self-resolved from one that requires the guidance of a trained marital therapist? What are the key signals of emotional stalemate between spouses? When is it foolish, or even dangerous, to ignore them and insist on continuing to try to "work it out ourselves"?

There is one guideline that can help to provide a basic answer to these questions. It is embedded in a concept called *marital balance,* which was described by Dorothy Fahs Beck, Director of Research for the Family Service Association of America, in her analysis of thousands of couples counseled by Family Service caseworkers. Marital balance describes the dovetailing of each spouse's needs with the other's ability to meet them over the long run of a marriage. According to Dr. Beck, conflict begins when this equilibrium is disturbed . . . when one partner feels he or she is giving more than the other . . . that the rewards are not worth the cost.

Most people assume that the severest marital stress occurs at a time of crisis. But counselors know that while a crisis often brings stress to its breaking point, the stress itself is due to a gradual erosion of the marriage rather than to any one special event. This erosion occurs, says Dr. Beck, when the balance of a marriage begins to tip. That is the start of "spiraling conflict." Couples usually try to ignore, disguise, or obscure this incipient mutual hostility, hoping the problem will go away. Sometimes—rarely—this works. Most often the build-up of irritations and resentments leads to increased tension. Sooner or later a new development tips the balance even more and triggers open conflict. "The actual trigger," writes Dr. Beck in her report, "may be unwanted pregnancy, a new baby, a financial crisis, the arrival of an unwelcome in-law . . . Whatever it is, something felt as threatening suddenly reactivates earlier dissatisfactions or noticeably undercuts the gratifications that have been received . . . [spouses] cannot satisfy each other's needs. The added stress triggers some dramatic new—and perhaps ill-advised—action. This unexpected action precipitates an open clash or blowup . . . To the most unaware partner this may seem incomprehensible—'a bolt out of the blue.'"

At this point one of two things may occur. The clash may clear the air and force a couple to take steps to improve their marriage. Or the conflict may simply restabilize itself at another level of

avoidance and denial. The couple are still off-balance, but have
made an uneasy truce. Counseling may well be helpful at this early
stage, Dr. Beck suggests. Without therapy, however, the conflict
spiral picks up speed when the next trigger event sets off another
confrontation. Says Dr. Beck: "Each round of attack and counter-
attack, each increase in demands, each session of increasingly hostile criticism leaves a residue of smouldering anger and a bitter af-
tertaste . . . Any search for new solutions is blocked. While some
husbands or wives make repeated and even frantic attempts to
reach out to the spouse, reconciliation is usually temporary. After
an interlude, the quarrels begin again . . . The positions of the opposing camps become more rigid and polarized, and less subject to
negotiation and compromise. Eventually, the erosion of rewards is
so great as to destroy completely the marital balance and make the
continuation of the marriage untenable . . ." The couple at this
point frequently report hurts so deep that they have no desire to
try to work on their marriage.

Clearly, a couple who reach this stage are in no condition or
mood for self-counseling. And even professional counselors find it
difficult to help restore the balance of satisfactions in the marriage,
or to stop the conflict from escalating. Sometimes a person's hurt
or rage is so overwhelming that he or she is less interested in solutions than in revenge. At the least, a trained counselor may be able
to help avert the total destruction of whatever is left. Such was the
case, for example, with a woman who found out that her minister-
husband was having an affair with an attractive young widow in
his congregation:

WIFE: I wish I could hurt him as much as he's hurt me. I want
    him to suffer the way I have.
MARCIA LASSWELL: I can understand that you feel that way. The
    thought of revenge can often make you feel better. And if
    you are going to end your marriage, actually getting revenge
    could be a possible course of action. However, if you are
    going to work out a way to stay together, revenge may be the
    last thing you want.
W: Why is that? I'd think if we evened the score, we could start
    out again on an equal footing.

ML: Equally destroyed, you mean? (Wife is silent) What is your fantasy of what you'd do to get revenge?

W: I've thought of all sorts of things. I'd tell his superiors in the church, and all the men he has to work with and deal with. I'd spread it to all the parishioners. And I'd tell his mother, she thinks he's so marvelous! And our friends. Imagine how he'd squirm!

ML: Let's suppose you did all this, and your husband survives it without retaliating against you. Now, do you want a husband whose reputation has been ruined? Who is held in low esteem by his church, his family, your friends? Think your revenge through to its logical conclusion. Do you want to destroy the man, or do you want him to be strong and effective if you stay married to him?

There are half a dozen specific circumstances—in addition to marital imbalance—in which self-counseling is likely to be at best nonproductive, at worst counterproductive. For these, professional therapy is necessary:

When a marital problem is too deeply rooted in or inextricably linked to neurotic personality patterns. Any self-help program must assume that those attempting it are indeed able to help themselves. Thus, a self-counseling couple must be reasonably stable and free of severely neurotic behavior and personality patterns. These can include chronic drinking, severe depression, suicidal tendencies, acute nervousness, deep feelings of insecurity or inadequacy, and character disorders such as constant lying or compulsive gambling. For example, a case in which self-counseling failed involved a man who was so insecure that he had little emotional energy available to work on the problems his wife saw in their marriage. Depressed and apathetic, he willingly blamed himself for his wife's unhappiness but then never followed through on the solutions they formulated. This combination of self-abasement and inaction infuriated his wife. But, of course, the more she berated the man, the greater his sense of inadequacy became. The couple were trapped in a downward spiral that required professional therapy to stop.

When marital conflict goes on so long that it hardens into rigid confrontation, and spouses are unable to budge from their inflexible positions. This situation is one of the most difficult a marital therapist can encounter, because the couple behave as if they have a vested interest in rejecting change. Counselors find that such a couple will often end the marriage rather than give up their unyielding ways. It is no wonder self-counseling is rarely successful in these cases.

In one such disturbed marriage, each partner held dogmatic and unrealistic viewpoints and each refused to admit there could be merit to any perspective but their own. The couple did not even seek help for their marriage; they entered counseling when their son developed problems. The wife, strict in her ethical and religious beliefs, was also a firm disciplinarian. She expected the boy to be completely obedient, a top student, to perform regular duties at home, *and* to earn money from afterschool jobs. Naturally, the boy rebelled against these exorbitant demands. The father, meanwhile, gave lip service to his wife's standards but subtly sided with his son. When the boy protested that he had too many responsibilities and no time for fun, the father would say, "Yes, you're only young once." He would comment with pride about how "my son is learning to hold his own with his mother." The boy skillfully played the parents against each other, and they in turn used him as a pawn in their arguments over "right" and "wrong."

One day the boy was arrested for shoplifting. His mother was horrified, his father excused it as a "little scrape." A few weeks later the youngster was arrested again for petty larceny and this time the court's probation officer recommended family therapy. The counselor soon realized that the boy was "acting out" against a difficult home situation: his mother and father were subconsciously using him as a battleground on which to fight out their own war. It took many sessions—including individual, family, and marital therapy—before progress could be made. (It's useful to remember that problems with children often reflect marital problems, and that clearing up the latter often helps solve the former.)

When a couple are unable to move toward a solution of their difficulties—or to reach out to each other in understanding and love—without the guidance and support of a neutral "outsider." Typically, this can occur under three separate sets of circumstances: a) when one or both partners seem unable to forgive a past hurt no matter what or how hard they try; b) when there is a definite imbalance of power—one spouse really does *need* the most, *love* the most, or have the *fewest resources*—and the other partner takes advantage of his or her position; and c) where either or both partners are afraid of intimacy or commitment, afraid to be open or trusting because long-standing hurts have left them gunshy. Occasionally a marriage may involve a combination of these factors, and the couple may make headway in one area only to founder in the others:

HUSBAND: I really have been trying to even out this "power" business between us since I realized how dependent Margaret felt. But, damn it, now that she's feeling stronger, she's really getting bitchy. She dredges up things that happened years ago and wants to fight about them now.

The husband's reaction is to go back to being totally controlling in order to shut off his wife's attack. A professional counselor can give support to both spouses, letting them ventilate their feelings in a nondamaging way to keep the marriage from exploding:

MARCIA LASSWELL: Margaret, you have been storing up anger and resentment for years and now it is surfacing. It needs to come out. You need to "ventilate" before you can forgive. But I think it's going to come out pretty harshly at first, and we don't need to put Don through that. I'd like to see you alone for a few sessions. If some of your complaints are relevant to what's going on now between you two, we'll settle on a way to tell Don that won't make him defensive.

Professional counseling is needed when a marriage has deteriorated to the point where a spouse feels he or she must resort to a dramatic, climactic gesture: leaving home, becoming physically violent, attempting suicide. Any such act is clear evidence that the person can no longer be reached except by a skilled therapist. Even if the disturbed spouse will not agree to go to one, a counselor can help the other partner to handle both the situation and his or her own pain. For example, if one partner is in the throes of a life-cycle crisis and is behaving strangely, counseling usually can help the other to understand what is happening, and to endure until the crisis passes. A counselor's objective support is particularly helpful when a husband or wife is trying to wait out a partner's extra-marital affair.

When communication between a couple is so incessantly (or exclusively) hostile that it becomes what we call "the conversation of divorce." This pattern has been noted by many therapists and specialists in communication: an escalating series of violent verbal exchanges—accusations, insults, criticisms, recriminations, threats —which eventually climax in marital breakup. Just as declarations of love strengthen feelings of love, so words of animosity intensify negative feelings. When this happens, a spouse often has a depressing sense of puzzlement over why the marriage seems to be at the end of the road. For instance, a husband says:

> Ann and I quarreled a lot. At first we always managed to kiss and make up. But as the fights got more intense they ended in silence, withdrawal. One night we had a particularly bitter battle. Ann said maybe we ought to get divorced. I should have just shut up, but I was too angry. So I agreed, maybe we should. I was stunned to hear myself say that. I think Ann was shaken up, too. But neither of us was willing to back down.
>
> After that our quarrels got harsher, and they always ended up with one of us threatening to leave "for good," or to "see a lawyer in the morning." One day Ann *did* see a lawyer—I don't think she really wanted to, but she had to make good on her threat. A few weeks later she moved out, and then filed for divorce. I still don't know *why* it happened.

Or this from a woman whose marriage recently ended under similar circumstances:

> Oh, we had problems all right. "But who doesn't?" I

used to say. He would say, "You just want to avoid
talking about them." And maybe I did . . . but *he*
insisted on talking about them. Only instead of trying to
figure out what was wrong and do something about it,
he kept bad-mouthing the marriage: "Why are you
afraid to admit we don't get along?" "You shouldn't
want to be with someone who doesn't want to be with
you."

I tell you when somebody says things like that often
enough you begin to agree. I would say, "I love you."
And he would say, "It's no use, we can't go on this
way." After a while he convinced both of us enough so
we began talking about divorce. Once you both begin it
is almost impossible to turn back.

What makes the conversation of divorce so fiendishly effective?
For one thing, emotional boiling points get so low that it takes less
and less to set off each successive quarrel. For another, the arguments themselves become tension-releasers. For a third, hostile
talk helps a spouse to build a self-justifying image: Every word is
chosen to defend one's self and tear down one's spouse. To stop
the cycle, both partners would have to demolish the self-images
they put so much effort into creating. The result is that—almost by
definition—self-counseling becomes an impossibility. Professional
therapy becomes the only avenue through which a couple may be
helped to learn how to defuse hostile conversation and gradually
replace it with constructive talk.

*When a couple has made a substantial degree of self-counseling
progress, peeling away many layers of difficulty, but find that
they cannot deal successfully with the core problem in their relationship.* As self-counseling solves many of the minor differences
that plague marriage, it may open the way for major differences to
come more clearly into focus. That is why one couple who had
coped with most of their surface problems through self-counseling
turned to professional therapy for the basic problem they now
could see existed:

WIFE (to counselor): Bill and I are getting along better now than

we have for years. We used to quarrel a lot over things that
we now know how to handle. But since we get along so well
now *out* of bed, we've become aware that our sex life isn't all
that great.

HUSBAND: I used to blame the sex problems on other things, like
being angry with each other or "holding back" to get revenge. Now we realize we've got a real problem in this area.

MARCIA LASSWELL: Sometimes this happens. There are certain
problems self-counseling doesn't help. Usually they are either
very emotional—like sex—or they involve rock-bottom values.

W: You're right about this being an emotional issue. It was even
hard for us to talk enough about it to decide to call you.

ML: I'm glad you decided to come in. Most couples wait too long
and the problems get worse.

Knowing *when* to seek professional guidance is the first step in
the transition from self-counseling. The second is knowing *how to
get* the most effective help available to you.

"No longer is it possible—if, indeed, it ever was—to say 'Marriage counseling is . . .' and proceed to describe [it] in simple,
precise terms," writes counseling psychologist William C. Nichols,
Jr. As a president of the National Council on Family Relations, he
should know. As a result, Nichols continues, "It is exceedingly
difficult to ascertain what one can profitably use from among the
array of services being offered."

The range of marital therapy has been greatly expanded. There
are today counselors of various therapeutic persuasions and backgrounds; there are dozens of new and improved counseling techniques. But this very progress has created its own problems. With
many options open to them, how can a couple decide which kind
of counselor will serve them best? How can they tell which therapeutic method may be most useful in dealing with their particular
situation? Perhaps most important, how can they know which
combination of counselor-and-techniques may be most emotionally
acceptable to them?

These are hard questions to answer. And the difficulties are
compounded because most husbands and wives avoid confronting
them until the marriage has reached a crisis point. Then, under
great stress, and very likely willing to grasp at promises or to seek

instant solutions, a couple is even less competent to make wise decisions. Moreover, one cannot "shop around" for a counselor—sampling the variety of personalities and methods available—for every interview costs time and money, and meanwhile the conflicts intensify, the problems persist. Nor can one simply pick, as from a smörgåsbord, whatever looks good at the moment; an uninformed choice of counselor can turn out to be disastrous. But there are guideposts a couple can use to help them make intelligent judgments and arrive at reasonable answers to the questions: To whom should we go? For what kind of help?

WHAT YOU SHOULD KNOW ABOUT A COUNSELOR'S BACKGROUND AND QUALIFICATIONS

The basic training standards for a qualified marriage counselor have been set by the professional organizations in the field. Membership in such organizations is one of the surest criteria for determining who is adequately trained. The listings in the telephone directory's Yellow Pages under "Marriage and Family Counselors" usually will provide you with names of counselors who belong to the American Association of Marriage and Family Counselors. This organization's standards require that a counselor should have a graduate degree in one of the "helping professions"—medicine, law, social work, psychiatry, psychology, the ministry. He or she should *also* have had special training in marital and/or family therapy. Many universities and clinical institutes now offer graduate programs in marital counseling. To be considered for membership in the AAMFC, a therapist must also have had three years of clinical training and experience under the supervision of a senior counselor. In six states (at this writing California, New Jersey, Utah, Nevada, Georgia, and Michigan), a counselor must pass oral and written tests to get a license to practice. It is illegal for any person without this license to advertise as a marital therapist in these states.

In other states only a minority of those who do marital counseling have gone through maximum training. Since counseling is still an emergent field that crosses many academic disciplines, rather than a separate profession with its own special rules and standards, counselors come like old-fashioned penny candy—in a mixed assortment. At one end of the scale are the highly skilled, clinically trained practitioners; at the other end are sketchily trained "lay" therapists (or, worse, incompetent quacks and charlatans); and in between is a wide range of responsible professionals of varying degrees of skill and training. Any couple seeking marital therapy should not hesitate to ask about a counselor's background, to dig into the details of his or her qualifications. This means asking whether the person has had special training in marital counseling; where it was obtained and for how long; whether the counselor had clinical supervision as an "interne" in a counseling clinic or a graduate-school program. Inspect the diplomas on a counselor's office wall and ask questions if there is anything unclear or odd about them. Reputable therapists won't mind these questions at all.

You should also be aware, however, that competent and valuable help can come from a minister who has been trained in pastoral counseling; from a sociologist who specializes in communications techniques; from a trained sex therapist; from a social caseworker or psychologist who combines emotional sensitivity with substantial practical experience. But you will still need to be careful in choosing a therapist who does not hold membership in a suitable professional organization or a license to practice marital therapy.

A wise choice of counselor depends, moreover, not only on his or her qualifications but also on your problems, and on the intangible emotional interplay between the counselor and both spouses. A couple may find a highly qualified, skilled, and ethical therapist. Yet, unless there exists a current of trust and empathy between them, the couple may have difficulty accepting the insights and guidance the counselor offers. Sometimes the only way to learn whether a therapist will be one with whom you feel you can work is to go for one or two visits to see what happens.

Many troubled couples naturally think of talking to their minister, priest, or rabbi. And counseling of all kinds has traditionally been considered an integral part of the clergy's responsibilities. Despite this, some couples shy away from going to the clergy with a marital problem. They sometimes fear being faced with a moralistic stand; or they are embarrassed to discuss personal concerns with someone they consider a spiritual adviser. In recent years seminaries of all faiths have set up courses in pastoral counseling with special emphasis on marriage and family therapy. Many clergymen have also taken clinical training in major secular counseling centers. An inquiry at the headquarters of a denomination will tell you if your particular faith has counselors trained in marital therapy.

Lawyers occasionally become involved in marriage counseling as an outgrowth of their work with divorce and separation cases. So do some doctors, as a result of seeing patients with sexual or emotional problems. But comparatively few lawyers or doctors are particularly interested in marital counseling, or trained for it. These two professions are not the best places to look for marital advice. Physicians and lawyers may, however, be able to suggest a counselor, as they are usually aware of reputable sources of help in the community.

The shortage of qualified counselors leaves a vacuum which poorly trained persons or outright quacks rush to fill. Some are well-meaning but misguided folk who "want to help people in trouble." Some are professional people who, though untrained for counseling, try their hand at it anyway. Some are lay counselors who range from competent to useless to actively dangerous. Charlatans deliberately cash in on human suffering. They can usually be identified by their blatant self-advertising. (Legitimate counselors are restricted by their ethical codes from doing anything more than listing themselves in the classified telephone directory with a short descriptive line identifying their speciality.) A quack usually promises "prompt relief" for whatever ails your marriage. He or she tends to promulgate pseudo-scientific theories or gimmicky devices; may insist on a client "signing up" for a specific number of sessions; and either refuses to give details of training or tries to overwhelm you with phony "diplomas" from phony "colleges."

HOW LONG SHOULD COUNSELING TAKE?

There is no way to tell. A simple difficulty may be cleared up in a few sessions. (A session is usually fifty minutes once a week, but some counselors prefer to meet with a couple more frequently to maintain continuity or momentum.) A serious marital conflict may require a year or more of therapy. Most counselors set a tentative schedule or deadline so that the client knows there is a goal, that counseling is not an indefinite proposition.

Increasingly, counselors are concentrating on what is wrong with a marriage "here and now"—on what is going on at the moment—rather than delving into a couple's childhood backgrounds or their unconscious motivations. Thus, the trend is more and more toward short-term therapy. Some counselors make a "time contract" with a couple. In effect, they all agree upon a certain number of sessions in which to reach an agreed-on goal. These contracts may be extended, shortened, renewed. New goals and new contracts can be established.

Whether a time limit of any kind on counseling is a good or bad idea depends for the most part on how a couple react to it. Some husbands and wives are distressed or flustered by pressure. Others are challenged by it to work harder and more realistically to solve their problems. Thus you should ask yourselves: Do we work well or poorly under a deadline? Do we respond positively to time pressure, or do we resent it? Can we get to the point of a difficulty quickly, or do we need time to get ourselves geared up, able to talk about it? Would we feel that we had failed if we did not reach the preset goal in the scheduled time?

WHAT YOU SHOULD KNOW ABOUT COUNSELING THEORIES

Marital therapists have widely varying approaches to their work. Counseling has sometimes been called "a practice without a theory," but the fact is that it has many theories. And a couple seeking help should know—are *entitled* to know—which one is going to be applied to their problem.

For example, a counselor whose primary background and training are in certain schools of psychiatry or psychoanalysis may believe marital conflict stems chiefly from neurosis in one spouse or the other. A part of this theory is that a neurotic person will have a neurotic marriage. Restoring the partner to emotional health, it is believed, is the first and most important step toward improving the marriage. Such a therapist might deal solely with the personality problems of one or both spouses. If in helping to clear *them* up the counselor does not improve—or actually damages—the marriage, that would be unfortunate. But it is always a risk as a by-product of this school of therapy. For such a counselor there is really no such thing as "marriage counseling" per se. There is only the theory that removing a spouse's neurotic problem may *incidentally* have a good effect on the marriage. If not, it will at least be of benefit in any future marriage.

This approach to marriage counseling is a minority one. Most marital therapists today believe their function is to treat the *marriage,* not only one or the other partner in it. It is the *relationship* between the spouses that is at stake; and it is this relationship that the counselor explores, studies, and attempts to heal or strengthen. Obviously marital conflicts cannot be arbitrarily separated from the personality patterns of the partners. The *inter*action between spouses is, in a sense, the "flip side" of their intra-psychic life. A skilled counselor will look at both sides. But his or her main concern will be not with the individual, but with the relationship and health of the marriage.

One of the best summaries of how a trained therapist who thinks this way approaches a case was spelled out for us not long ago by Esther Oshiver Fisher, a special consultant in counselor training: "First I try to calm a couple's emotions so we can begin to find out how their conflicts occur and repeat themselves. This 'truce' is a starting point where we can begin to see what a husband and wife are doing to each other, and why. Next, I deal with the emotional problems of each spouse separately, and with the way they manifest themselves in the marriage. A counselor works on many levels—sometimes all at once—but the focus is on the marital relationship." In a sense, every counselor has three clients: one husband, one wife, and one marriage. The paradox is that the sum of the whole is greater than its parts.

No couple can be expected to take a crash course in counseling theory before they choose a counselor. But a couple should, at least, make use of their right to a general explanation of how the counselor sees his or her task. At best, a couple can be *aware* that many different counseling theories and approaches exist, find out which one the therapist uses, and then sort out their reactions to it.

WHAT YOU SHOULD KNOW ABOUT COUNSELING TECHNIQUES

In the past few years there has been an explosion of innovative techniques for dealing with marital conflict. They range from "transactional analysis" to "communications therapy" to "behavior modification." In addition, counseling methods that were considered experimental only a decade ago—such as group counseling and conjoint therapy—are now widely used.

The most popular of the newer techniques today is *conjoint marital therapy*. Instead of working with one spouse only or with one at a time, the counselor sees husband and wife simultaneously. The method has several advantages. To begin with, it may be the first thing the couple have done together for a long time. Spouses unable to talk to each other out of fear or anger can vent their feelings under the emotional protection of a counselor's presence. Nor do they have to worry that one partner is privately telling lies or secrets about the other, or that the counselor is taking sides. Everything that's said is out in the open. Another advantage is that the counselor can *see* the couple interacting, which is more useful than merely hearing a possibly distorted version of something that has happened between them. He or she can correct their misunderstandings—the "my wife never" and "my husband always" charges —on the spot. The therapist can observe the progress they are making and call it to their attention. For example, one couple in their first conjoint session sat in such a way that they couldn't look at each other. As the weeks passed they gradually changed from an almost back-to-back position to one that was side by side. Finally they turned face to face. They had not realized the significant change in their posture until the counselor pointed it out.

There are variations of the conjoint method. If a couple are intensely antagonistic, a counselor may begin by seeing both people separately (*concurrent therapy*), and then gradually bringing them into joint sessions. In *collaborative therapy* two counselors see one spouse at a time, or both spouses together, and then exchange views about what they have learned and observed. Still another offshoot is *conjoint co-therapy,* sometimes called "TCC"—treatment of a couple by a couple. In this method a male and a female counselor work together. TCC costs more per session (to pay for the second counselor's time). But since a counseling team can often pick up behavioral clues a therapist working alone might miss, and since they bring male and female insights to bear, progress may be faster in the long run. TCC not only avoids the possibility of a therapist's sex bias, but it also gives couples the opportunity to learn to talk comfortably with a member of the opposite sex. In many cases a woman can benefit from speaking to an understanding male therapist, and vice versa.

Group marital counseling, once experimental, is now a common form of therapy. Several couples meet to talk about their problems under the guidance of one or sometimes two counselors. You may wonder whether a couple can air their intimate concerns in a circle of strangers, or whether strangers can care enough about one another to give emotional support. But the fact is that marital groups do develop a remarkable degree of mutual trust and sensitivity.

In addition to certain practical advantages—lower fees and a shorter waiting period—group counseling holds therapeutic advantages for certain kinds of people. A husband who might feel "threatened" in a face-to-face session with an individual counselor may feel more comfortable with other men (or couples) who have similar problems. A person who would bridle at certain comments from a counselor can take the same remarks calmly when they are made by others in the group. One of the biggest advantages of group counseling is that an unhappy couple can get a new perspective on their situation by seeing and hearing other unhappy couples with their guard down. In a group, husband and wife need not confront each other directly. One can make a sort of end run around the other's defenses. They get through to each other by what they say to the group.

Moreover, the insights one gets into another person's situation are often transferred to one's own. People become aware of the defenses and fears of others in the group long before they can be aware of their own. Eventually this sensitivity gets carried over to one's own situation. For instance, a man in one marital therapy group was silent for many sessions, and the wife complained constantly about his "passivity." One evening, to everyone's pleased surprise, this man began to talk about his ideas of happiness. While he was talking his wife's face became more and more contorted. Finally she couldn't contain herself any longer. "See how he leaves me out!" she cried. And so *she* revealed not only her own need for attention but her hidden fear that if her husband became more assertive he would not need her any more. Another woman in the group suddenly leaned forward and in a flash of empathy said: "I know what you are going through." From that moment on *both* these couples made rapid progress.

Sometimes groups are composed only of husbands *or* wives, but usually four or five disparate couples make up a group. It can be compared, perhaps, to a giant test tube. If only one chemical is poured into it, nothing will happen. If different kinds are mixed, there will be reactions that will produce changes. But you should be aware of certain cautions. One can lose oneself in a crowd and group therapy may not be wise for anyone who tends to use it as a cover-up for his or her silences. Nor is it recommended for persons who may feel rejected if the group ignores them, or shattered if the group attacks them.

Within the over-all structure of these various new methods, counselors draw on an ever-growing variety of *specific* therapeutic techniques: transactional analysis, rational-emotive, Gestalt, contract negotiation, behavior modification, symbolic interaction—to name just a few. An exploration of these methods would require a book of its own. Just as one example, however, let's look at behavior modification, which is fast growing in popularity with counselors.

Its proponents believe that if you can stop one spouse from doing even one small thing that annoys the other, that is an important step toward improving the over-all relationship. For instance, if a husband's constant television-watching annoys his wife, she and the therapist work out a simple method to get him to cut down. Usually it consists of tempting him to substitute some other activity he enjoys, or offering to do something he wants in return for his doing something that she wants. By "modifying" the annoying behavior, the theory runs, a roadblock in the path of marital harmony is removed.

There is a good deal of debate about the value of this technique, however. Some counselors believe behavior modification merely deals with symptoms and does not come to grips with basic attitudes. Others question the morality of trying to "manipulate" another's behavior without his or her knowledge. Those who favor the method believe its results are quick and practical, and that so long as the marriage gets better the methods are justified.

Some couples who seek professional counseling are unaware of this great variety of available techniques. Other couples insist that the counselor use a specific one. Neither approach makes much sense. Both therapist and clients need to agree on the technique that seems most suited to the situation.

Perhaps the most important ingredient of successful therapy is *self-knowledge*—the understanding of your own attitudes toward professional help. Since there is no magic in therapy, much of what it can accomplish depends on the couple involved in it. To get the best results, then, any couple must ask these serious questions of themselves:

• *To what extent are we committed to trying to solve our problem?* That means not just how much time and money you are prepared to invest, but whether there is a firm personal resolve on the part of both of you to stay with counseling long enough for it to have a real chance to work. The depth of this emotional commitment by both husband and wife is probably the single most important factor in counseling success.

• *What do we expect ultimately to get from counseling—what goal or goals do we have in mind?* A couple have the right to be told fairly early by a counselor how—and how much—he or she thinks they can benefit from counseling. It is well to keep in mind, however, that the counselor, too, will be limited by the clients' own hopes and expectations. Some spouses enter counseling already knowing—consciously or not—what end result they want. One of our colleagues, Elizabeth Kraft, says, "There are two kinds of couples who come to marital therapy: those who want to stay married and those who do not. The real problem comes when one partner *does* and the other *doesn't*." Clinton Phillips, a veteran marital therapist and director of the California Family Study Center near Los Angeles, observes that "when a person starts out by saying, 'This is the end of my marriage, *isn't it?*' I can see that he or she hopes I will agree." A wife who has made up her mind that she wants "out" of her marriage may select a counselor she thinks approves of divorce, or one she thinks will take a more "liberal" view of her behavior. Conversely, if the wife wants to keep her marriage going she may take her problem to a minister, feeling that he is more likely to try to hold a marriage together. Few counselors actually have such preconceptions or biases, though some people think they do.

• *How honestly and freely can we express our feelings?* Most people are not able to talk openly at first. Counselors don't expect them to, and have ways of drawing them out in time. But if a couple know that one or both of them have serious difficulty in communicating, they may decide to choose a counselor who specializes in opening up discussion between spouses. Unless a couple can be frank about their emotional relationship, a counselor cannot accurately understand their actions or interpret their feelings.

By developing these insights into your attitudes toward counseling, you are doing two important things. First, you are preparing yourselves emotionally for the counseling process. Second, you are setting up practical guidelines that will help you make a wise choice of a counselor.

WHAT YOU SHOULD KNOW ABOUT FINDING A COUNSELOR

Referrals are made to trained therapists in specific areas of the country by the American Association of Marriage and Family Counselors (225 Yale Avenue, Claremont, California, 91711). The National Council on Family Relations (1219 University Avenue, S.E., Minneapolis, Minnesota, 55414), an organization of family life experts, will also suggest names of legitimate counselors in your community. Social agencies, primarily those affiliated with the Family Service Association of America (44 East Twenty-third Street, New York, New York, 10010), have skilled caseworkers who do marital counseling at fees geared to family income.

To locate a qualified counselor you can write to any of these organizations. Or you can check the listings under "Marriage Counseling" in your local classified telephone directory. It usually lists social agencies, church counseling centers, and therapists in private practice. (Remember that legitimate counselors are prohibited by professional ethics from doing more than listing their name and address, and perhaps an area of special expertise. Many choose not to list a specialty at all.) You can also ask your clergyman or physician for a referral to a counselor; check with such community organizations as United Fund; or contact the sociology, psychology, family life, or public health departments of a nearby college or university.

WHAT YOU SHOULD KNOW ABOUT THE CHANCES FOR COUNSELING SUCCESS

When financier J. P. Morgan was asked one day by an investor what the stock market would do, he replied: "It will fluctuate." That may seem to be a supercilious or disdainful answer. But it is, in fact, the only possible correct one. Much the same is true of marriage counseling. If you were to ask, "What are the chances that therapy will solve my/our marital problem?" the reasonable answer would have to be: "It depends."

It depends, for example, on the answers you make to the questions we suggested you put to yourself. It depends on at what point in the marriage you bring your difficulties to a counselor. It depends on whether both spouses are willing to co-operate for the necessary length of time. It depends on how determined you are to make your marriage work.

Even so, there is no true yardstick that can measure "success." If a couple leave a counselor today blissfully arm-in-arm, yet are battling about the same old thing a year from now—is that success? If a couple are helped by counseling to see that they are trapped in a marriage that is beyond repair, and that the least painful course is to end it and start anew with their new insights—is that success? Experts estimate that about two thirds of all clients are "helped" by counseling, that about a quarter of them show little or no change, and that the rest—roughly, 7 per cent—find their relationship has grown worse.

At best, successful counseling releases enormous amounts of

energy for constructive use. It improves communication, often results in a happier sexual life, restores real parents (and a positive view of marriage) to children. At worst—even if success is minor or totally absent—counseling can alleviate the pain and bitterness of hostility or of divorce. It can make a couple aware of the effort that is required to make a marriage work. It may help them to find happiness in a future marriage.

Does Seeking Professional Help Mean That Your Efforts at Self-counseling Have Been Fruitless?

Having tried on your own—even if you have failed—will prove to be a valuable experience for several reasons:

1. You have gained experience in confronting problems and in developing some skills for dealing with them.

2. Chances are that you have worked through a number of minor or subsidiary difficulties, and added to your knowledge of each other. With that foundation, a professional therapist is able to start work with you at a higher "level" of counseling. You will be able to convey more quickly the essence of your problem; in turn, he or she will be able to communicate better with you.

3. With a better understanding of the counseling process, you will be able to work more efficiently with the therapist —saving time and money, avoiding blind alleys, being more emotionally ready to accept new insights and more willing to try new approaches.

It was the astronomer Galileo who observed that "You cannot teach a person anything . . . You can only help him discover it within himself." He was talking about the miracles his telescope found in the skies, but his principle holds true for the miracles that can be found on our inner horizons. Self-discovery is the key to a happier and more productive married life.